PRAISE FOR
THE COURAGE TO BE YOU

"Cheryne Blom's *The Courage to be You* mind-maps the thread of insight and dives into the internal dialogue swirling around the toxicity of fear to help readers discover their true essence. Using her own story, a series of lists, diagrams and exercises, Blom encourages readers to peel back the layers of their toxic onions and watch the petals of their inner lilies bloom with the sweetness of happiness."

—**CAROL JEFFERS**, author of *The Question of Empathy: Searching for the Essence of Humanity*

"*The Courage to Be You* is the perfect title for Cheryne's book as it rests on her personal story, the courage she has demonstrated in leaving a stuck relationship and reinventing herself, and the courage in sharing even the raw and vulnerable aspects of her journey so openly and honestly. Her commitment to her growth, her big compassionate heart, and the wisdom she has gained along the way shine through in this book."

—**LILIANE GRACE**, author of *The Mastery Club®, Quest for Riches* and *Wanted: Greener Grass*

"Cheryne Blom's latest book, *The Courage to be You* engages the reader with her compelling personal story of breaking down, breaking free and breaking through to become her authentic self. With years of experience as a self-empowerment coach and mindfulness teacher she expertly guides the reader to self-discovery and self-mastery. Very helpful and amazing!"

—**MARTHA THOMPSON**, author of *The Oxygen Mask Rule* and *Giving Paws: Having a Service Dog for a Hidden Disability*

"Cheryne's book shows great courage and conviction. Courage to share her most intimate stories and conviction to put this into a universal practice to assist folks in need of her intimate journey. Her wisdom and insights provide a framework for those who wish to do the work involved, and a basis to achieve what she has achieved; to be in control of their lives and move forward with confidence."

—JENNY NEWTON

"I have just finished Cheryne's book *The Courage to be You*. It was one of the best coaching books I have read. It talked to my deeper self and aroused feelings in me that were long forgotten. I will be rereading it again, and sharing it with my adult kids. Cheryne has packaged in one book what I have been looking for, for most of my adult life."

—JACK KAGAN

"Thank you Cheryne for the wonderful gift that is, *The Courage to be You*. It has to be the most comprehensive yet succinct guide to understanding the process of who am I today based on past experiences and how I can re frame those experiences to become the woman I want to be going forward. I look forward to making *The Courage to be You* my new bedside bible; a gift I can continually refer back to as I continue to learn life through love."

—MYLEE COLLINS

"*The Courage to Be You,* is a book one needs next to your bed and in your bag at all times! Each time life throws one of its curveballs at you, you will certainly find something in this beautifully written inspirational and motivational book to guide you to become a better YOU through love and life. Loved this book. Highly recommended. A 'must have' in your life coaching library! Thank you Cheryne."

—VALMA ZINN

"No matter what others say, you are good enough to be the person you were meant to be. In *The Courage to Be You*, author Cheryne Blom will give you the steps to empower your best self and leave negative thoughts and worries behind. Change begins with you, but a guide is invaluable. Let Blom's practical tips and life stories guide your journey. She's living proof that these ideas work."

—**B. LYNN GOODWIN**, owner of Writer Advice and author of *Never Too Late: From Wannabe to Wife at 62* and *Talent*

"Cheryne has written a guide for the person who is searching for true healing. She has a gift that balances loving guidance with honest self-confrontation. *The Courage to Be You* allows us to challenge our negative core beliefs, explore our authentic self and create a freer, more whole version of the person we are meant to be. On top of that, she gives us a set of tools to keep using on life's journey to maintain our growth. Thank you Cheryne, I will use this guide and share it with anyone who wants to become the best version of themselves they can be!"

—**ANN BILLINGTON**

"I've read many books on my quest for self-improvement and inner-wisdom. Cheryne Blom's *The Courage To Be You* is one that will stay with me for a long time. I felt a new surge of inspiration as I delved deeper into the book. I was reminded of a really important fact. My past doesn't have to define who I am today. It's easy to get sucked back into old mindsets and fears that no longer serve us. Cheryne's easy narration and practical advice have renewed my self-awareness and given me the courage to once again step out of my comfort zone and see the truth of who I am. It is a gifted coach who can teach from the pages of a book. Written with authenticity and speaks to the heart of the reader. I loved this book! I'll be paying it forward to my girlfriends, and my adult daughter."

—**MARCIA ABBOUD**, author of *Every Shitty Thing*

"Cheryne leads the way like a true warrior. Undaunted and unapologetic, she lifts the veil that masks our fears and shows us what could be if only we dare to embrace our true self. After all, fear is a learned behavior and courage is truly a choice that burns deeply within. A highly recommended read if you are committed to living your authentic life."

—JO-ANN LIM

"Cheryne's book *The Courage to be You* is filled with wise words interspersed with practical exercises and narrated through personal experiences, making it a joy to read and an invaluable tool on your own journey of self-discovery. This book is the perfect gift for yourself or a loved one. Thank you Cheryne for this wonderful and insightful book!"

—SYLVIA SCHWALL

"'By allowing ourselves to feel, we enable ourselves to heal.' *The Courage to be You* is a guide to healing and personal transformation. Cheryne offers easy to implement tools to help us move beyond the difficult thoughts and behaviours that hold us back. We all know that vulnerability is key to living an authentically courageous life. But knowing how to be vulnerable and moving beyond our inner limitations is the hard part. This book gives us the how. I will use this book as a personal guide as well as with my coaching clients.

—**SHANNAH KENNEDY,** life strategist. author of
The Life Plan

"Thanks to Cheryne's honesty and vulnerability displayed throughout *The Courage to be You*, I realized that I am not alone in my own personal struggles. I am now aware that my thoughts and fears are normal. Thank you Cheryne for the courage to be me!"

—ANDREA ASH

"*The Courage to be You* is a powerful book. It has helped me understand the deeper meaning, and the 'why' behind subconscious behaviour and conditioned reactions. Cheryne gives realistic advice, as well as clear and practical solutions to universal problems that hold many of us back. Cheryne gained my trust immediately when she wrote of the painful times she encountered in her own life. She showed great strength and courage, and now shares with us the valuable tools she learnt on her path to personal freedom. Cheryne has a powerful voice in her area of expertise and I felt that she was speaking directly to me as I turned each page. After reading *The Courage to be You* I feel that I can live the rest of my life in a more authentic way. I can't wait to hear more from this author."

—LISA BENSON

"*The Courage to Be You* is such a wonderful roadmap to help you discover more about who you really are with all the layers peeled back. It is beautifully written, engaging and delivers a practical way to be the best version of yourself."

—LUCY VAN DER RIET

"Thank you, Cheryne, for creating a book that so gently takes our hand, and navigates us through the challenging steps to unveiling our truest essence. Taking the courage to get rid of our 'goo' is a choice one must make to live a life of true happiness, inner peace and personal freedom. Thank you for explaining this self work process so eloquently in your book—and may you lead many readers to a beautiful journey back to their truest selves."

—NICOLE SALINGER

"Only once in a while do you come across a book that reaches you to the core. It's like Cheryne was inside my head. She understood me in ways the closest to me don't and that helped me rediscover the woman I once was and need to be today. How Cheryne explains, the accurate and brilliant analogies she draws to help the reader get a deeper understanding of her message, is pure gold. Genius in fact."

—**BRIGITTE BENGE**, business coach

"This book has helped me dig deep within myself and articulate those feels and thoughts which are difficult to express. Cheryne had the courage to share her vulnerabilities and her inner demons which gives this book great integrity. Many people will resonate with the feelings and challenges she overcame to become a great example to have the courage to be you.

"When realizing I was not alone to in having these feelings in my own challenges, it kept me engaged in the book in discovering attitudes and angles to commence self-examining and discovering my inner me.

"I realised that by being a people pleaser as my first reaction towards others for most of my life gave me short-term gratification but, in the long term I found it chipped away from my authentic self. I now feel ready to pursue what I want in life without guilt.

"I recommend this read to those who feel they have lost themselves. Understanding that following the truth within you not only creates fulfilment for yourself, but also creates a positive energy around you and uplifts those close to you.

"This is the information people should read and know of in their teenage years and be a reference in their journey of life as a guide to being true to yourself to achieve genuine fulfilment and happiness."

—**LOUIS ANTHONY**

This book is for anyone that wants to press reset and create a new life OR level-up in their current life. Cheryne will be your guide as you muster up the courage to dig deep and strip back the self-limiting beliefs and behaviors that have been holding you back from living your best life. We all have two voices inside and at times it can be hard to decipher which one to listen to. *The Courage To Be You* will not only explain how to decipher the two voices, it will help you discover which voice is your truth. With the help of Cheryne, you will discover how to live life being your truth and as a result feel inner peace and happiness. It is a soul-nourishing read which will give you the tools to make this a reality—LIVING YOUR BEST LIFE. Anything is truly possible if you find the courage to be you!"

—SARAH FINDLAY

"Cheryne manages to beautifully balance storytelling, theory, practical tools and resources in this book, it's all here. Her generosity of spirit in sharing the wisdom in her own story is a gift. She uses delightful analogies to explain complex theories as she gently guides us step by step out of our 'stories' and into our 'bliss.'"

—SUZIE MCMILLAN

"*The Courage to be You* has helped me realise who I am in my feminine essence. I feel I am able to let go of that which no longer serves me and live in my truth."

—ANNE BARNETT

"Authentic happiness. This is a phrase many creatives yearn for, yet spend their lives reaching for, mostly in pain. We just want to be comfortable, rid ourselves of doubt, pity and self-destruction. Cheryne guides you past the confronting reality of our minds to a place where we can 'unstick' ourselves. We can act from love, not fear.

"I am blessed to have met Cheryne at a time of creative ruin. As we delved deep into my purpose, I embraced the soul I am and the only soul I have. I have since published 15 books, authored many and incredibly created and designed them all. That can only come when you put ego aside and you remove self-limiting beliefs.

"There are still moments of fear. But this book, incredibly, and beautifully, has grounded me, once again. I can hear Cheryne's words of reality. Her questioning truths. Her way of reaching into your heart and drawing out who you are meant to be. As I read this book, I had a sense that this was going to be one of those books that redefined the definable; that spoke to thousands, if not millions, to reach higher, to create a better planet.

"And, I was right. As tears of joy fell down my face as I absorbed the depth of her wisdom she was courageous enough to share, I knew that this woman and the space she had created for these words had nailed it.

"This book will shake your core where it needs to be shaken. It will send tendrils of uncertainty while offering up safety. This is your incredible journey. Let Cheryne help you discover how amazing you really are."

—**CLARE MCALANEY**, Create-a-Vision

"Life is full of blissful meaning but most people never discover their life's true meaning and this is unfortunate! There is a solution to this tragedy and, *The Courage To Be You* holds one of the pieces that we all need to properly piece together our life's exciting puzzle. Courage has so many elements but without *The Courage To Be You*, you will live out your entire life as a copy of someone else's dreams rather than being the original you. *The Courage To Be You* helps you to discover your true-self while convincing you not to waste your life's precious time being someone else because if you aren't being you, than who is going to be you? Cheryne's book has the ingredients to help you live on purpose and to cure the debilitating nemesis of fear."

—**ISAAC SAMUEL MILLER**, entrepreneur, author of *Just Get Up: And Manifest Your Inner Genius*, sales coach, motivational speaker, minister, licensed fitness trainer

To Ashleigh, Jason & Jai

The Courage to be You

by Cheryne Blom

© Copyright 2019 Cheryne Blom

ISBN 978-1-63393-846-5

All rights reserved. No part of this publication may be reproduced, stored in a retrieval system, or transmitted in any form or by any means—electronic, mechanical, photocopy, recording, or any other—except for brief quotations in printed reviews, without the prior written permission of the author.

PUBLISHED BY

GRACIOUS COURAGE
PUBLISHING

11 CLARENCE STREET
BENTLEIGH EAST, VICTORIA
AUSTRALIA 3165
WWW.GRACIOUSCOURAGE.COM

THE COURAGE TO BE YOU

CHERYNE BLOM

BENTLEIGH EAST
VICTORIA, AUSTRALIA

TABLE OF CONTENTS

ABOUT THIS BOOK	VIII
INTRODUCTION: Breakdown, Break Free, Breakthrough	1

PART ONE: SELF-REFLECTION — 8

Chapter 1	The Mirror Never Lies	9
Chapter 2	The Two Sides of Self	17
Chapter 3	Shining Light onto Our Blind Spots	26
Chapter 4	The Hidden Agenda of the Ego-Self	35
Chapter 5	The Conditioning of the Ego-Self	41
Chapter 6	The Terms and Conditions of our Self-Worth	52
Chapter 7	The Four Ugly Gremlins	61
Chapter 8	Twelve Self-Defeating Mindsets	69
Chapter 9	The Science of Fear and Stress	77
Chapter 10	Love, Money and Health	83
Chapter 11	Ego Personification	102
Chapter 12	A Summary of the Ego-Self	108

PART TWO: SELF-DISCOVERY — 112

Chapter 13	The Courage to Change	113
Chapter 14	The Art of Letting Go	120
Chapter 15	Three Rules for a Growth Mindset	127
Chapter 16	The Anatomy of the Essence	137
Chapter 17	The Pathway to Essence	149

Chapter 18	Twelve Self-Empowering Mindsets	156
Chapter 19	The Essence of You	161
Chapter 20	Living with Purpose and Passion	181
Chapter 21	The Science of Calm	186
Chapter 22	Embodying the Essence	191
Chapter 23	A Summary of the Essence	196

PART THREE: SELF-MASTERY — 200

Chapter 24	A Delicate Balance	201
Chapter 25	The Happiness Formula	208
Chapter 26	Question 1	213
Chapter 27	Question 2	222
Chapter 28	Question 3	226
Chapter 29	Question 4	230
Chapter 30	Implementing and Practicing the Happiness Formula	237
Chapter 31	My Blessing for You	239
Chapter 32	Additional Resources	242

ABOUT CHERYNE	247
ACKNOWLEDGMENTS	248
PUBLISHIZER PATRON SUPPORT	249

ABOUT THIS BOOK

Who are you?

Who are you *really*?

Beyond the roles you play, beyond the mask you wear, beyond the person you have been conditioned to be, how would you define your authentic self?

When I ask many of my clients this question they answer, "I am me." When I ask, "Well, who is me? How would you define who you really are?" they reply, "I'm not sure—I actually don't know. I don't know how to put that into words. I have never stopped to think about it. I am not sure if who I am is enough."

You may not have thought about that before either, but perhaps you have asked yourself, *Who am I, what is my truth and what is my purpose*? Right now, you may be feeling lost, stuck or frustrated. You may be feeling disappointed because you seem to let yourself down time and time again. You may be exhausted from pleasing everyone around you or comparing yourself to others.

I know those feelings. That is how I felt when I had my breakdown and hit rock bottom. As my knees hit the ground I felt I would never have the life I yearned for. I could not see beyond my negativity and pain.

When I peeled myself off the floor and began my quest of self-discovery, what I learned most of all was this: We are all born with unique virtues that reveal the essence of who we are. You simply need to look into a baby's eyes or watch a young toddler playing to see the purity of their personality. That spark is lost way too soon. And those virtues are the ingredients gifted to us at birth that enable us to actualize our full potential.

There is a moment in time, very early in childhood, when the certainty of our world is threatened. In these moments of shock and confusion, we begin to question ourselves and often develop self-doubt. If we become caught up in that cloud of doubt, we forget who we truly are and become the person other people need us to be, or, more specifically, the person we need to be to fit in or feel accepted. In these moments we develop a 'story of limitation'—a disempowering inner dialogue that keeps us playing small and safe.

My whole life I have felt the existence of these two sides to my personality. As if there were literally two sides to me: one side being truly authentic, a confident, self-assured me, who knows what she wants and what she offers the world in her own unique way; and then a darker side—a side filled with self-doubt and self-pity standing in the way and blocking my greatness.

This duality of being I also observed in many clients I worked with in my life-coaching business. One part of them spoke of their dreams, their vision and a deep desire for happiness and greatness. The other side spoke of their fears, doubts and obstacles holding them back. The latter was influenced by a series of beliefs that limited the way they each perceived themselves and their world.

As we worked through these two contrasting mindsets, they gained greater self-awareness and clarity. They discovered who and what they needed to return to in order to achieve their goals and live their lives with passion and purpose. As we worked through their fears, we cleared out the beliefs that they had absorbed from their childhood. Beliefs that in fact belonged to the people who had the greatest influence on their upbringing. Beliefs that were blocking them and no longer served any purpose. As we challenged their conditioning, we reframed these limiting thoughts into positive and empowering beliefs that would not only support them but also build them into the best version of who they could be. The result: each experienced greater levels of inner peace, personal freedom and authentic happiness.

This book is about helping you return to your essential nature and rediscover your true self—to remember who you are—because your true self harbors your gifts, your talents, your strengths, your creativity, your authenticity, and the unique purpose you hold for this lifetime. You know you are connected to your *essence* when you feel happiness, peace, joy, bliss and personal freedom.

Even though you may not be able to see these aspects of yourself right now, trust that they are there. I have seen this transformation in myself and in hundreds of my clients. I have watched them go from broken to brilliant, from shamed to sensational, and from confusion to clarity.

If you have ever been to a chiropractor, you are familiar with the feeling of being "clicked" into place. Through the stories I share from my own experiences, client anecdotes and practical lessons, and my own formula for personal transformation, I hope to help "click" you back into alignment so that your mind and body no longer hold you in a posture incongruent with your truth. That is exhausting. Once aligned, you will feel reconnected to your internal source of power. From this place of empowerment, you will feel calmness, clarity, and confident courage. In your core you will feel *core-ageous*: the courage to be your core self.

You will learn that your essence is not your conditioned self. It is not self-doubt, self-pity or self-sabotage. It is not your personality or the identity you present to the world. It is not the limiting story narrated by your inner dialogue. It is not judgment or criticism, and it knows no fear. You will reunite with the forgotten parts of your true self that were shut down in the face of fear. This conditioned self develops as a result of trying to be the person we think our environment needs us to be. Once you are aware of these two sides, you have a choice: do you want to be the person who needs to fit in, or do you want to be your own person, and a person with purpose?

This book helps you answer the following questions:

What beliefs are breaking me and what beliefs are building me?

What beliefs belong to me and what beliefs did I take on from my upbringing?

What is at the core of my fear?

How would I define my true self?

How can I stay connected to my true self and maintain a level of empowerment?

How can I trust myself, accept myself and discover my true purpose?

Together we will travel through three stages of growth. I aim to challenge you to move beyond your conditioning, beyond your comfort zone, so that you can rescript your inner dialogue and upgrade the way you perceive your world. We will begin our journey in the space of *self-reflection*, where you can learn how your self-doubt and personal limitations were imprinted, and uncover the core fear of this limited self. We will then move into *self-discovery*, where you will have the opportunity to define who you are as an essence and explore how you can align your thoughts and behavior with your authentic self. This will equip you with the language to express your essence to others. Lastly, we will evolve to *self-mastery*, where you will learn a process for navigating through your fear and negativity, and even maintaining a sense of empowered confidence in those moments that challenge you the most.

You will notice that throughout the book I have included splashes of my own personal story. I hope that by disclosing the most vulnerable aspects of myself, you will be inspired to explore your own sensitive areas. I hope you will learn how to recognize your own *story of limitation* and how to flip from fear into freedom.

With the knowledge of who you are in your essential nature, you will be able to share your truth with the most important people in your life. Your essence will come across in your communication as you will now have the courage to be vulnerable and authentic. You will feel energized by your own enthusiasm and passion. You will feel free because you are doing what makes you happy and what you ultimately want and need. You will have greater self-acceptance, self-belief and self-love. As you ignite your inner light, you will help others ignite their own light. Imagine our world when we are all lit up from within! You can be the game-changer and the way-shower.

Thank you for choosing this book. I acknowledge your bravery in the decision to break free from your past. Change is possible, especially when we are committed to ourselves, our dreams and our growth. Sometimes all we need to know is *how* to make that change. Take my hand and let's dive into your inner world, shed the parts of you no longer needed, and awaken the courage for you to be you.

INTRODUCTION:

BREAKDOWN, BREAK FREE, BREAKTHROUGH

On the eve of my thirty-fourth birthday I had an emotional breakdown. I felt depleted and depressed. My body, once bursting with energy and vitality, had become a shell encasing a numb soul. On the surface, everything appeared perfect. On the inside, I felt as if I was dying.

Honeymoon photos of me and my husband "Shaun" reminded me that, back then, my eyes had sparkled with hope. I had promised myself on my wedding day that I would make this marriage work, even though the night before walking down the aisle I had fought a sickly feeling that this relationship was not right for me. I'd pulled myself together, zipped up the dress I so desperately wanted to show off, and said yes with a torn heart and a half smile.

I was not going to desert a family as my own father had deserted me. I was not going to let people down. My husband Shaun had two children from his first marriage whom I had grown close to. How could I hurt them? I was emotionally invested in this marriage. There was no turning back. My chaotic childhood, disrupted by change and loss, taught me to be adaptable. I believed my ability to bend in order to fit in was one of my greatest strengths. My default was to slip into this mode unconsciously and automatically.

Eight years after our wedding day, I had molded myself into a position I could no longer tolerate. We had two of our own children, a family business, and my dream house. I also had scarred feet from walking on eggshells. All my energy went into trying not to cause another argument. My life felt more like a circus act than the blissful fairy tale of happily ever after. Each day I would paint on a happy face and juggle all my *shoulds*, *musts* and *have-tos*. "I must get dinner on, I have to go and do the pick-up, I should really play with the kids more, I should have sex with him tonight." I had become a well-trained performing people pleaser, putting everyone's needs over my own.

With insomnia keeping me awake into the wee hours of my thirty-fourth birthday, I stared at my eyes in those photographs, hoping they would somehow ignite desire in me once again. Mulling over possible choices, I kept coming back to the decision I knew I had to make. I felt sick at the thought of it. How could I be the one to hurt my family? How could I put myself first? Was that right or wrong or selfish?

I hadn't always been such a pathetic version of myself. There were days when I honored myself and had the courage to go after what I wanted. The shining example that stood out in my mind was when I left my family in South Africa at the age of twenty-one and went to Australia with my fiancé at that time. After our split eighteen months later, I decided to courageously stay on in my new life—alone. I was working on an exciting business idea called GO GIRL CLOTHING. I envisioned a funky clothing range for the sassy girl of the nineties—the girl with attitude! The independence and confidence I felt at the time inspired me to be a role model for other young women. I had a burning desire to contribute to a society hungry for change. From an early age, I knew I wanted to make a difference. And I had been honoring my empowered self until I caught the love bug.

At twenty-four I met beguiling Shaun (tall and charming, built like a rugby player) at a singles party—the Saturday night "find your match" event in the pre-Tinder dating days. He reminded me of the boys I crushed over in high school: the ones who bullied me, teased me and used me sexually, and the ones I thought a girl like me would never win. Our instant attraction aroused a deep craving within me. He said he loved me. I desperately wanted "us" to work. I gave up everything. It was the least I could do for him.

Shortly after we met, I shelved my business plan and joined him in his business. Spellbound, my independence quickly turned to neediness. And instead of pursuing my passionate purpose, I did everything I could to enable and support *him*. I thought I was on the path to what I wanted, but I was, in fact, on a total detour from my own truth. I was a million miles south of who I knew I could be and wanted to be. My thoughts were frazzled as I rushed from role to role—mother, stepmother, housewife, business partner. An inner restlessness pushed through my fatigue. My short temper distracted me from my frustration. Where had my "go-girl" gone?

The truth is my bliss bubble with Shaun popped a year after our wedding when I was pregnant with our first child. By that stage I was already entrenched in martyrdom, immersed in the family business, caring for my stepsons, taking care of a household, and adjusting to the hormonal changes pregnancy brings. I could no longer give him the attention he needed, especially sexually, and he was quick to express his disapproval. At the beginning of my final month of pregnancy, I woke up one morning to find the whole right side of my face paralyzed. My first thought was that I had been bitten by a spider, but it wasn't that simple. I was diagnosed with Bell's palsy, a virus that attacks a nerve in the face. Looking in the mirror at my lopsided face, I thought, *Oh my God, am I going to be like this forever? I am a monster.* What a great way to introduce myself to my first child.

My body was trying to get my attention, but I was too numb and disconnected to listen. It took almost two years to recover. However, with the birth of my daughter, my confidence grew. I suddenly had a clear identity: I was Ashleigh's mum. But still, it was easier for me to submit than to argue. As the days and months turned into years I thought about leaving so many times. But when our son Jason was born five years later, I convinced myself that I had to stay for the sake of my children.

Everyone else's happiness was more important than mine—my kids', friends', family's and customers' happiness all counted for more than mine. Seeing their contentment validated me and made me worthy. But the daily hustle masked a loneliness whose whispering voice began to amplify in the silent hours as my household slept.

My body held onto excess pounds of post-baby weight as fuel so I could deal with the busy chaos of life. My joints were swollen with repressed anger and unexpressed words. I had learned to avoid disturbing the peace at all costs. In an argument, I would shut down rather than stand up for myself. The pain of Shaun's backlash was far greater than that of not speaking up.

My mind often replayed one of our most tumultuous arguments, an argument that took place shortly after Ashleigh's arrival. It was a chaotic day in our gift-basket business. I was in charge of sales, overseeing production, sourcing products offshore, managing local suppliers and much more. I pretty much ran the business on my own. That day we were on a tight deadline and everyone was tense. On my way out to see a major customer, I left instructions for a newly recruited factory assistant to wrap the pallets. I arrived back in the factory a few hours later to mayhem.

"Shaun is looking for you," Rosie, one of the production girls, muttered without looking up from her work. The next moment Shaun stormed through the building like a hurricane. He was in my face, virtually frothing at the mouth.

"What the fuck were you thinking?" he barked. "How could you be so stupid?" I stared at him, shell-shocked. All I could hear was something about the pathetic way the pallets had been wrapped. I was conscious of the production team watching us. Sandy, our youngest team member, ran out, shaken by the violence of his attack on me. His rant over, Shaun torpedoed out the way he came in. Feeling like a scolded child, I gazed at my team in humiliation, then ran to my desk and cried. Perhaps it was the stress, perhaps it was the embarrassment or the injustice or the disrespect, but this episode represented hundreds of other small lashings that were building up within me and breaking my spirit.

A few days later, I packed a small suitcase, put Ash in the car, and drove off. With no extended family to run to and too much pride to turn to friends, I returned a few hours later like a naughty, contrite puppy, apologizing, of course. I suffered through many similar arguments in silence. I was like a trapped circus animal, surrendering to my master. Some nights my despair was so dark I would pray to God to take me. People often die spontaneously. Why couldn't I? As each night passed, I continued to lose my strength. As my mid-life crisis drew closer, I could only see two choices ahead of me: death or divorce.

In the midst of my darkness, the universe sent me a catalyst. A man I worked with began to flirt with me. Our attraction stirred a stagnant life force deep within me. My feelings toward him highlighted the emptiness in my marriage. My cells tingled with desire. Was it possible for me to put my own needs first? I was torn. It was easier to wrap myself in despair than make a decision.

Then came the night that changed everything. Two months after my thirty-fourth birthday, I was woken up at the ethereal hour of 2 a.m. by what felt like a cosmic slap. I sensed a higher presence shaking me from my slumber. I sat up, suddenly awake. One word instructed my next movements: "Enough!"

I went straight to my study and searched for an apartment online. I submitted an application then and there, and moved out of our family home one week later. I took only the necessities my two children and I needed. Eight boxes. No more. *A light ship can weather any storm*, I remember thinking.

I will never forget my first night of freedom in what my daughter called our "little cave." I lay in a fetal position on my borrowed mattress, weeping as if my body was purging years of pent-up anger, frustration, loneliness, disappointment and sadness. As I let go, I felt a release and a space opening within me. In the silence and solitude, I suddenly saw the parts of me that had been lost in the chaos. Now I wanted my confidence back. I wanted to regain my courageous edge and rekindle my passion for life.

But I also wanted to understand why I had lost it in the first place. What was it that made me lose my power to a man?

My new "single life" offered quiet space to self-reflect and feel my pain. Instead of running from my emotions, I faced my wounds. As if I were a surgeon slicing into my pain, I discovered scar tissue left from childhood trauma. My father's abandonment when I was nine years old was still raw. The years of humiliation at Shaun's hands had deepened the wound of my perceived worthlessness. But this time of my life could not be about a man. I had to attend to my pain and ensure I did not repeat the same mistakes.

Although in those first few months of separation I pined for my children on the days they were with their father, divorce offered me the gift of me time. I returned to my deepest passion—studying human behavior. I had my bachelor's degree in psychology, but in my twenty-one-year-old haste to go where my man went, I had become busy in my Australian life and never furthered my studies.

Looking back, I see that the hiatus was perfectly timed. While I was drowning in family and business commitments, healing modalities such as life coaching, positive psychology, neuro-linguistic programming and mindfulness took off in a big way. I had needed to wait for the right time to reenter the education sector. Perhaps, too, I had needed to suffer more myself in order to be able to understand and guide others.

What I realize now that I did not know then is that I was being groomed. It was as if the higher presence that lifted me out of my slumber the night I decided to leave my marriage had heard my prayers and was responding. "Death and divorce" were apparently not my only options. My whispering voice of guidance was preparing me for the next, most important stage of my life.

As if the hands of my broken compass had returned to north, I was put back on the path my soul wanted most: the path of purpose. I had no idea at the time that this experience, which felt like rock bottom, would become the foundation of all my life's work in the years to come.

*"I am trying to free your mind, Neo.
But I can only show you the door.
You're the one that needs to walk through it."*

The Matrix

PART ONE: SELF REFLECTION

Authentic happiness is not for chicken shits.

Authentic happiness is not for the faint-hearted, nor for the ones who wish to stay in their comfort zone. It takes immense courage to *sculpt yourself happy*.

Experiencing this happiness requires a desire to take control of yourself and your life and let go of whatever is preventing you from experiencing peace, freedom, bliss and empowerment. The resultant transformation and change will include moments of discomfort and vulnerability and even pain. And there may be tears. And that is all okay.

Pain is a signal that highlights where change is needed. Pain tells the body that something is wrong; it forces us to listen. Pain lets us know where we are out of alignment. Pain forces us to stop and question and begin a search for meaning. Pain is necessary.

For the explorers brave enough to dive into the waters of uncertainty, authentic happiness requires the ability to step into your inner world and search out patterns of behavior that stem from fear. Developing this ability will enable you to break the habits that no longer serve you.

This courageous artistry begins with *self-reflection*, the ability to step into a *mindful* mindset and observe your internal landscape with compassion, acceptance and a desire to change and grow.

Self-reflection involves turning the lens through which you view the world inward, and asking yourself key questions to activate new levels of awareness. Without awareness, you will continue to run on autopilot, oblivious to what is motivating you and confused about where your life is heading.

- *Who are you?*
- *How have you become the* you *you are today?*
- *What do you truly desire?*
- *What obstacles stand in your way?*
- *What does it really mean for you to reach your full potential?*

We will explore these questions and many others through the pages of this book!

CHAPTER 1

THE MIRROR NEVER LIES

*"Mirrors reflect back to us our feelings about ourselves.
They show us clearly the areas to be changed
if we want to have a joyous, fulfilling life."*

Louise Hay

I stared into my own eyes, dumbfounded, searching for answers.

Did I seriously let this happen to me again? My teary eyes stared back at me as I reflected on the destructive intent of my continued self-sabotage. There was nowhere left to hide. The mirror never lies.

Mirror work was a new self-help tool I was committed to, an essential daily habit I learned through the teachings of Louise Hay. Mirror work involves standing in front of the mirror for a few moments each day and noting the thoughts and feelings that arise as you gaze into your eyes. Instead of running, you face the truth of your feelings and listen to your self-talk so you can attend to the parts of you that need healing.

My personal growth became my focus as I settled into separated life: not only was I learning how to be a life coach and empower people, I was working with healers to empower myself and dissolve patterns of behavior that no longer suited the person I was growing into.

A tsunami of tears had swept through my first few months of solitude, uprooting emotions and feelings lying dormant in the soil of my being. A storm of that magnitude clears a path for new life, and with each tear I shed a part of myself that I no longer needed and hadn't realized was holding me back. Years of suppressed anger and unexpressed needs floated to the surface to purify me so I could be present to the next chapter of my life. With each tear, I released an inauthentic part that belonged to the person who wanted to please rather than be a person with purpose.

Meeting "Mr. Catalyst" helped me make the decision to leave my marriage, and although he disappeared out of my life as fast as he came in, he served his purpose: to get me out of there so I could start living my truth!

As the tides of the ocean move, so did my moods ebb and flow. "High tide" brought days of anxiety, emotional restlessness, tears, uncertainty and confusion. "Low tide" brought calm clarity.

Eighteen months of separation helped me gain new levels of self-awareness. There was a visible contrast between who I had been in my marriage and who I was in my new single life. I was learning what I needed to thrive. I sifted out friendships that were draining me, and focused on building my own business, eating well, exercising, enjoying my kids, and surrounding myself with positivity. My body effortlessly dropped twenty pounds of weight. It was as if, in married life, I had puffed up in a shroud of self-protection. Being on my own allowed me to manage my energy more effectively and ensure I was not taking on anyone else's stuff.

I had a new rule for myself. All I had to do was be fully present to the opportunities in front of me, follow my intuition, and choose what felt right for me. This rule helped me transform and avoid repeating past patterns. My past insecurities belonged to the old me. I had grown. I now understood my essence and my purpose in this lifetime.

The day I opened my full-time coaching practice was, besides the birth of my children, the most fulfilling day of my life. I did it! Miraculously, everything had lined up to support my move. Our family business was sold and purchased by a close friend from my twenties. They employed me to run it and Shaun was not to be a part of it. This blessing gave me the first step toward financial independence. I was able to earn my own money for the first time since my single days and finally make my own choices, which included studying life coaching.

My career split into two possible pathways: one offering the comfort of a paycheck and one speaking to a deeper calling from within. Once

I received my divorce settlement, I made the bold decision to leave the business and take my life-coaching business (and my two clients) full time. *Build and they will come,* I thought.

Diane, a massage therapist and new friend, invited me to take a look at the space she worked from. As I stood in the empty office, the buzz up my spine told me it was mine. I signed a lease on the spot. Some called it insanity; I knew it as inspiration.

I flourished until I was introduced to what I now know was my next soul challenge.

On my kid-free weekends, as if I were reliving my twenties, I would join friends at a trendy bar. On this particular day I had my hair and makeup done and was feeling confident. As my girlfriend and I walked into the bar, there was my warrior.

He stood out like Thor. Tall, blond and chiseled. A dynamic presence. With cells tingling and heart skipping a beat I called upon my newfound confidence and initiated a conversation.

I became fascinated by his journey. He had battled through the war zone of drug addiction, come out the other side, and had opened his own rehabilitation center. As if we had danced many lifetimes together, we connected quickly.

Intoxicated, we jumped in like two hungry addicts devouring a fix. He moved in to my apartment and our lives became enmeshed. As a sort of social experiment we decided to abstain sexually for our first three months together. We were curious to explore how a relationship could build without sexual influences. Intuitively, together we discovered what we later found out to be Tantra: the sacred union of two souls joining through the heart. The most breathtaking occurrences began to take place. With my Thor, I experienced a multitude of spiritual awakenings.

One exercise we found was to sit very closely, place a hand on each other's heart, and stare into each other's eyes. At first we giggled like school kids! It was so hard to focus and not feel self-conscious. But as we continued, we lost ourselves in the stare, which took us into a deep meditative state. In this altered state of consciousness, I connected with him on a soul level. Memories of what felt like past lifetimes flashed through my mind. It felt as if we had spent many lifetimes together in different forms to enable each other to learn our highest lessons. I dreamed of us working together, traveling the world as inspirational speakers, empowering people with our spiritual insights.

Throughout these months of connection, the voice of my intuition screamed at me. "Something doesn't feel right! Remember how far you have come and that your life is now about you and being true to yourself. Don't make it about a man. Don't lose your focus."

My intuition had emerged soon after I separated. She awoke from her slumber the moment I decided to stop putting other people in front of my own needs. She had been buried under my fear of being selfish and letting everyone down. The more I learned to choose me, the more I heard her voice.

She tried so desperately to keep me centered, but there was still a void. There was still a hunger within me searching for ways to satisfy a deeper craving. Her guidance did not offer any fun, so I was lured into the adventure.

Feeling wanted by this new man stirred up deep cravings. I felt nudgings from my "wise woman" as she reminded me that I had turned my back on her once before, but my inner need was overwhelming. Instead of honoring myself, I moved to needing him and pleasing him. By putting him first, I lost myself . . . yet again.

We celebrated our three months of celibacy in Byron Bay, Australia's spiritual center. The moment we had sex everything shifted. As if we had broken the purity of our connection, unresourceful behavior patterns returned in both of us. I felt myself slipping back into the patterns of the codependent people pleaser, needing him and wanting to put him first. The Thor mask he showed the world began to slip.

He was not sober and began to disappear for days on end. He had also lied to me about his own marriage breakdown. To this day I still do not know the truth. I was compassionate about his drug addiction, but his lies and deceit poked at pain trapped in my emotional scars.

Three months after our Byron trip, we decided to split. I stood staring into my own eyes in the mirror, desperate for answers. With my hands pressed against the glass, I leaned into my reflection, getting as close as I could. I searched within the shades of blue as if they were mysterious oceans. What was at the heart of this craving and need? Why was it still robbing me of my strength? It was hard to endure my own reflection. Discomfited by my inner bitch and her critical disgust, I turned away to pick up my phone and listen to my voicemail.

"I'll be there at five to pick up my shit," his voice said for the twenty-seventh time. Did I somehow think that everything would suddenly change on the next redial? And why on earth was I still listening? I turned back to the mirror. I now stood about a foot away from my reflection so I could see all of me.

As I searched for guidance, my mind and heart were at loggerheads, and two voices spoke to me. The pathetic, needy me groveled for love, and my wise woman tenaciously held onto my power. Now I was being put to the test. Would I revert back to my old ways or stand in my power?

"I'll wait for him outside. When we see each other, everything will go back to normal," Pathetic Me justified.

"I can't believe you are going to forgive him!" Wise Woman exclaimed. "He's lied to you, he's hurt you more than you have ever been hurt before. I can't believe you would even consider it. Please think of yourself."

"I need him. I want him. I don't want to be alone. I'm happiest when I'm loved by a man," Pathetic Me begged.

"That sort of happiness is self-betrayal."

"I want to honor myself here, I want to put myself first, but how can I let go of this desperate need in me?" I anguished.

"You need to love yourself more than you need him to love you," Wise Woman said.

Ouch. Those words hit home. I repeated them in my mind. *Love yourself more than you need him to love you.* I needed to let that one simmer.

My mind felt as if it was going to explode. I knew what I needed to do: Take this basket of his clothes, still smoking from me ripping them off the hangers, and leave it on the front porch. Switch off my phone, get into bed, and hide under my blankets.

My life was not just about me anymore. I was a single mother with a practice full of clients, and both roles required me to be the best version of myself. My self-discoveries would not only heal me but would also help my children and my clients to discover the tools to greater happiness and empowerment. I knew that the lessons I was searching for would ultimately lead to my breakthrough.

I desperately wanted to understand this internal contradiction. It was not only my battle. I witnessed my clients struggle with this same issue. I had to understand why we thrived in certain areas of life and repeated patterns of chaos in others.

I reflected on a client who was recently promoted to train other managers in her field. She spoke of how she felt loved and supported by her husband and her family, but as soon as she got in front of a group of managers, her nerves took over and she would lose her focus and often her voice. I reflected on another client who achieved success in her career but could not say no to anyone or create any personal or professional boundaries. She found herself people-pleasing to the point where she would burn out and collapse in a state of overwhelm. Why do we lose our power? What motivates this internal conflict?

I wanted to break up with not only every man who had hurt me in the past, but also the part of me that had let them in. I had to get to the core of the issue. If I could transform myself, I could transform others. If I could shed this part of myself, I would be living proof that true empowerment is possible.

Cradled by my wise woman, I summoned all the strength in me and dumped his belongings on my front porch. Then I collapsed into bed. Enough was enough! I did not split up my family to get myself into another pathetic mess. Perhaps sleep would give me clarity. And it did.

A gentle whisper woke me as dawn broke. Scrambling through the drawer of my bedside table, I searched for a pen and paper. I had to capture what was in my head. I felt as if I was receiving a download of information, a transmission of insight that would answer my questions.

No lights, a blunt pencil and my journal caught an internal monologue of inspiration:

> *There is only one toxin in the world. And it is not what people think. It is not drugs, nor alcohol, nor chocolate, nor coffee . . . This toxin is blocking us and creating darkness and despair . . . It is like a black cloud that enters the natural effervescent bubble of our being. As we let it in, it seeps into our Essence and clouds our clarity, leaving us feeling heavy. It depletes our energy and lowers our vibration. It leaves us feeling depressed, anxious, restless and stressed. It drains our self-belief and pollutes the purity of our thoughts. It fills us with self-pity, self-doubt and self-sabotage.*
>
> *As we let this toxin into our consciousness, it takes over our perception of reality. We lose ourselves in this intoxicated state and forget who we truly are.*
>
> *It has created damage and destruction in our world. It has*

caused unrest, fighting and war. It feeds off our insecurities and demands power. Like a parasite draining its host, it weakens the body and shakes us to the very core of our being.

This inner leech is often hidden under layers of self-protection. Most people are unaware of this intoxicated state. Most people blame something outside of themselves as the core of their stress or power loss, but it is this internal substance that is weakening mankind.

This toxin causes a split in personalities. Because we forget our truth, we develop a persona to mask our pain. It is what fuels the ego-self.

This toxin that exists within each one of us is fear. Fear is at the root of addiction, sadness, depression, anxiety and chaos. People need to learn how to let go of fear if they are to change their thinking. A pure mind will create a pure heart, and a pure heart experiences personal freedom and empowerment.

As an agent of transformation, my role is to help people gain self-awareness and recognize the fear within them. Once they notice the effects of fear, they can detach and purify themselves from this inner poison. And in this awakened state they will find their purpose and live courageous lives.

I fell back onto my pillow and let the steam of these words sizzle through me. Fear. Yes, fear was draining me. Fear was leading me to need a man. Fear was in the heart of Pathetic Me. Fear clouded the clarity of her truth and weakened her self-esteem. It stripped her self-respect and dignity and led her to be the person she thought she needed to be rather than her authentic self.

But what was this fear really about? How did it come to be, and how can we purify ourselves of this toxin? These questions and many more ignited a fire in my belly to travel into the heart of fear and deconstruct this crippling emotion.

I had been called to attention and I was listening. I mind-mapped the threads of insight I had received. Ego, essence, fear and purpose were the components that stood out to me the most. How did they piece together?

I have since spent over a decade observing and researching fear, and have woven my findings into the tapestry of thoughts I offer you in this book. The upcoming chapters present a model of transformation, designed to help you break up with the part of you standing in the way of your full potential. Together, we will journey into the space of self-reflection where you will gain new levels of awareness. We will detox your mind and body from fear and discover a pure essence that has been patiently waiting for your return. As you reconnect with the natural state of your being, you will discover your authentic virtues—virtues that enable you to be the best version of you.

So sit down and buckle up as we dive into the core of your fear, turn it into blazing courage, and activate your true life purpose!

CHAPTER 2

THE TWO SIDES OF SELF

There is an ancient Cherokee parable that describes an internal battle we all experience. A grandfather is teaching his grandson about life. "There is a fight going on inside me," he says. "It is the same fight that is happening in you and inside every person too. It is a fight between two wolves. One is dark and evil. He feels anger, disappointment, hatred, self-pity, self-loathing, resentment, guilt, embarrassment, pride. The other is light and good. He feels peace, love, faith, trust, belief, kindness, empathy, compassion, gratitude, benevolence, humility, grace, truth and joy."
The boy turned to his wise elder and asked, "Which wolf will win?"
His grandfather answered, "The one you feed."

I was driven to make sense of the guidance I received about the toxicity of fear. As an agent of transformation, I made the commitment to be a courageous coach. This meant having the courage to take people into the depths, into the most vulnerable parts of themselves. I would travel with them to the core of their unconscious world, as if we were deep-sea explorers searching uncharted waters, and help them identify fears hidden beyond their blind spots so they'd be able to discover the thought patterns holding them back from achieving their deepest desires. This awareness would offer them the first step toward realizing their life goals and ultimately achieving greater happiness, fulfillment, inner peace, purposefulness and personal freedom.

Each client had a personal catalyst for investing in self-development.

Some were stuck in an unhappy relationship; others lacked direction and focus, could not find a partner, or suffered from anxiety and depression. Their stories mirrored my own struggles, so I listened to them with empathy. As clients entrusted me with their thoughts, my senses sharpened. I noticed recurring themes and recognized the same story in different bodies. Our conversations took on a recognizable pattern.

Almost each coaching conversation began with this cry: "I am so stressed out! I need calm! I want to change things, but I don't know how." Each client had his or her own stress triggers, be they children, partner, work, finances, friends, health or parents.

We began to explore this stress, and their thoughts and feelings. I noticed that while they were aware of their emotions, many did not recognize what triggered their emotional reactions. Instead of blaming the external stress trigger, I guided our conversations inward, aiming to unravel what was at the root of their distress.

This process involved taking them back through the layers of their awareness to what was stored in the "cave" of their unconscious. As we journeyed through their internal landscape toward the source of pain, we stumbled upon a divided belief system, a "circuit room" with various "compartments" containing beliefs that built them and beliefs that broke them. The latter limiting beliefs revealed emotional wounds. These wounds, not the stressor, instigated an emotional reaction.

One client, for example, spoke of her husband being the source of her anxiety. "He will be the death of me!" she cried. "He is so selfish, always doing what he wants and never wanting to spend time together."

"How is his behavior making you feel *about yourself*?" I asked.

"It makes me feel hurt and frustrated," she said.

"And how do *those* feelings make you feel?" I inquired, gently taking her deeper into a more vulnerable compartment.

"It makes me afraid that he doesn't love me," she sobbed.

Below that fear we discovered a belief she had not been consciously aware of: the belief that she was not lovable.

Almost all client conversations arrived at a similar destination. I saw three distinct limiting beliefs planted in the unconscious mind of each client: *I am not loved, I am not good enough,* and/or *I am not worthy.* These beliefs also showed up in a blended form, such as the belief "I am not good enough to be loved" or "I am not worthy of being loved."

Having learned how the unconscious mind automatically governs

95 percent of our behavior, I realized that these beliefs and the wounds they cause are at the core of disempowerment. I was quickly reminded of the cosmic guidance I received. These three beliefs represent the toxin of fear "blocking us and creating darkness and despair." They are toxic seeds buried in the soil of our being and taint the way we see the world. Imagine placing a tinted filter on a camera. This filter would distort the view of the lens. Instead of seeing an object clearly, the world would appear darker, duller. Think of the filters we play with on social media websites: we can Photoshop an image with a filter to enhance the image or completely change it. By doing so, we distort the viewer's perception.

These three beliefs of not being loved, worthy or good enough in turn distort our view of the world around us. We do not see the world as it objectively is; instead, we see a distorted world. My client's *belief* filtered the way she viewed her husband's behavior. Because she did not believe she was loveable, she *needed* her husband to love her. When he did not want to spend time with her, she felt hurt and frustrated. As we enhanced her feelings of self-worth and replaced her "not-worthy filter" with a "self-love filter," she began to feel less needy, more independent, and more empowered to pursue her own interests and fulfill herself rather than being totally dependent on him meeting her needs.

These three beliefs metastasize just as a tumor does. They spread into other areas of our lives, controlling how we construct our identity. We therefore become the person we believe we need to be in order to prove our worth, feel loved or feel good enough.

The more we reinforce this identity, the more we come to believe it is our real self, and the more we lose touch with our authentic self. We forget that we have resources and beliefs designed to help us navigate challenges and build our potential, and instead, we become fixated on limiting beliefs.

With an improved filter, clients have been able to reconnect with their dreams, desires, creativity, and passion, and, in turn, activate their life purpose. My role became crystal clear: If I helped people to eliminate the clouds of fear, they would be able to actualize this potential. They could return to their authentic self and be the best version of who they were born to be.

I became as curious about this empowered dimension as I was about the limiting part. I began to understand that the personality could be viewed as having two distinct aspects. When these two parts are well integrated, we function successfully. When they become disconnected through the process of forgetting our *authentic self*, we experience internal conflict.

One of those parts is fear-driven, while the other is trusting. One is stuck in self-doubt while the other flourishes with self-belief. One is our lower self and the other is our higher self. These two sides of the self explain why we thrive in some areas of life and struggle in others. My battle between "Pathetic Me" and "Wise Woman" is a good example of how I expressed those two aspects.

THE ESSENCE OF SELF

The authentic side of self is our *essence*. It is the essential nature of who we are. It holds the blueprint of our true self, and offers an understanding of our unique strengths, values and individual purpose. Our essence is our inner knowing of who we are and what we require to be happy. It is our wise self.

Imagine a curious child exploring the world with zest and vitality. A child does not necessarily think but rather feels its way through the world with a sense of joy and enthusiasm. Children are free-spirited and playful. Their goal is fun, lightness and laughter. Likewise, our essence is curious about the world. It is wired for happiness and is in search of personal freedom.

The "anatomy" of the essence is trust, belief and faith. When we experience a feeling of freedom, we know we are connected to our essence. Our essence has its own inner compass that directs us through the voice of our intuition. When we are connected and listening to our intuition, we are guided to what makes us truly happy. The essence has a deep desire to share its gifts and individuality with openness and grace.

My inner wise woman is how my essence expresses itself. Her voice guides me to stay true to myself. She is the voice of my personal power. When I listen to my essence, I am drawn to my true path and feel a sense of calm, confident freedom. This sense of bliss affirms my decision to honor myself.

We will delve into the essence in greater detail in the second part of this book, where we will discuss how to connect with and define your essence, the part of you that holds the key to your freedom.

THE EGO-SELF

The *ego* has long been a central theme in the study of human behavior. Many experts have offered descriptions and definitions of this complex aspect of our character. Sigmund Freud, the father of psychotherapy, explained that the ego is formed as we begin to interact with and make sense of our outside world. It is necessary to ensure our survival. Carl Jung saw the ego as the conscious awareness of our existence. He believed the ego could be viewed as a hero on a journey to find its best self, a process he named *individuation*. Eric Erickson said the ego's responsibility is to form our identity. Buddhist psychology explains the ego as "the mind creating a story about itself and how it relates to the world." Spiritual leaders such as Deepak Chopra define the ego as our self-image—the mask we wear. Eckhart Tolle defines the ego as a dysfunctional relationship with the present moment.

My explanation of the ego is an eclectic combination of these various schools of thought. My focus is on how fear affects the ego and disrupts its full potential. Let me offer you my take on this complex "compartment" of our humanness.

Structurally speaking, the ego is the part of our mind and nervous system that is constantly searching for meaning. It judges, analyzes and assesses our environment to ensure we are safe. Just as the spines of a sea urchin constantly monitor its environment, so too does our ego aim to protect us from any possible threat. Once the ego has identified a threat, it will create defense mechanisms to protect itself from danger. The meanings our ego attaches to events become an internal story that the ego tells itself over and over. This story is known as our internal dialogue.

Problems arise when we identify with these stories and hold them as absolute truths. Once we attach meanings to any object or situation, we form beliefs and attitudes that establish our mindset. This mindset affects how we feel. Instead of perceiving the world objectively, the ego clouds itself with thoughts tainted by fear. This fearful ego mindset is what I call the **EGO-SELF**. It strives for safety but with a distorted perspective of itself that complicates matters. We will explore this ego-self in the first section of this book, our goal being to see the world through a clearer, less scary lens.

The ego-self is created in childhood the moment we feel threatened by our outside world. A significant emotional event—a new sibling arriving, a parent yelling at us, a kid on the playground saying something mean, a teacher humiliating us in the front of the class—shakes the certainty of the essence and we begin to feel alienated from our environment. These significant emotional events imprint our belief system, thus forming our conditioned self. They are as impactful as a meteorite crashing to earth.

This imprint wounds the emotional body and leaves a trail of pain. Fear, therefore, can be understood as the body's memory of pain. Where the essence is wired for happiness, the ego is designed to conceal pain and keep us safe. As our ego-self starts to question itself and the world around it, we forget who we really are and get stuck in the pain of that emotion. Our personality modifies itself as a means of self-protection.

Imagine the essence as a pure and effervescent bubble of energy floating high in the sky—light and free, in full expression. Now imagine a fearful thought as black goo (let's call it e-goo). Every time we perceive a threat and feel fear, we let this e-goo into our clear consciousness. The purity of our consciousness becomes clouded and its lightness denser, as if a tinted filter is applied to our perceptual lens. This filter changes our perceptions of the world and affects our own sense of identity. The more impure our bubble, the greater the darkness. Instead of floating light and free, our bubble becomes heavy and shrinks. Clarity becomes confusion, expression becomes depression, and greatness becomes smallness.

Without interference, the essence will blossom into full expression and greatness. But it is dependent on the soil it grows in. When that soil is lacking in nutrition (unsupportive, scary, barren), the ego develops protective layers, blending, adapting and molding itself to fit into its environment. Like chameleons, we learn to survive instead of thrive.

There are amazing animal adaptations that demonstrate the power of self-protection under threat. The hairy frog of Central America cracks its own bones, shoves them through its feet and grows claws to attack predators. An opossum has an involuntary mechanism enabling it to play dead and release a foul-smelling odor. A basilisk lizard can run along water for twenty meters before sinking, and the mimic octopus can take on fifteen different forms of marine life in a bid to protect itself.

We too develop adaptations that alter the blueprint of our essence. We adapt to our environment, which means becoming the person we "need to be" in order to feel safe, rather than continuing to confidently express our essence, which is striving for happiness. This process of adaptation is called *conditioning*. We become conditioned to think and behave according to a certain set of "rules" influenced by society. This process of conditioning leads to a sort of forgetting of who we truly are. We think that who we are is the identity we reveal to the world, evident in our choices and behavior. We think this is our truth. However, this conditioned ego-self is a false self. It is an adapted version of our essence. When we become aware of another way of being, we can challenge our *e-goo-ic* ways.

By rediscovering and reconnecting with our essence, we begin to find our way back to the light of who we are.

THE DUALITY AND INTEGRATION

The difference between the ego and the essence can be likened to an onion and a lily. The onion originates from the same family as the lily, so in its origin it holds the same potential and beauty. It is an inspiring paradox to observe how something so pungent can have emerged from the same source as something so sweet.

The onion develops hard layers around its core. Cutting through the tight, protective layers that enclose its center releases the onion's pungency and literally brings us to tears.

Alternatively, the lily develops beautiful, sweet-smelling petals that open as they receive light. These petals, like the layers of the onion, enclose a sensitive core, yet the lily's intention is to open and reveal rather than to close and protect.

Classical yoga philosophy defines the word *yoga* as a union or act of conscious connection. This beautiful philosophy highlights the intention of our two sides. They are not supposed to be in conflict. They are supposed to function as two opposing forces that seek balance and integration. At least two elements are required to achieve balance.

Our basic goal is to integrate these two sides through a purification of the ego-self. When we clear ourselves of the fearful, limiting beliefs tainting our perceptions, we can then view the world through the lens of the essence. This process is both transformational and very healing because, as we let go of the emotional pain blocked in the body, we reclaim the forgotten parts of our authentic self and become whole again. Our purpose, therefore, is not to eliminate the ego because it is a necessary part of our being. We need the discernment of the ego for our survival. But there is a difference between caution and fear. Fear is disabling, whereas caution alerts us to possible threats and helps us seek solutions to minimize risk.

When the ego-self and essence are in conflict, we experience chaos, a battle between the head and the heart. When they are in harmony we experience calm. When they are out of accord—when the heart says one thing and the mind says another—we feel an internal split that causes turbulence and restlessness. This internal wobble creates tension and an inner struggle that we label stress, depression, or anxiety.

We need both these forces to thrive, so it's important to learn how to integrate them. "Teach the heart to think and the mind to feel," my spiritual teacher, "Eagle," once said. As we begin to see how our daily challenges and conflicts serve us, we effectively open our minds to appreciation and our hearts to a thoughtful response. We are truly "dancing with duality." When integrated, when the mind is *feeling* and the heart is *thinking*, the ego serves us in a positive way; confidence and clarity return when we purify the ego of its fearfulness.

Metaphysics describe the ego as a servant obeying our dominant thought. When we indulge our limited fearful beliefs, the ego must carry out those beliefs. However, when we produce healthy and resourceful beliefs such as the following, our ego can express itself by carrying these beliefs out:

- I was born to serve the world in a great way.
- I have everything within me to survive and thrive in my world.
- I will always land on my feet; everything will always work out as it needs to.
- I am a good person who can make a difference.
- I am able to express my thoughts and creativity openly and honestly.
- I can move with the changes of life because I know there is a plan for me.
- I am human; I will not always be right or know everything because I am constantly growing.
- I empower my life one thought at a time.
- I am strategic and organized with my goals and desires.
- The more I learn, the more confident I become.
- I am curious to know the truth. I never assume.
- I endeavor to always be grateful for everything in my life.

The first step toward self-empowerment is an awareness of these two sides of ourselves: the ego-self, often creating an inner struggle and story of disempowerment, and the essence, creating lightness, inner freedom, peace and enlightenment. In fact, we need this duality because we cannot find our light *in the light*. We find our light (our power and our truth) in the contrasting field of darkness. It is an intriguing paradox of the universe.

From this crossroad we are left with a choice: to express our ego or our essence

Whichever story we engage with will determine the choices we make and the actions we take. If we attach to fear, we will experience a fearful reality. If we attach to our authentically confident self, we will experience an empowered reality. The story we buy into represents the wolf we are feeding.

How was your ego-self conditioned, and what safety habits have you created to adapt to your environment? Let's dive deeper.

CHAPTER 3

SHINING LIGHT ONTO OUR BLIND SPOTS

"The greatest hunger in life is not for food, money, success, status, security, sex, or even love from the opposite sex . . . The deepest hunger in life is a secret that is revealed only when a person is willing to unlock the hidden part of the self."

Deepak Chopra

The process of self-reflection can be broken down into two steps: *self-inquiry* and *self-awareness*. Self-inquiry is about knowing how to question ourselves so that we penetrate more deeply into our unconscious world. Achieving that level of awareness helps us move beyond our blind spots and emotional blocks. We can peel away the layers of our emotional onion that have been holding us tightly in order to protect us. If we want to achieve sustainable healing, we need to get to the core of our emotional makeup. As we ask questions, we gain new levels of self-awareness, such as how we have been conditioned to become who we are today.

We delve into our emotional layers with the purpose of finding the three toxic beliefs that taint our ego-self. Most of us realize we are experiencing stress, but in the majority of cases we are unaware of the fears that perpetuate those beliefs. This debilitating story lies in the darkness beyond our blind spots and creates a hidden agenda that influences our behavior and increases our stress. In order to peel away these layers and question ourselves, we need to turn the lens of our awareness inward and face our deepest vulnerabilities.

Self-reflection requires us to dive into our unconscious thoughts and bring them to our conscious awareness. When we are aware of what thoughts are hindering us, we can make the necessary changes. Without awareness, we will continue to repeat the same behavior over and over again. Repeating those behaviors while expecting a different result is, according to Albert Einstein, the definition of insanity. In order to change, we need to understand exactly how our beliefs were formed and conditioned. We need to divulge the ego's hidden agenda and reveal what is at the core of our dysfunctional thinking and subsequently generating pain, self-doubt and fear.

The problem is that facing our self requires us to face our feelings, and as Sigmund Freud put it best, *we will do more to avoid pain than to seek pleasure.* The mind and nervous system search for the pathway of least effort, or more specifically the path of less pain. In fact, in order to avoid pain we do one or more of these three things: *distract, react,* or *contract.*

We are masters at **DISTRACTING** ourselves from our feelings. This explains addiction statistics. Drug addiction, alcohol addiction, sex addiction, food addiction, drama addiction, and shopping addiction all stem from a need to distract ourselves from emotions that make us feel vulnerable. We focus on our external world and avoid our internal world at all costs. The more we focus on the external, the more "comfortably numb" the internal becomes. Most people would rather reach for their phone first thing in the morning than meditate and be present with their thoughts and feelings.

Another way of avoiding our feelings is to **REACT:** to surrender to that great human weakness of taking things personally. Like a toddler having a temper tantrum, our "fight" response will kick in. We will cry, scream, punch a fist through the wall, bite back or self-harm. These violent reactions are often further complicated by shame or guilt.

The third way we avoid feeling pain is to **CONTRACT,** which means withdrawing, "fleeing," shrinking or shutting down. Just as a stepped-on sea urchin coils into itself for protection, we retreat within ourselves. We close up in an effort to protect ourselves and we internalize our emotions.

By allowing ourselves to *feel,* we enable ourselves to heal. We open ourselves up to change and transform our inner toxicity into a greater sense of empowerment. The caterpillar's metamorphosis into a butterfly is a symbolic demonstration of the art and mastery of transformation.

When ready, the caterpillar wraps himself in a cocoon or chrysalis. He creates this dark and private space trustingly, knowing it is a part of his life cycle. For humans the transformational process can feel dark and lonely and very confronting. Our lives are so much more complex than a caterpillar's that we often lack trust in the process. It's also riskier. Unlike the caterpillar, whose process is simple and almost risk-free, for humans there is a definite possibility of making decisions that do not serve us and instead deepen our pain and trouble.

The caterpillar experiences an extraordinary transformation. His entire body literally dissolves and turns to black goo. He loses his identity as a caterpillar and for a period of time lies in total uncertainty. But some part of him knows that, when ready, he will grow his wings and fly. He does not rush the process, nor try to control it. He allows the process to unfold. He allows himself to go through the necessary stages. He patiently surrenders because he knows that soon he will see the world through the eyes of a butterfly and will fly with freedom.

He surrenders. He endures and embraces because he accepts his cycle of change and growth. Lao Tzu said, "What the caterpillar calls the end, the rest of the world calls a butterfly." The caterpillar's focus is not on what he is losing or on what he is moving toward. He is simply present with the process.

The same process of transformation occurs in the release of the ego to our essence. As we peel away layers, we expose inner vulnerabilities that we naturally want to protect. We become aware of thoughts and behaviors preventing us from blossoming into our full potential. We can go into the darkness and let go of the self that no longer serves us and "dissolve" because, unlike the caterpillar, we know we are going to grow wings and fly.

We face our feelings by moving *into* and through them, rather than avoiding them. As we move into our feelings, we can get to the core of what is causing them, and we can challenge them. We challenge imprinted beliefs by asking questions that take us deeper into our unconscious world. Like a submarine sinking below the surface, we can dive into our hidden world. When we are in that zone, we can break through the layers of beliefs that create a protective armor. Each layer we shed takes us deeper to our core. This gives us greater clarity as to what unconscious thoughts are programming our behavior. More than 95 percent of our behavior is controlled by unconscious processes, so this deeper awareness is very empowering.

This preponderance of unconscious thoughts explains why transformation can be so difficult. As thought travels faster than the speed of light, we are unaware of the hundreds of thoughts we experience in each moment. In fact, researchers believe that we may have around 60,000 to 80,000 thoughts per day. A few of these thoughts filter into our consciousness while the vast majority is stored in the intricate layers of our inner coding. Although we think we are aware of and in control of our choices and behavior, this unconscious matrix decides what filters through and what we store.

Renowned psychologist Mihaly Csikszentmihalyi, the genius behind *flow*, the focused mental state, suggests that roughly two million bits of information come at us each second. Other researchers have identified information transmission rates of each of the five senses: the eyes are thought to perceive ten million bits of information per second, the skin one million, the ears one hundred thousand, smell one hundred thousand and taste one thousand.

The majority of this information is compressed into our unconscious because the conscious mind can only process around fifty bits per second. This means that we are unaware of a plethora of detail. Like a pool filter, our brain centers choose what thoughts are tossed into our "rubbish bin" and what we keep in our awareness. We will delete, distort and generalize information that we perceive to be irrelevant to us. The coding of our belief system determines how and why we filter certain information.

Imagine asking ten people to enter the same room. If we then asked each one to recall what they observed in that room, we would most likely get ten different answers. Each person notices details relevant to *their* perceptual lens. If another person brings something new to their attention, they will then be able to notice it and add it to their "conscious collectables."

The same process can be applied to our belief system. Every experience we have is filtered through a part of the brain called the reticular activating system, which distinguishes between information it deems worth noticing and information that can be filed away. This values-and-beliefs-driven system is why we tend to notice things that we perceive to be important or relevant to us, such as noticing red Mazdas just after we've purchased one, or noticing people who appear to be criticizing us, if that's our belief, and fading out the people who are supporting us.

Another example: If our partner is mindlessly letting off steam, our default position may be to take it personally. As their harsh tone hits the receptors of our senses, it triggers a myriad of stored pain and inner beliefs we are unaware of. Our automatic response, driven by thousands of thoughts, will be to protect ourselves. We express that through our stress response; we either shut down and retreat in self-defense or fight back aggressively. Why is taking it personally our default or knee-jerk response? What happens within us to trigger self-protection?

It is essential to get to our core beliefs because we are then able to observe the intention behind our decisions and behavior. If our intention is rooted in a fear, it will have toxic effects. If we plant toxic seeds, we grow toxic plants. The same applies to our beliefs: If we sow toxic thought-seeds, we will reap toxic behavior. If we become aware that we are fueled by fearful thought-seeds, we become motivated to purify our thoughts, intentions and behavior. And as we shift our intention, we alter the way we filter information. We expand our awareness and widen our perceptual lens, giving us a panoramic view rather than a selfie. Greater clarity and insights can follow.

The three fears of not being loved, not feeling worthy, and not feeling good enough are the toxic seeds we plant in the soil of our unconscious. As we water them with our focus, they grow into pestilential perceptions, programming our senses with paranoia. These beliefs create an illusion of reality that we take as our truth, unaware that we are stuck in a delusional awareness.

These three toxic fears not only explain our emotional responses, they also define more specifically the hidden agenda driving the ego-self. It is essential for us to gain awareness of these three toxic beliefs (our "story of limitation") and how they impact us. With awareness, we can remove them from our blind spots and see them clearly. This gives us the opportunity to heal them. The following client conversations demonstrate the "peeling of the emotional layers" that uncover the three toxic beliefs and hidden agenda of the ego-self.

THE THREE TOXIC SEEDS OF THE TAINTED EGO-SELF

I met my client *Michael* on the eve of his fiftieth birthday. When I asked him what he hoped to achieve from our sessions, he answered, "My whole adult life I have seen the same patterns repeating themselves. I keep getting into bad relationships, my business never fulfills me, I feel lost and I desperately want to make change and have better relationships, but I do not know how and do not understand why I keep making the same mistakes."

When I asked him what was standing in his way, he said, "I always know what I want, but something stops me."

"What stops you?" I asked.

"I end up sabotaging it."

"How come?"

"Something happens in my head. I know what I want to do but feel unable to make that choice. Like, I may want to approach a woman I feel attracted to, I can even see myself doing it. But then I choke. Can't get words out."

"What are you afraid of?"

"I'm scared she will reject me."

"How would it make you feel if she rejected you?"

"I would feel like I've failed. Just like I fail at everything in my life."

"Are you fearing failure?"

"Yes, I guess that's it in a nutshell."

"Oh no," I answered. "That is only the shell of the nut! What's within your fear? What is this really about?"

Silence. His tapping foot said it all. Clearly we were stepping into the swampy goo of his ego-self. We began to peel through the layers of his buried emotion, right into his blind spots.

"What do you mean by what's within my fear?" he asked.

"Well, what would it mean for you to fail?"

"It would mean that I can never do anything right. It would mean that I always let myself down. It would mean that my father would win."

"How would he win?"

"He always told me that I would never amount to anything. He told me that I don't have what it takes to be successful."

"How old were you when you first heard those words?"

He searched through the files of his memory. "I think I was six."

"And when you heard those projected words, what did you decide?"

"I didn't think I decided anything."

"Think about it . . . as a child, absorbing the world around you, unaware that every word you hear scripts your inner coding. What did you make it all mean?"

"I guess I made it mean that I am not worthy of success . . ."

"So then, at the core, what is your actual fear?"

"I guess it is a **FEAR OF BEING WORTHLESS, OR NOT BEING WORTHY.**"

***

Julie came to see me as a result of being stuck in depression after her relationship breakup. When I asked her what she hoped to achieve from our sessions she answered, "My focus has always been on a man and having a relationship. I want to be free from that need. I want to find myself again and I want to love myself without a man."

When I asked her why she needed a man to love her, she answered, "Because it makes me feel whole."

"In what way?"

"I feel a man fills an inner void."

"Tell me about the void."

"It feels like this empty space in me, like a big black hole."

"Has it always been there?"

"For as long as I can remember." She gazes at a spot in front of her as she searches through her inner world. "There were times early on when I felt full. Before my parents split, I felt whole."

"What happened?"

"My dad left. I was five or six. I never saw him again."

"How did his leaving affect you?"

"I remember waiting by the front window, waiting to see if he would come back. Everything felt so chaotic."

"In what way?"

"Mum broke down. She would cry all the time. We had to move into a smaller house, and she went to work full time. I spent a lot of time alone."

"What do you remember feeling in those moments alone?"

"I replayed the days before he left. Tried to understand what I did wrong. Tried to understand why he had to leave. I was so sad at school.

Eventually no one wanted to play with me, so I spent most of my time alone. I think being alone was safer."

"Because . . ." I nudge, helping her go deeper.

"Because I did not have to worry about anyone leaving. No one would abandon me again."

"How does your wound of abandonment make you feel?"

"Like no one will ever love me."

"So what, at your core, are you fearing?"

"I FEAR I AM NOT LOVED."

***

Sam came to see me because she was completely burnt out. She had the onset of chronic fatigue and major digestive issues. She took three months off to rest and invest in her self-development. She desperately wanted to understand why she pushed herself the way she did.

"I have this need to prove myself," Sam said in our first session.

"How come?"

"Not sure. It feels like it's always been there. Maybe it's working in a male-dominated environment? Maybe it was the competitive sport I played when I was younger?"

"What are you scared of?"

"I don't think I'm scared. I mean, I push myself every day—I make bold decisions, I show up, I get out of my comfort zone. I fight every day to get to where I want to be."

"How come?" I asked.

"Because I don't want to let others down; I don't want to let my team down."

"How would letting others down be a problem for you?"

"I would disappoint them."

"And if you disappoint them, how would that make you feel?"

"I would feel judged; probably rejected too."

"Can you explain how you arrived at that conclusion?"

"I remember doing a large project at school. I put so much work into it. I thought the teacher would love it, but when I got up and showed my project to the class, she did not look happy. I had misunderstood the instructions and hadn't done the project correctly."

"What do you remember hearing?"

"I think she said something like, 'Sam, this is not like your usual work. I am disappointed in you.'"

"How did hearing that make you feel?"

"I remember looking around the classroom and seeing the group of mean girls smirking—like they were happy that I did poorly. I was so embarrassed."

"What do you remember saying to yourself?"

"I must have said that I was stupid and not as good as the other kids."

"So, what do you think is the limiting fear at your core?

"I BELIEVE I AM NOT GOOD ENOUGH."

***

The deconstruction of these client conversations offers greater insights into the makeup of the ego-self and what exists beyond our blind spots. As we peel away the layers of our emotions, we will always come back to the same three toxic core beliefs: I am not worthy, I am not loved, I am not good enough. Because these three limiting beliefs reveal our deepest vulnerabilities, the ego-self operates to keep us in a comfort zone of safety. How can we recognize this "hidden agenda"?

CHAPTER 4

THE HIDDEN AGENDA OF THE EGO-SELF

"Worry pretends to be necessary but serves no useful purpose."

Eckhart Tolle

When the ego-self perceives an external threat, it instigates a response to keep us safe and avoid pain. These responses are sneaky behavior patterns that all have a hidden agenda. We have hundreds of these patterns (agendas) that help us avoid or mitigate risk.

These behaviors protect us from feeling deep emotional wounds. An emotional wound is the scar tissue (the memory) left in the body after a painful event. The memory is the "story" we made about the painful event. It represents the meaning we assigned to it in a split second. This story causes the wound. These wounds also stir up a craving for attention, acceptance, certainty, validation, recognition and approval. When we have certainty or feel accepted and validated, we feel safe.

I have identified the following six wounds:
- Rejection
- Abandonment
- Betrayal
- Uncertainty/Change
- Judgement/Criticism/Humiliation
- Failure

These emotional wounds act as pain buttons that rest over the three limiting beliefs of "I am not worthy," "I am not loved," "I am not good enough." When I ask people how being rejected makes them feel, they answer, "It makes me feel unworthy or unlovable." How does a fear of judgment affect us? If we are judged, we feel that people don't like us, which affirms the limiting belief of not being loved or good enough. Abandonment will affirm the belief of not being worthy of being loved. Likewise, not belonging or being accepted will make us feel that we are not good enough.

A person or event "out there" pushes this button, setting off our pain response. The button corresponds to an inner wound. Having our button pushed will usually result in us feeling threatened or even attacked. The ego proudly steps forward to save us from the illusion of threat. We will blame the other person or situation for making us feel the way we do. And herein lies our problem: Our inner conditioning is so deeply hidden that we do not realize that the issues do not actually lie with the other person or external trigger but rather with our state of fear. When there is no fear, and we have attended to our wounds, there is no button and we can no longer be triggered.

The ego-self will do its best to help us avoid the pain of feeling these wounds at all costs. Shyness is a perfect example of a hidden agenda. Being shy helps to ensure that we do not say or do something that others may not approve of. The potential threat of being judged or rejected by others is motivating our "choice" to be shy. The pain of rejection then validates the limiting belief of not being loved. Therefore the desire to be more confident instead of shy will be slim, because from such a fearful mindset, the perception of the perceived pain (rejection) is too great.

If we look back at the three client conversations mentioned in Chapter 3, we can observe how these inner wounds have an effect on our behavior. Michael was apprehensive about approaching a woman because of his perceived fear of rejection, failure and judgement. These wounds were a result of the decisions (and beliefs) he had made about not being good enough for his own father. Once he attended to those beliefs, he was able to stop "playing safe" and meet the love of his life.

Likewise, Julie's wound of abandonment caused her to need a man and try to ensure that he would never leave her. Sam's fear of judgment and failure influenced her lack of personal boundaries. She would push herself and compete in order to avoid letting people down.

We now see that the ego-self is not necessarily motivated by our authentic happiness. It is more concerned with our safety. In order to protect us, the ego-self develops an array of *safety habits*. Our safety habits can also be known as our stress responses: the way we respond to stressful triggers. Our stress response makes us more emotionally reactive to situations because we are not fully in the present moment. We are reliving past pain that is trapped in our emotional wounds.

These safety habits demonstrate the adaptations we make to our essential nature—in other words, the changes we make in order to be accepted and prove our worth. It is important to remember that our goal is not necessarily giving up our safety habits; bills still need to be paid, and we will always want to avoid shame. The key point is how we balance and integrate our ego and essence so that we can feel safe without jeopardizing or compromising our happiness.

We also want to know how to nurture the sensitive aspects of ourselves. If, for example, we have an injured leg, we would have to make adjustments to the way we walk and to our posture. We would have to be sensitive to our injury (our wound) and have realistic expectations. The same applies to our emotional wounds. We need to be aware, accepting and gentle toward ourselves. This means knowing what your wounds might be and how you can nurture them as opposed to being emotionally reactive because of them.

I asked a dear client to identify the difference between what we called her *safety habits* and her *happiness habits*. These habits include the beliefs we hold, what we say to ourselves, and the actions we take. Her happiness habits are based on what makes her authentically happy. With her permission, I have included her summary here, as a perfect example to demonstrate the drive of the Ego-self.

SAFETY HABITS	HAPPINESS HABITS
These represent the beliefs and behaviors we choose in order to keep safe. These are influenced by fear.	These represent what we believe and what we do from our authentic self. These represent who I can be without fear.
<ul><li>I must be financially independent</li><li>I won't let myself make the same mistakes as Mum made</li><li>I won't put myself into "unsafe" situations—for example, being in a group where I feel uncomfortable</li><li>I guard myself when in a group of people</li><li>I try to avoid/prevent other people from seeing my flaws and thinking I'm not a very nice person or a good friend</li><li>I need to be pragmatic/action-oriented to prove that I am productive and achieving success</li><li>I am only interested in outcomes</li><li>It's difficult for me to trust others/life</li><li>I don't feel that who I am is enough</li><li>I judge myself and beat myself up over small things</li><li>I get angry with my husband and become distant</li><li>I am defensive and feel resentful</li><li>I hold onto things because they validate my inner fears</li><li>I bottle my emotions because I don't feel safe expressing my feelings</li><li>It's important to me to please people</li></ul>	<ul><li>I trust myself</li><li>I have an inspiring vision for my life and believe I am the conscious creator of what I want to experience</li><li>I let go of my fear and take risks</li><li>I let my heart lead</li><li>I feel confident to express my true self</li><li>I know that who I am is enough</li><li>I am free and independent</li><li>My spirit is free</li><li>I am easygoing</li><li>I trust the process of life; I know I am safe</li><li>I accept myself—my weaknesses and my strengths</li><li>I have a clear purpose and am here to contribute</li><li>I am able to put my needs first</li><li>I hold my boundaries</li><li>I feel positive and happy</li><li>This state of mind feels like an inner warmth/glow that is empowering me</li><li>I feel whole and complete</li><li>I express myself passionately</li><li>I am committed to what I feel is my purpose</li><li>I believe I can make a difference to people</li><li>I have the courage to further my studies</li></ul>

SAFETY HABITS	HAPPINESS HABITS
- I don't have personal boundaries - I don't take time out for myself; I think that is selfish - I need to be in a well-paying job even though I hate it - I have learned not to speak up and instead hold my opinions to myself - I am strict with my kids and get overwhelmed by my mothering duties - I feel stuck and lack confidence to make change. I would rather keep things as they are as that feels safe - I don't think I am a nice person and don't share myself openly - I do not know how to make decisions for myself - I take everything personally - I give up when things feel too hard - I do not feel like I have much to offer - I often feel anxious and have so much to juggle	- I have the courage to open my own business - I am present as a mother and as a wife - I am playful, carefree and fun - I listen compassionately to people and understand them - I share my thoughts easily - I am a good friend - I am committed to my self-care and wellbeing - I am transparent with my feelings (I have dropped my guard and opened my heart) - I know I have the resources within me to manage my life - I feel calmer and I accept who I am - What I get done every day is enough. I know how to balance my time and am less demanding on myself and others

Our safety habits are based on the decisions we made in difficult moments. In every situation two forms of meaning are constructed: objective meaning and subjective meaning. The objective meaning is the actual facts of the events such as time, place, and the people present. Subjective meaning is the personal meanings we attach to the event. Our decisions are based on these subjective meanings, and they form the foundation of our belief system. It is within our belief system that our story of limitation (our story of not being good enough) began. Although this subjective story feels truthful, it is in fact a delusional reality. Our limiting beliefs have distorted the perception of our experiences. When we remove the toxic seeds from our unconscious, we can awaken to an entirely new way of responding to stress and life in general.

How have these belief systems been formed, and how have they influenced our perceptions of the world—our own subjective reality? Let us explore this process of conditioning in the next chapter.

CHAPTER 5

THE CONDITIONING OF THE SELF

"Pain is certain, suffering is optional."

Gautama Buddha

How has our story of limitation been formed? How have we been conditioned?

The tainted ego-self and its safety habits are the result of a detailed conditioning process influenced by our genes, our environment and our experiences. Every decision we make, every belief formed, lays the foundation for the lens through which we view the world.

This is our perceptual lens that determines our attitudes, our values, our choices and our behavior. Just as no two fingerprints match, it is improbable for two people to have the exact same perceptual lens. Having the same lens would mean having the exact same experience and forming the exact same meaning, which is unrealistic. Even twins growing up in the same environment have unique perceptual experiences.

The first ten years of childhood are known as our *imprint years*. During these formative years, the narrative of our belief system is written. This narrative is known as our inner dialogue or self-talk, and is made up of positive and negative thoughts. We form millions of beliefs. Many will be helpful and contribute to our growth. However, the formation of our story of limitation hinders our growth. It is these limiting beliefs and thought patterns that we aim to reframe and heal through the process of self-development. When we change our beliefs, we change our thinking. In changing our thinking, we alter our attitudes and transform the way we respond to life.

The process of conditioning occurs like this:

First, a significant emotional event takes place. This is a *defining moment* in time that shocks us emotionally. In this moment we *perceive* something through our five senses and then *internalize* our perceptions with a thought and/or a feeling. From those perceptions we attach meaning and make a *decision*. This process can be mapped out as follows:

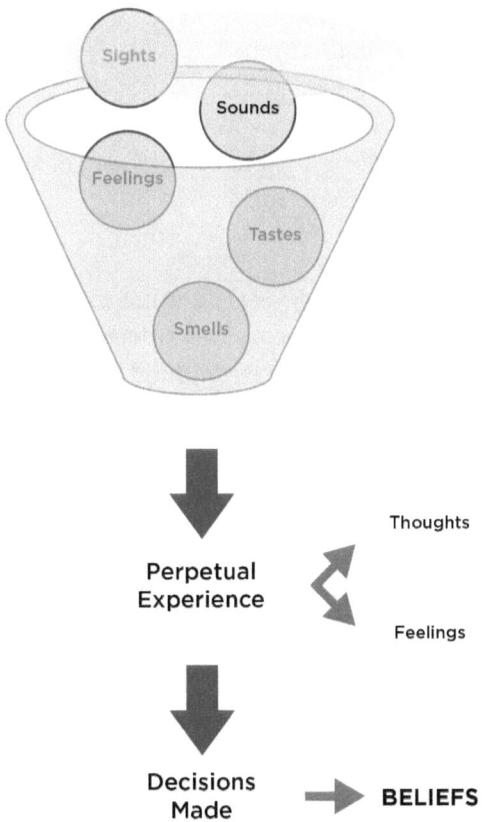

Conditioning of Belief System

Imagine, for a moment, a three-year-old child who overhears his parents arguing. The loud voices make the boy feel scared or worried. Given the limited understanding and experience of a three-year-old, he will attach his own meaning to what he is observing. Since children are egocentric, he may instantly conclude that *he* has done something wrong and his parents are shouting because they are angry with *him*. He may think they are going to leave, or he may fear physical harm. From his feelings and the meaning he has attached to their behavior, he makes decisions like these:

- I am a naughty boy.
- I must be a good boy to ensure I don't get yelled at.
- My parents don't like me.
- My parents don't like each other.
- I don't feel safe in this home.
- Relationships are dangerous.
- Relationships are unpleasant.
- You have to argue or fight to be heard or get what you want.
- I must be strong like Dad/Mum.
- This is the way you treat a woman/man.

In a split second his three-year-old mind makes major decisions that direct him for life. These decisions will determine what he believes about his parents and how he behaves around them, and will influence his choice of relationships, how he acts in his own relationships, and how he speaks to women or allows women to speak to him. These feelings and thoughts, more importantly, will have an effect on his self-worth. He has formulated a belief system that will govern his behavior until one day when he finds himself an emotionally broken thirty-seven-year-old lying on a therapist's couch, desperately trying to keep his marriage together.

Okay, that ending may be a bit drastic; however, that sequence of events exemplifies what I have heard from many clients, both male and female.

When we have a positive experience, physical sensations are positive, and we decide that we feel good. For example, holding a crying baby soothes her distress. The parent's touch feels good and the baby will feel calm. The mind forms a positive association to being held, and the baby will seek more of what feels good. The more positive associations we form, the safer and happier we will feel. We will develop a greater sense of security, stability and confidence, all of which enable us to build supportive beliefs about ourselves, others and the world at large.

Our attitudes and values are influenced by the "dominant theme" of our personal story. This includes what we perceive in our family, school, religion, culture, friends or media. Everything we perceive around us influences how we feel and think. If, as children, we were exposed to stories such as Cinderella, our belief system will include the meanings we attached to those stories. We wait to find our Princess or Prince Charming. We dream about our "happily ever after." We may decide that we have to be or look a certain way in order to secure our prince or princess.

If we return to the example of the parents arguing, and imagine that the child heard them arguing about money, then this perception in turn will influence his attitude toward money. Possible beliefs he might form are "Money breaks up families" or "Money is hard to earn" or "Money is the source of all pain." If he comes from a religious family, that belief might be further layered like this: "Money is the root of all evil." We take these beliefs into adulthood as our *money mindset*, and they influence our choices (and hence behavior) around how we spend, save or earn money. We may become tight, conservative or risk-averse with money. We could become controlling toward our partner's spending money or work really hard to ensure we have a lot of money and never have to struggle.

Cognitive behavioral therapy is one of my favorite modalities to explain how the beliefs we form determine our thoughts, feelings and behavior. A *core belief* causes *automatic negative thoughts* (ANTs). The negative thoughts create feelings, and those feelings define our behavior. The beliefs can happen in isolation or they can overlap; for example, we may not feel good enough or worthy to be loved.

We each hold these limiting beliefs to some degree as they are conditioned into all of us throughout our childhood. If we have defining moments that validate our inner fears, they will dominate. If we have a supportive environment and a solid base that makes us feel safe, these beliefs will be less amplified. The reality or the behavior formed can apply to each of the beliefs.

I have mapped them out as follows:

CORE BELIEF (I.E. THE CORE FEARFUL THOUGHT)	AUTOMATIC NEGATIVE THOUGHTS (THOUGHTS GENERATED AS A RESULT OF THE CORE BELIEF)	FEELINGS (FEELINGS GENERATED IN THE BODY AS A RESULT OF THOSE THOUGHTS)	BEHAVIOR (HOW WE BEHAVE AS A RESULT OF THOSE THOUGHTS AND FEELINGS)
I am not good enough	• I can't do anything right • I am not smart enough • I have no value • I don't bring anything to the table • I always fail • Nothing ever works out • Nothing I do will ever be enough • I wish I had what others have • I am pathetic • I hate my body	• Anxiety • Sadness • Depression • Worry	• Acting stressed, fearful, withdrawn, insecure • Comparing ourselves to others • Being ambitious • Being disempowered • Demonstrating performance anxiety • Showing excessive need for recognition • Being overwhelmed • Showing inability to take responsibility • Showing a lack of confidence • Indulging in excessive worry/anxiety • Feeling separate from others • Keeping self small • Playing safe • Always wanting more • Self-sabotaging • Indulging in self-pity • Indulging in self-loathing

CORE BELIEF (I.E. THE CORE FEARFUL THOUGHT)	AUTOMATIC NEGATIVE THOUGHTS (THOUGHTS GENERATED AS A RESULT OF THE CORE BELIEF)	FEELINGS (FEELINGS GENERATED IN THE BODY AS A RESULT OF THOSE THOUGHTS)	BEHAVIOR (HOW WE BEHAVE AS A RESULT OF THOSE THOUGHTS AND FEELINGS)
I am not loved	• Something is wrong with me • I have nothing to offer anyone • I am unlovable • I am ugly • I can't trust anyone • I can't trust myself • I am different • I don't fit in or belong • I am alone • I don't deserve happiness • I am invisible • No one sees me • No one understands me • I need someone to love me • No man/woman will ever want me	• Loneliness • Emotional guardedness • Neediness • Insecurity • Jealousy • Despair • Sadness	• Social isolation • Social anxiety • Promiscuity • Frigidness • Sexual dysfunction • People-pleasing • No personal boundaries • High expectations, demanding • Neediness • Needing attention • Needing acceptance • Needing control • Codependence • Counter-dependence • Possessiveness • Addictive behavior • Fear of abandonment • Fear of rejection

CORE BELIEF (I.E. THE CORE FEARFUL THOUGHT)	AUTOMATIC NEGATIVE THOUGHTS (THOUGHTS GENERATED AS A RESULT OF THE CORE BELIEF)	FEELINGS (FEELINGS GENERATED IN THE BODY AS A RESULT OF THOSE THOUGHTS)	BEHAVIOR (HOW WE BEHAVE AS A RESULT OF THOSE THOUGHTS AND FEELINGS)
I am not worthy	• I am worthless • What I say does not matter • I need to prove myself • I need material possessions to feel worthy • I don't deserve success • I am not worthy of being loved • Who am I to want this? • I am a fraud • I am nothing	• Pressure • Stress • Anxiety • Anger • Resentment • Despair	• Feeling stuck • Competitiveness • High expectations on self • Perfectionism • Negative self-talk • Overriding intuition or gut instinct • The need to prove one's worthiness • Fatigue/burnout • Frustration or self-doubt • Fear of being judged • Seeking pleasure and avoiding responsibility

When I began my own process of self-reflection, I finally understood my pattern of losing myself in a relationship. Uncovering my limiting beliefs and how they were formed offered me greater awareness of where I needed to heal and transform. I would love to share my imprint years with you now as an example of how to locate your own defining moments and how to access the vulnerability required to do so.

I was born in Johannesburg, South Africa, and spent the first years of my life playing in our beautiful garden. My world was safe, fun, playful and imaginative. I had a magnificent nanny who would tie me to her back with her colorful African scarf. The warmth of her care cradled me with love and protection. My parents were connected, loving and present. Why would I ever want anything to change? I had safety, security, freedom and happiness.

The certainty of my world was completely shaken when I was four years old and my family moved to Los Angeles, California. From the moment we landed at LAX, life as I knew it was never to be the same again. LA was electrifying—loud, busy, crowded, and, although exciting, I was out of my comfort zone. Everything I had known was taken away. The crowds and chaos sent shock waves through my body like a defibrillator to the heart. My body felt things it had never before experienced. Part of me was excited and loved the adventure, but another part of me felt scared. I felt that I needed to protect myself from my new environment.

This duality became more apparent on my first day of kindergarten. My innate sense of playfulness, enthusiasm and excitement went hand in hand with a sense of trepidation as I entered the classroom. I wanted to play and explore, but my excitement was soon replaced by pain. No one appeared to want to play with me.

"You have funny hair," I remember one of the kids commenting on my frizzy mop.

"Your accent is different to ours," another observed.

Those words sent further shock waves through me. More need to protect myself. More evidence that this was a scary place.

The perceptual lens of my four-year-old self led me to form this conclusion: "Everyone looks the same here and I look different." I layered this neutral, factual observation with emotion: "They all look like Barbie, with their long blond hair. How come I don't look like that? Is that why they don't want to play with me? What's wrong with me?"

This distorted perception made me feel I had to adapt myself to fit in and be accepted by everyone. I formed dysfunctional beliefs like this:
- I am different.
- If I am different, then I am ugly.
- If I am ugly, then no one will like me because only pretty girls like Barbie get things.
- If I am not liked, then I need to prove to people who I am so they see beyond my looks.
- I have to work hard for the real me to be seen and heard.
- I will be strong, very strong. I will form a hard shell to protect me from feeling scared.

- I notice that people like me when I make them laugh, so I will do that. If they like me, then I can feel safe.

It took five years, until I was nine years old, before I finally adapted to life in LA. By then I had two best friends, attended dance classes, loved my roller skates and Venice Beach. My life once again felt calm and secure. And then another defining moment occurred.

It was Halloween and my father was home from one of his many overseas trips. Every year my best friend and I would dress up and trick or treat around the neighborhood with her father. Tonight, I proudly had mine with me, which added an extra special buzz to the outing. Looking back over my shoulder, I felt so happy seeing the two of them following us. I felt safer.

On our way home, my father and I made a stopover at our usual lookout point on Mulholland Drive. I always enjoyed our one-on-one time, which included visits to Tower Records, ice cream in Westwood, the horse rides at Griffith Park, and driving home along the twisty bends of Mulholland. I loved this particular LA hot spot. It felt as if I was on top of the world looking down on a divided city. To one side I could stretch my imagination far enough to see the twinkle of the carousel on Santa Monica Pier. The other side looked down upon the Valley.

I felt like such a big girl sitting up front. Not only was I the eldest, but I felt as if I was the most important. I propped myself up on my hands and stretched my neck to look even further.

"I need to tell you something, Cheryne," Dad said. The coolness of his tone broke my daydream. My nervous system rose to attention. *What now?*

He continued, making a statement that was not only an eighties cliché, but also an inappropriate communication to a nine-year-old: "I need to go and find myself, Cheryne. I will be going away, and I need you to take care of things while I am gone."

I am not sure what he said after that as my erupting emotions skewed my thoughts. I was suddenly drowning in a hot orange sea. My breath was trapped in my throat and my heartbeat thumped through my ears.

What just happened? What do you need to find? What don't you have here? Why am I not enough for you?

His words scraped through my being like the San Andreas Fault through California. Through the distorted perceptual lens of my child's mind, this development could only mean one thing: I was ugly and unwanted. This validated the belief that no one wanted me, not even my own father. If I were beautiful, he would have stayed. Not even my own dad loved me enough to stay! Who would ever want me if he didn't?

At that age I did not have the wisdom or the know-how to see the situation beyond my limited perceptions. I was not able to go deeper into understanding what he was going through or what he needed. All I could feel was my own pain. My pain confirmed my distorted beliefs about myself—it was all the evidence my mind needed. I applied the old trusted remedy: adapt and move on.

I needed to try even harder to be liked and accepted. I needed to be what people needed me to be. I would do anything to please others and protect myself from that awful feeling of rejection. The fear of being alone or abandoned ensured I would build a personality strong enough to never let that happen again.

From that point forward my mind sought further evidence to support these limiting beliefs. My ego-self developed a multitude of safety habits to protect me from feeling the pain of rejection. I shut myself down, dimmed my light, and put up a guard to ensure no one could hurt me. The carefree child sank into a stupor. It was as if my essence, my authentic self, lay down and went to sleep. I lost the ability to hear her voice or engage with her playful imagination. As time moved on, I took my "ugly" story into adolescence. Intoxicated with pain and anger, and caught up in a distorted perception of reality, I sought love in all the wrong places.

This tendency to arrive at limiting beliefs and then live in reaction to them has been apparent in all of my clients. All those beautiful souls were able to locate a moment in time when they separated from their essence and made decisions about who they needed to be to feel safe in their world.

As we repeatedly act out this limiting story, the ego-self becomes our conditioned self—the person we have learned to be, the person we have adapted to be in order to survive in our world.

The freedom, curiosity and playfulness of our inner child morphs into a desire for safety and acceptance. Our moment-by-moment choices are motivated by this desire to protect ourselves in whatever way works for us individually.

The more we lose touch with our carefree child, the more likely we are to move away from our truth, forget who we truly are and adapt into the person we "need to be" to cope in our perceived environment. The conditioned ego-self becomes the personality we present to the world, a mask we wear to hide our pain and protect us from being too vulnerable. Our perceptions are tinged by this inner story, senses programmed by dysfunctional language created by dysfunctional meanings.

What are the defining moments in your past? Which experiences imprinted the way you view the world? Take yourself back to your earliest memories. Think of those moments in childhood where you may have created limiting beliefs about yourself, and note how you perceived the event that occurred at that time.

What were the decisions you made in those moments, and how have they influenced your life? How have those beliefs shaped the person you have become? Is this your true self?

CHAPTER 6

THE TERMS AND CONDITIONS OF OUR SELF-WORTH

Good deeds bring good results.
Bad deeds bring bad results.
Your own deeds bring your own results.

The Teachings of Buddha

How, specifically, is our story of limitation motivating our behavior?

The Law of Cause and Effect states that for every effect there is a cause, and for every cause there is an effect. Everything in nature works on this principle of causation. We reap what we sow. If we plant a seed and nurture it, we will grow a plant. The plant, in turn, will return nutrients to the earth. We learn very quickly in life that anything we do has a consequence or reaction. The same principle applies to our thoughts: what we think, creates our reality. As Ralph Waldo Emerson said, "Man becomes what he thinks about all day long." Our thinking (our self-talk) is the cause, and the choices we make as a result of our thinking are the effect (consequence).

Therefore, everything in our life can be seen as a result of choices (decisions) we make based on the beliefs (meanings) we hold. Change the meaning and the way you perceive a situation and you change your reality. Wayne Dyer put it best when he said, "When we change the way we look at things, the things we look at change."

Through repeated exposure to stimuli in our environment, we build mental and emotional associations that ultimately form conditioned (learned) responses. Every time the mind attaches a meaning to something, we have formed an association. A baby playing with a toy, for example, will learn that when he presses the red button, the red ball pops out. We have millions of associations linking neural superhighways in our brains. When someone uses harsh tonality, something must be wrong (or we have done something wrong). If someone smiles, they are probably happy. If the sun is out, it is daytime. If the moon is out, it is nighttime. If this, then that.

These associations shape our behavior, causing us to respond automatically to the elements that trigger us. If you've ever played a game of mind association, you will notice the associations you have with certain stimuli. Notice the first word that comes to mind when you think of the following words:

- Happy
- Angry
- Love
- Relationships
- Money
- Religion
- Food

The first thought or image to pop up in your mind is the meaning your mind holds for that word.

Our self-worth works on the same premise as the law of causation. We learn that if we behave in a certain way, people will like us, approve of us, validate us, and we will, in turn, feel good enough, loveable and worthy. The choices or decisions we make in every defining moment result in us forming a "contract" with ourselves. This contract is an agreement or understanding regarding who we need to be and how we need to behave in order to feel safe and operate successfully in our world. This internal contract acts like a legal contract to protect our best interests and keep us safe. I refer to this inner agreement as the terms and conditions of self-worth (our Ts and Cs).

Our Ts and Cs explain what motivates our behavior and answers the following questions we often ask ourselves:

- Who do I need to be in order to be accepted, liked or successful?

- Why do I do what I do?
- Why do I have certain needs?
- Why do I have certain expectations?
- What is ultimately driving (controlling) my choices?

In order to feel safe and accepted in our world, the mind (ego) prioritizes this internal contract over being authentic because the true version of who we are does not seem good enough or because the true version does not seem to fit in with what is required. We make decisions that to us mean operating successfully in our world, even though that success might not be true success and is more about survival. Most people experience more pain in being rejected than pleasure in being true to themselves, so they organize their lives to avoid pain. The fact is that we do not get what we desire in life; we get what we believe we are worthy of. Understanding the Ts and Cs of my self-worth helped me to understand what motivated my relationship choices and how I gave my power away.

I remember the precise thought I had when I met Shaun. I was twenty-four and had been living in Australia for three years. After the relationship that brought me to Australia dissolved, I enjoyed the single nightlife Melbourne offered. My friends and I arrived one evening at a singles party, each with high hopes of finally finding a man.

By midnight I was bored, disillusioned and ready to call it a night when the "man of my dreams" came up to speak to one of my friends. He was charming and good-looking. We connected instantly. Within five minutes of our introduction, numbers were exchanged and a date planned.

After the party, I came home flooded with a rush of excitement and flopped into bed, my mind racing with possibilities and dreams. And here came the thought:

"OMG! He is just like the boys in high school. The ones who teased me, called me names, told me I was ugly and only good for sex. The ones I thought were not made for girls like me. *If he likes me, then I must now be good enough to love!*" His interest in me was the measure of how far I had come since my awful high school years. *I must now be physically attractive and worth something because this desirable guy wants me!*

What I know now that I didn't know then is that this man mirrored my self-worth conditioning. My Ts and Cs dictated what I felt worthy of, which in turn reflected what I could receive. After a few months, when the cracks in our relationship began to show and my intuition was screaming at me to run for dear life, I chose to override my gut because I could not bear the thought of feeling rejected and alone again. Years of conditioning drove me to uphold this internal contract, even though it was in desperate need of an overhaul.

Every defining moment or emotional event I experienced added more evidence to support my internal contract. My "ugly story" amplified with puberty, which decided to bless me with its presence early—around my tenth birthday. By twelve I was already fully developed and looked more like a voluptuous woman than an insecure girl trying to accept and understand herself. This made me the perfect target for bullies.

It took me a long time to piece my confidence back together after my father left us. I still craved love and desperately wanted to fit in and belong, so when I heard comments like, "The only good thing about you is your tits," I began to believe that boys liked me when I was sexual with them. But behaving like that felt wrong, and anger began to blaze through my bloodstream.

I was angry with my father, who had left California and moved to another state with a new woman. I was angry with my mother: My warped perception was that if my father chose another woman over her, then she was not good enough. I was angry with the boys at my school for teasing me. I was angry with the girls I'd thought were my friends who were excluding me.

I had no tools to express my anger, so I kept it inside, and over time my unexpressed toxicity turned into depression. I shaved my hair, turned more heavily to marijuana and alcohol, and offered myself to any boy who showed me attention. Then, in what felt like the blink of an eye, everything changed.

A month before ninth grade started, my mother, who was struggling on her own with three girls in Los Angeles, lost her house. In a matter of two weeks our possessions were packed into boxes and put into storage, and we moved into my cousin's one-bedroom apartment in Santa Monica. I remember falling asleep on a mattress on her floor with my two sisters next to me, staring at six suitcases piled up in the corner. Whatever we had left to show for the past eleven years of life was squeezed into those six suitcases.

I started ninth grade at a new school. Although I was devastated by all the loss and change, this school move proved to be my greatest blessing. It was as if the universe threw me a line of hope amid the chaos. I found a group of friends I fit in with, who seemed to like me for me. For the first time in a long time, I began to feel confident and happy. Then, just two months into finding my feet again, life in the USA came to an end.

My mother decided to move us back to South Africa. By comparison with everything I had gone through, this move back to South Africa proved to be by far the most traumatic. I returned to my place of birth and happiest memories, but now as a complete misfit with a massive chip on my shoulder.

The life I'd built had once again been ripped away from me, and I was forced to reinvent and redefine myself once again. The confidence I thought I'd developed over the last few months quickly faded as I met with new bullies who simply had different accents.

I wanted my life back and had no idea how to blend into this new world I had just landed in. I blamed my father for ruining my life—"If it weren't for him and his stupid choices, I'd be happy," whined my inner victim. "If he hadn't left us, I'd still have the life I loved."

South Africa in the late 1980s was a very different place to what it is today. Apartheid was still in place, and global sanctions created a protective, almost naïve state of mind. Compared to the wild, trendy life I had been exposed to in Los Angeles, I felt as though I had traveled back in time. In February 1987, fourteen-year-old me and my shaved hair (which I thought was "eighties cool") showed up at a very conservative Jewish day school in Johannesburg.

My lack of self-belief and persistent self-loathing perceived the looks and comments to mean that I was some sort of a freak show. My shattered confidence attracted more bullying and isolation. I had no idea who I needed to be to fit into this world. Because I had no inner power or strength, I lost myself as I tried to adapt to what this world needed me to be. My repressed and unexpressed anger turned into a deeper depression, and for many months I contemplated checking out. The only way to numb myself from social anxiety, feeling misunderstood and that I didn't belong anywhere, was to drink alcohol. To feel accepted and loved, I offered myself sexually to boys.

Luckily, there was always something within me—the whisper of my essence—that kept pushing me through, or I might not be here today.

But I did fall very low. For example, the time my friends and I went out clubbing and I arranged to be picked up at 2 a.m. by my latest crush—let's call him Mr. GTI. He was known as the bad boy and a player, and when he showed me attention, it melted the small amount of self-respect I still had. My friends left, and I waited outside the club until 2:45 a.m. Finally, resigning myself to the fact that he was not showing up, I went back into the club and called a cab to take me home. I had told my mom I was sleeping at a friend's place and I'd be home after 9 a.m., so I couldn't go home too early. Instead, I stumbled into the small mailroom adjacent to the front gate of our townhouses to hide there until morning and see my lie through. I wrapped myself in my jacket, and fell asleep on the cold white tiles, waking up on Sunday morning, cold and stiff, surrounded by one hundred mailboxes. Luckily, when I finally let myself into our apartment, everyone was still sleeping, so I was able to quietly get into the shower and wash away my shame.

As I got out of the shower I caught a glimpse of myself in the mirror.

"I hate you! You are such a loser," I spat at my reflection.

Shame and embarrassment were written all over my face. I could see the pain of my four-year-old self who thought she was ugly. I saw the pain of my nine-year-old self who thought her father had left because she was not good enough. I saw the pain of my fourteen-year-old self who felt mocked by her peers for being fully developed. As I glared into my eyes, I hated everything in front of me. I scanned my body. *You are so ugly! Your hair, your features, your body, your hands, and your feet—everything is repulsive.*

I hated how lonely and sad I felt. I wanted desperately to be loved by a man. Unbeknownst to me, my choices were being defined by an internal contract I had made that defined my self-worth.

A few examples of the terms and conditions of my self-worth were as follows:
- I am worthy if I have a guy in my life.
- I am worthy if a guy thinks I am beautiful and wants to be with me.
- If I am sexual with a guy, then he will like me.
- If I am pretty, boys will like me, and I will feel worthy.
- If I can make boys happy, I will feel good enough.
- If I have a boyfriend, I will be just as good as "the pretty girls."

My Ts and Cs defined who I thought I needed to be, how I perceived men, how I perceived relationships, money, religion, and every other construct. The basis for those Ts and Cs was clear: if a man wanted me, I was good enough to be loved—a simple case of cause and effect.

This belief gave rise to needs and expectations both of myself and of the people around me. I not only needed a man in my life to feel whole, I needed him to be attentive, affectionate and validating. I expected him to be with me all the time, to be loyal, and to take care of me. If these expectations were not met, disappointment and depression would follow.

A more in-depth exploration of my Ts and Cs revealed the following:

- I need to ensure I have a man to take care of me.
- I need to put a man's needs above my own so that he stays with me.
- I also need to be independent in case he leaves me.
- I need to be successful in order to feel validated.
- I need financial status to prove I am successful.

This set of beliefs reveals the decisions we make in order to be accepted and fit into the world. These are the adaptations we make to our authentic essence because we do not trust or believe that who we are is enough. We become the person people need us to be rather than the person we are. Because we do not feel worthy, we need to prove our worth. Because we fear we are not loved, we need to be loved. Because we do not feel good enough, we need to mold ourselves into the person we need to be in order to feel accepted.

When we satisfy false needs like these, we feel safe because we have validated the three toxic beliefs of the ego: the car means *I am good enough*, the job proves *I am worthy*, the relationship affirms *I am loved*.

My Ts and Cs also, of course, drove my choices. Why do we want the car we want? Why do we need the house we desire? Why those shoes? Why that job? Why this relationship?

These internal agreements drive our ego and shape every decision we make.

In the ego's defense, such contracts (safety habits) serve to protect us from pain and help us feel safe in our world, but they stem from toxic beliefs. If we had to defend those beliefs in court, our legal representative would plead temporary insanity.

Even worse, this contract defines our identity.

When I started taking myself through this process, I realized that every relationship I entered was based on my Ts and Cs. My internal contract motivated my attraction to those men. I was not necessarily attracting my heart's deepest desires. I was attracting a reflection of my ego-self. Each of those men was as wounded as I was: our pain drew us together. As I reflect on them today, I can accept them as soulmates, because I now know we attracted each other to heal our inner pain—to purify our toxic beliefs and express more of our essence.

With greater awareness of my true self, this internal contract became null and void and I scripted a new agreement with myself:

- Because I am worthy, I want a kind loving man to share my life with.
- Because I love myself, I deserve a man who treats me well and accepts me for me.
- Because I accept my appearance as beautiful, I can show my true self to the world.
- Because I no longer fear rejection, I don't need to people-please.

As a result of my updated contract, new men—and men I probably would not have noticed before—began to appear in my life. My moment-to-moment choices were based on a different set of perceptions where I no longer needed to conceal my fear but was instead motivated by a need to be my true self. I will go into more depth about this in Part Two as we begin to discover the "anatomy of our essence."

Meanwhile, what are the terms and conditions of *your* self-worth? How would you complete the following sentences?

- I am loved if . . .
- Because of my need to be loved in a relationship, I need . . .
- My expectations of my loved ones are . . .
- I am good enough if . . .
- Because of my need to feel good enough I need . . .
- Expectations of myself that make me feel good enough are . . .
- Expectations of others that make me feel good enough are . . .
- I am worthy if . . .
- Because of my need to feel worthy, I need . . .
- Expectations of myself that make me feel worthy are . . .
- Expectations of others that make me feel worthy are . . .

Not only is it essential to know which of our Ts and Cs keep us stuck in ego, we also need to know how this story of limitation shows up in our behavior. There are four distinct behaviors that reveal how ego shows up in our lives. Let's explore those "four inner gremlins" in the next chapter.

CHAPTER 7

THE FOUR INNER GREMLINS OF THE EGO-SELF

"No one has ever seen the face of ego. It is like a ghost that we accept as a controlling influence in our lives . . . The ego is only an illusion, but a very influential one. Letting the ego-illusion become your identity can prevent you from knowing your true self. Ego, the false idea of believing that you are what you have or what you do, is a backwards way of assessing and living life."

Wayne Dyer, *The Ego Illusion*

Once we are aware of our ego, we begin to notice how the three beliefs of not being good enough, not worthy and not loved have shaped our perception of ourselves, others, and life itself. We begin to see how that inner conditioning has influenced our behavior. Once we begin to notice the effects of ego on our behavior, we can stop fear in its tracks.

There are four distinct behaviors that stem from ego. I call them the *four ugly gremlins*, and they can help us see how ego shows up in our lives. These behaviors stem from the three toxic core ego fears.

Who are the four ugly gremlins of the ego? Let me introduce you! Their names are *Compete, Compare, Compromise* and *Control*.

- We **COMPETE** with others to feel worthy and prove our worth.
- We **COMPARE** ourselves with others to show that we are good enough.
- We **COMPROMISE** ourselves by people-pleasing and placing other people's needs over our own so that we can feel accepted and loved.

- We **CONTROL** our environment, people, outcomes, and ourselves in order to feel safe.

GREMLIN #1: COMPETE

When we compete, we push ourselves to be better than others.

Doing our best is part of living an authentically happy life, and it is our birthright to maximize every opportunity in order to realize our full potential. I refer to this natural desire to succeed as *authentic ambition*. Here, behavior has a positive intention: to actualize our gifts and share them with the world. However, when we need to be better than others *in order to feel good enough*, then the motivation for that behavior is not truth (essence) based; it is fear or ego based.

It may be hard, at times, to identify the difference between authentic ambition and competition. Authentic ambition is our genuine need to grow and develop ourselves, but when we are fueled by competition, our behavior is based on a need for validation, recognition, approval and acknowledgment. Recognition makes us feel worthy.

Children have an innate tendency to be motivated by their authentic ambition, but once they enter the schooling system, their passion, creativity and enthusiasm for their authentic ambition often drain away in that competitive environment. Instead of staying in the joy of their passion, their motivation shifts to winning, achieving and gaining awards. Competitive sport reinforces this competitive nature even further.

When children are able to maintain their authentic ambition and stay connected to the fun and pleasure of their prime interest, they thrive and can use contests to embrace challenge and extend their skills. However, fear-based competition can quickly drain innovation and creativity and replace it with a judgmental inner critic who begins to play safe rather than expand. The pressure often results in anxiety and depression.

We can recognize competition in our language:
- I should do everything I can to succeed!
- I must win!
- I must never fail!
- I have to get that promotion!

- I have to come first!
- I have to be better than her/him!

Whenever we hear ourselves start a sentence with *I should, I must, or I have to*, we know that we are being motivated by our fear and need for approval, attention, or validation, all of which affirm our worthiness. We can also recognize competition in our feelings, as we feel more pressured, stressed, panicky and impatient. We have a greater sense of urgency and a fear of failure or a fear of success.

Authentic ambition, on the other hand, stems from a deeper calling or purpose. It comes straight from the heart and is inspired by a desire to contribute in a significant way. By comparison with competition, authentic ambition feels joyful, playful, gracious and collaborative. There is a greater sense of patience and presence, and we are fueled by enthusiasm and passion.

Sonia is a client who came to see me because she was burnt out and needed a career change. She worked as a scientist in a male-dominated industry where she constantly had to prove herself. When we did some inner child work, Sonia discovered a limiting belief within herself that she was not as good as a man and had to prove herself and compete with men to get ahead.

As we searched through her inner coding, we came across a memory from when she was around two years old. In this defining moment, Sonia remembered playing on the floor with her brother, who was six months at the time. Sonia asked her mother for something to drink, and at the same time, her brother began to cry. Sonia's mother gave her younger brother his bottle before giving Sonia her drink. Sonia, in her toddler's naivety, could not understand why her brother came first. In this moment of confusion, she concluded that her mother loved him more; that boys get more; that she was not as good as her brother and would have to compete with him to get attention. Forty years of competing for her space in the world had led to her inevitable burnout.

When she connected back to a deeper purpose and meaning in her career, she found a renewed energy and passion for her work. She felt more present and more focused, and worked with greater ease and a sense of inner peace. Over time her purposeful focus resulted in her having a major scientific breakthrough in the field she worked in.

GREMLIN #2: COMPARE

When we compare ourselves with others, we are coming from the belief that who we are is not enough, and that other people have more than we have.

"What do they have that I don't have?" is the question we find ourselves asking. We feel envy, jealousy or bitterness about the difference between what we have and what others have. Our inner critic constantly compares us to everyone else, and we beat ourselves up for not being as good as everyone else.

One only needs to spend five minutes scrolling through the Facebook feed to hear the voice of this gremlin, who typically has an acute case of *compare-itis*.

- "Oh wow, they're on another island holiday," says Gremlin #2. "I wish I could go on holiday."
- "If I were pretty like her, I would have married someone like him, and I'd be happier now."
- "Maybe things would be better if I were smarter/wealthier/fitter."
- "If I just had more time, I could achieve more."
- "Life would be easier for me if I'd had parents like them."

Do you recognize that voice?

This gremlin is insatiable. Nothing we do or have will ever be enough. We may feel content for a moment in time here and there; however, the moment we see something else that someone has that we don't have, the cycle of comparison kicks in again. (This gremlin is often accompanied by the competition gremlin.)

The mindset of comparison is a perfect breeding ground for developing unrealistic expectations of ourselves and others. Perfectionists are forever comparing themselves to others, and are consumed with worry over what people will think and how they might compare.

Based on my five-year-old self's "ugly story," I spent over three decades comparing myself to others. According to this delusional perception, other people got what they got because of their looks, while I struggled and needed to work harder because of mine. I sabotaged situations over and over again because of this unconscious belief that made me feel less deserving.

To slay this gremlin, we need acceptance and gratitude. The moment we accept who we are and connect back to a deeper inner purpose, we feel a greater sense of gratitude for who we are and what we have in our lives. Gratitude shifts our focus to how much is actually present in our life as opposed to what we do not have.

When I was studying to be a life coach, I shared my "ugly story" with the group of beautiful souls in my course. After my tale, another student came up to me and told me how much she loved my hair and that it made her feel good and happy. I had never thought of my hair as something others might enjoy! I always thought it was ugly, and I'd always felt judged and different. But when I understood that I was uplifting her (without even being conscious of it), my whole map of reality blew up. I began to reframe my story and accept my uniqueness. I realized that my hair supported my soul's purpose: to make people feel good.

Instead of the bitter resentment I felt toward myself, I suddenly felt grateful. I accepted my looks, which in turn led me to accept me altogether, and view myself through the lens of self-love. My world and the choices I made began to look completely different.

GREMLIN #3: COMPROMISE

When we **compromise** ourselves, we are driven by a desire to people-please.

The need to please others overrides the need to honor oneself. Instead of choosing what we truly want, we decide on what is better for others in a kind of self-sacrificial way. We hold no personal boundaries, have an inability to say no, and we people-please. Martyrdom offers us worthiness. The more we do for others, the more we please them, make them happy or fulfill their needs, the more we feel they will accept us and like us.

I love how Oprah Winfrey refers to this human illness as the *disease-to-please*. She points out that we have mostly been conditioned to be good children making everyone happy and putting everyone else's needs above our own.

When I think of past relationships and what drove me, I see that I often compromised myself and my truth to please a man. When I was being a martyr, I felt worthy. I could not have personal boundaries because saying no to others would make me feel that I had let them down or disappointed them, which would then make me worry that they might reject or abandon me. This distorted perception, in turn, validated my fear of not being good enough.

Now, you may naturally be a peacemaker and prefer to avoid conflict. Being a peacemaker can be part of your essential character. Again, like authentic ambition, it might very well be your purpose to bring peace to the world. However, the distinction between the two is also intention-based.

When your behavior stems from a desire to be peaceful, graceful and loving, it is flowing from your essence. But if you compromise yourself in order to be liked or gain acceptance, then your behavior is motivated by your ego needs.

For me this was a major learning experience as I realized how much of my behavior was controlled by my need to be accepted rather than being an expression of my truth.

Think about what you do to fit in and be accepted. Are you being true to yourself? Do you have personal integrity? Are you able to say no easily? Do you have healthy boundaries?

GREMLIN #4: CONTROL

Nothing drains our serenity more than the need to control people and our environment, and very often we have no idea that we are desperately trying to control and micromanage every aspect of our existence in order to feel safe.

Now, there is a difference to being *controlling* and being *in control*. When we are *controlling* we have no control over ourselves and are so fueled by fear and emotions that we feel the need to control others and events. Being *in control* means we have the power to step back, observe ourselves, and be *in control* of our reactions and responses.

This need to control takes us out of a state of flow and out of the present moment because we create expectations, assumptions, predictions and anticipations of people and our future. Because we need people or situations to be a certain way, we are attached to outcomes. If things do not go our way, we feel that we are out of control.

There are many ways we can notice ourselves trying to control others' behavior. The big clue is that just below the surface of all controlling behavior is fear and defense mechanisms protecting us from our core wounds. We are scared of being judged, scared of being abandoned, scared of failing and looking bad, or scared of uncertainty. When we recognize the underlying fear in our behavior, we can begin to make changes at our core.

- A person with an eating disorder, for example, may be desperately trying to control at least one area of their life.
- A possessive or jealous person desperately tries to control the whereabouts or behavior of their partner so they can avoid getting hurt.
- A controlling parent will be very strict or discipline too rigorously out of the fear of something happening to their child, or perhaps of appearing to be a bad parent.
- An employer will control employees and have a need to micromanage their team out of fear of looking bad or failing.
- We tightly control our finances out of the fear that we will lose our security and appear to fail.
- We fight to be right or have things our way to achieve a sense of control when everything feels uncertain.

All of these attempts to gain control ultimately reinforce our belief that we are not good enough.

The antidote to being controlling is *flow*. When we let go, we let flow. We embrace uncertainty because we trust and are detached from an outcome. We allow ourselves and others to have freedom and be themselves without needing everything to go our way.

You may feel challenged right now, as you begin to reflect on your own behaviors and perhaps see all of these gremlins at work in your personality. Or perhaps you can particularly recognize one or two of these gremlins in your behavior and see how they affect your moment-by-moment choices and behavior.

To fully see the ego fear functioning below the surface requires you to humble the chatter of your ego and look honestly at what motivates your behavior. This requires courage and a desire to express your truth rather than your ego. It is motivated by a desire to feel authentic happiness and serenity rather than fear. It means letting go of the limiting story that has dominated your life and asking yourself if the current version of the movie of your life is how you genuinely, deeply want it to be.

When I recognized the destructive unconscious beliefs running my behavior, I became aware of how my fear of not being good enough or worthy of love had created an addiction to being loved. This love addiction caused me to lose myself to a man, to lose my focus, to give up my goals, to compromise my essence. It led me to embarrassment, failure, sadness and intense anxiety because I continually compromised myself and my truth.

Once I gained these insights, I was able to challenge the old mindset and release the unresourceful part of myself. The more awareness I gained, the more clarity I gained, and the more confidently I sought and affirmed my true essence.

As I began my journey toward my essence, toward self-love and truth, I began to recognize the personality traits that motivated those four gremlin behaviors. I observed twelve disempowering mindsets that, like Achilles' heel, kept me stuck in an egoic reality. Let's explore these in the next chapter.

CHAPTER 8

TWELVE SELF-DEFEATING MINDSETS

"Don't give in to your fears. If you do, you won't be able to talk to your heart."

Paulo Coelho, *The Alchemist*

In addition to the four ego gremlins—Compete, Compare, Compromise and Control—there are twelve *self-defeating mindsets* that we default to when we are emotionally challenged. These twelve masks of the ego each have their own unconscious payoff, and without awareness of these behaviors, they drain our personal power. These self-defeating patterns act as our Achilles heel.

Achilles was a hero in Greek mythology who fought in the Trojan War. As a child, his mother dipped him in the Styx River for protection and immortality. She dipped his whole body except for one heel, as that was how she held onto to him, and his heel became his "mortal" or most vulnerable and weak part. Although he became a great and powerful soldier, Achilles was purportedly killed by an arrow to his heel, representing how this vulnerable area eventually led to his downfall.

Each one of these twelve self-defeating mindsets acts as an Achilles heel as they rob us of our power and make us vulnerable. These mindsets mask the deepest fears of the ego-self.

An important step to transforming our pain is to become aware of our Achilles heel. Awareness lifts our hidden beliefs out of our unconscious mind and brings them to conscious awareness. Rather than hoarding old limiting ideas the way we hoard our old possessions in case we need them again in the future, we can let them go and free ourselves for more fulfilled and productive lives.

Although we all experience each of these mindsets to some degree, they are problematic when they become a habit and the default mindset we resort to when challenged. When we are stuck in these negative mindsets, we tend to react unthinkingly and replay the same disempowering story, which blocks us from finding our strength and moving forward.

Which of these mindsets do you recognize as your Achilles heel?

1. The Self-Pity Ego Mindset
- We blame others and complain (victim mentality)
- "Poor me," "Why me?"
- We believe we are unable to meet our own needs; we seek help and pity
- We take no personal responsibility
- We feel overwhelmed and disempowered
- We take ourselves too seriously

2. The Self-Loathing Ego Mindset
- We have an extreme dislike and rejection of self
- "I hate myself"
- We have a stubborn inner critic who sets unrealistic expectations
- We feel shame, embarrassment and guilt
- We feel we are not good enough or worthy
- We push people away; our bad behavior repels them
- We display narcissistic behavior; we seek others' admiration to boost our self-worth
- We feel threatened by others
- We feel angry; we hate ourselves
- We often sabotage opportunities
- We may be jealous, insecure or possessive of partners or isolate ourselves
- We may neglect ourselves
- We may deny ourselves food, overeat, or use harmful substances to numb our self-hatred
- We may punish ourselves

3. The Self-Harm Ego Mindset
- We feel the need to punish or restrict ourselves
- "Screw me"
- We treat ourselves poorly and disrespectfully
- We follow a destructive path: poor food choices, overeating, starvation; addictive behaviors such as alcohol, smoking, drugs; we attract negative or destructive people; we work in a negative environment; we stay in unfulfilling or abusive relationships; we are promiscuous; we succumb to emotions; we criticize ourselves
- We fear we are not lovable, worthy, or deserving of success and happiness
- We blame and punish ourselves
- We starve ourselves of appreciation and pleasure
- We build shame, which erodes self-confidence

4. The Self-Righteousness Ego Mindset
- We believe our ideas are correct/best and that we are superior to others
- "I am right. You are wrong"
- We focus on proving ourselves, justifying our beliefs and defending ourselves
- We create conflict and power plays
- We need to be right at all costs, which is dangerous
- We become arrogant and egocentric
- We lack empathy for others
- We lack openness to others' points of view; we forget that others also have valid points of view based on their life experiences and beliefs
- We defend our opinion until we feel validated
- We can be very competitive; we compare ourselves to others; we can be very controlling
- We can be defensive instead of listening openly
- We need to prove ourselves
- We exacerbate anger and stress and prevent deep connections with others

5. The Self-Doubt Ego Mindset
- We feel the absence of self-belief and self-confidence
- "I can't," "I will fail"
- We forget our abilities and resources; we don't listen to or trust intuition
- We question ourselves and compare ourselves with others
- We become more confused and lose track of our right path
- We don't feel we are deserving, so we don't attract much good
- We experience "glass ceiling syndrome": limits to success (scarcity mentality)
- We lose our enthusiasm and give up on our dreams
- We lose energy and aliveness
- This mindset usually kicks in when we take on the beliefs, judgements or assessments of those around us

6. The Self-Sabotage Ego Mindset
- We limit, damage, destroy or undermine ourselves; usually unconsciously
- "I shoot myself in the foot"
- We block our own goals and dreams
- We cause problems in our relationships
- We behave in ways that will bring us shame
- We give in to addictions or vices
- We stand in the way of our own success and happiness
- We procrastinate
- We become perfectionists
- We unconsciously seek situations that will validate a lack of self-worth
- We expect or anticipate failure
- When successful, we feel like an imposter; success feels uncomfortable
- We sabotage to avoid being hurt or failing
- We break the diet, disrupt a good relationship, repeat behaviors that we know will bring us shame or disappointment
- We compromise
- This mindset promotes self-doubt, self-loathing and self-pity

7. The Self-Preservation/Protection Mindset
- We have a basic instinct to protect ourselves
- "I must play small and safe"
- We have a deep need for safety
- We are shy or withdrawn
- We are risk-averse and controlling
- We squash our potential and remain psychologically immature
- Our need for safety overrides the need for happiness; we retreat into a comfort zone, close down our potential, stay small instead of taking chances
- We are guarded; we shield our heart; we prevent people from coming close
- We become stuck at the emotional or psychological age when we first experienced pain (e.g. the pain of rejection) and decided to withdraw and protect ourselves rather than embrace opportunities and adventures
- We avoid situations that make us feel vulnerable or weak
- We are likely to be misunderstood because we are not being authentic
- We don't speak up even when we have good ideas
- We may eat to create a protective layer
- This constant defensiveness and guardedness is exhausting

8. The Self-Sacrifice Ego Mindset
- We deny ourselves happiness, joy, pleasure, success; we don't feel worthy of the sweetness of life
- "I must make everyone else happy"
- We have an inability to receive; we put other people's needs first
- We people-please
- We have a lack of boundaries
- We feel empty, bored, stuck in a rut
- We feel frustrated
- We gain pleasure from martyrdom
- We compromise
- Pain is more comfortable than pleasure
- We feel that it is easier to deprive ourselves than risk rejection by asking for what we want

- This mindset can result in depression
- It can cause overwork and burnout
- It can take various forms: an inability to receive a gift or a compliment; not giving to ourselves or making time for ourselves; hiding in the comfort zone of addictive behaviors, e.g. poor food choices through not valuing oneself, resorting to alcohol instead of dealing with the issue, staying in a relationship to not hurt a partner or children by leaving; not seeking a pay raise

9. The Self-Absorption Ego Mindset
- We have a preoccupation with ourselves to the exclusion of others
- "What's in it for me?"
- We exhibit extreme selfishness and self-indulgent behavior; we are egotistical
- We have a disproportionate degree of concern regarding how we appear to others or what others think about us
- We have grandiose ideas about ourselves and our importance
- We feel excluded and rejected and even paranoid
- We block our ability to give to others or be compassionate
- We have a need to prove ourselves rather than genuinely being ourselves
- We have an underlying lack of self-belief; we don't feel good enough or worthy
- We have a sense of entitlement
- We take everything personally
- We feel people are talking about us and judging us or can't live without us
- We have an inability to give from the heart
- We feel empty, lonely, and insecure; we need to feel special; we are hungry for attention
- We have Compete and Compare gremlins present
- This mindset isolates us from others, or others begin to avoid us
- This extreme focus on oneself can create worry, depression, anxiety, obsessive-compulsive disorder and other unhealthy states of mind

10. The Self-Indulgence Ego Mindset
- We enjoy an excessive and unrestrained self-gratification
- "I want more"
- We feel out of control and impulsive
- We have an insatiable need to fill the void
- We lose self-respect and self-confidence
- We indulge in vices such as food, shopping, alcohol, drugs, sex, gambling or excessive spending
- This mindset can breed guilt, remorse and shame
- It increases stress and anxiety as we cannot trust our own choices
- The lack of self-worth results in a need to treat ourselves to fill the emptiness inside, but these treats are not nourishing because they are motivated by self-pity and self-loathing

11. The Self-Withdrawal Ego Mindset
- We retreat/withdraw in an unhealthy way
- "I can't face it"
- We avoid responsibility
- We end up feeling immobilized and disempowered
- We feel different and that we do not belong anywhere
- We avoid confrontation and shut down any feelings or expression of personal power
- We feel as if we have nothing to contribute
- We are motivated by fear and opt to remain in our comfort zone where we feel safe
- We feel the persistent need to run away, hide or escape results in emotional numbness as we try to disconnect from this pain
- The isolation results in intense loneliness, self-pity and self-loathing
- Instead of facing and dealing with relationship issues, we look for an exit strategy
- Instead of voicing our opinion or standing up for ourselves, we remain quiet

12. The Self-Conscious Ego Mindset
- We are intensely aware that we are being observed, judged or even ridiculed by others

- "What if I humiliate myself?"
- We feel embarrassed, shy, lacking in confidence
- We often feel frozen
- We have trouble finding our voice
- We are so focused on how we look and come across to others that we focus on them instead of on our purpose or on being of service to them
- This mindset is at the heart of fear of public speaking and of fully stepping into our purpose
- The (mis)perception that we are being judged exacerbates the pain of not being liked or worthy
- Blushing is common

Each one of these egoic mindsets illustrates what causes human suffering. We all experience moments in these mindsets, and in fact they are necessary for our survival. However, when they validate our perceived lack of worthiness and keep us stuck in the ego-self and disconnected from our true self, we suffer. On the other hand, when they prompt us to choose better and reconnect with our essence, they serve their purpose.

Becoming aware of the twelve self-defeating mindsets helps you challenge your thoughts and behavior. Shift the lens through which you see the world, and instead of searching outside of yourself for validation, reflect on which of the mindsets most reveal your Achilles heel. You can challenge your ego-self and awaken higher levels of self-awareness. Most importantly, you destroy the delusion of limiting ego-thoughts currently narrating your personal story and can instead begin to script a new story of empowerment and purpose.

CHAPTER 9

THE SCIENCE OF FEAR AND STRESS

"We cannot solve our problems with the same thinking we used when we created them."

Albert Einstein

I trust the last few chapters helped you recognize the delusional story of your ego-self. We create a story and identity based on the early decisions we make during painful defining moments. Our story determines our belief system and the terms and conditions of our self-worth. Those Ts and Cs give birth to our need to compete, compare, compromise and control, which in turn lead to our disempowering mindsets, our Achilles heel. It is inside this prison of the mind that we lose our freedom as human beings. Our struggle emerges from these false perceptions because we allow ourselves to be intoxicated by three toxic fears.

One of the best definitions of *fear* is "**F**alse **E**vidence **A**ppearing **R**eal." Although the ego's story is a false reality (false evidence), to our existing belief system it feels frightfully real. This is because every thought we've had, every belief, every feeling, every decision and association creates neurological pathways that *code* our brain in a particular way. These pathways form a detailed communication network. Think of them as the roads and highways that all our thoughts and information travel upon.

The brain recalls our stored memories to decide how we think, feel and act. It fires off pathways to help us respond to situations. Without us knowing, we develop a fear pattern that is based on our neural programming.

The way we are programmed can be likened to computer programming. Take a look at this: <!DOCTYPE html><html lang="en-AU"><head><style>.cta{}.default-theme{}#dood{}.fkbx{}#fkbx-hht{}.fkbx-hht-s{}#fkbx-text{}.lhide-sf{}.init{}.left-align-attr{}.light-text{}.mv-dot{}.mv-dot-bg{}.mv-focused{}.mv-link-hide{}.mv-{}.mv-locgradient{}.

No, this is not gobbledygook! That is the computer language that lies behind the face of Google. On screen we see the Google logo and search bar, but below the surface is an intricate script of code, an algorithm instructing Google's functionality. The logical sequence of coding tells Google what to do. Any changes to functionality require new coding.

Just as a software developer can rewrite the computer code, so can we alter and update our neural pathways to function in a way that yields greater calm than stress. Modern neuroscientists originally believed that the brain was hardwired; they now understand that it is malleable—it can adapt to the environment it is exposed to. When we change our perceptual experiences and thoughts, we change the neural pathways. The brain can therefore update itself.

The more we separate ourselves from the ego's deluded story, the more we discover who we truly are and why we are here. We can let go of a story that was scripted by a scared child. That scared child can reframe the memories causing emotional blocks. True healing and transformation occur the moment we write a new story.

And so, there is a science to fear, which explains why we get "stuck in stress" and stuck in the ego-self. To understand this best, we first need to explore the way we handle stress. Our *stress response* is managed by the brain and nervous system. The following is a simplified explanation of how our mind and body manage stress.

We perceive our environment through our senses of sight, sound, touch, smell and taste. When the mind perceives a possible threat, signals are sent to a part of the brain called the amygdala. The amygdala is the emotional processing system—it acts something like a security guard working outside a nightclub. Let's call it Butch. Butch has the job of filtering every thought we have as if deciding which guests to allow entry. Butch assesses whether we are safe or under threat.

Our "nightclub" comprises two rooms: a "Pleasure Room" and a "Panic Room." These two rooms represent the two parts of our autonomic nervous system that receive alerts from the brain: the parasympathetic and sympathetic nervous systems. Butch sends positive thoughts to the Pleasure Room and negative thoughts to the Panic Room.

The Pleasure Room is our parasympathetic nervous system. This is also known as our rest and digest mode, or relaxation response. Positive thoughts that make us feel calm activate the Pleasure Room. In the Pleasure Room, we know we are safe, and we stay connected to our inner power, our essence. We'll visit the Pleasure Room in the next section of the book.

The Panic Room is our sympathetic nervous system, whose function is to put us into a heightened state of alertness so that we can manage a possible threat. The sympathetic nervous system, in turn, activates the adrenal system: our survival mode. The adrenal system release stress hormones (such as adrenaline and cortisol) that enable the body to manage stress. Our heart rate increases, muscles tense, breathing becomes shallower, and we become more alert.

This stress response is also known as our *fight, flight or freeze response*. These three modes define how we handle stress. In fight mode, we face stress head-on, verbally or physically. In flight mode we run, withdraw or shut down. In freeze mode, we are frozen in fear, unable to fight or flee. The three ways we avoid pain—*react, distract or contract*, explained in Chapter 3—also explain the fight, flight and freeze modes.

Each of us has experienced different levels of stress. For those who have been brought up in safe and secure environments, this stress pattern is less heightened. Although this stress response is vital to our survival, the problem comes when the body gets stuck in stress. When we are exposed to high levels of compounded stress, the amygdala can become enlarged and create hypervigilance and heightened sensitivity to pressure. Like a drug addict, the body gets addicted to the rush of adrenalin and we remain trapped in our fight, flight or freeze modes. As the adrenal glands fatigue, we receive less stress hormones, such as adrenaline and cortisol, and begin to feel that we cannot cope as much as we used to. Stress then presents itself as depression and anxiety, or even worse, as illness.

Some of the most common stress symptoms include:

Fatigue	Anxiety	Lack of focus	Lack of energy
Apathy	Irritability	Low libido	Sleep disorders
Depression	Restlessness	Busy mind	Food cravings
Emotional outbursts	Shortness of breath	Future/past focused	Muscle pain/headaches

Most of us do not even realize we are in a state of stress. Our stress response happens automatically because we passively surrender to our environment. We blindly accept our lives because we don't know that a completely different way of being is possible. Our story of limitation is so embedded within us that we do not realize it causes an undercurrent of fear. We become so familiar with the Panic Room that we are oblivious to the existence of a Pleasure Room. We go through our daily routines in a trance-like state, on autopilot.

Our automatic stress responses and the limiting glass-ceiling beliefs of our ego keep us locked into our lower, unevolved self—our outdated software. Like a caveman, we stay stuck in survival mode, searching for safety rather than self-actualization. Instead of tuning into our essence, we resort to disempowering behaviors and mindsets.

We think that we are stressed because of work, relationships, health or finances, but in reality it is the ego's story that triggers our pain buttons and in turn signals Butch to protect us. If public speaking stresses us out, we think it's because we fear being in the spotlight, but to the unconscious mind operating below the surface of our awareness, we are actually afraid that people will judge us or embarrass us. Below that level of fear is a memory of humiliation associated with the infamous *I'm-not-good-enough* belief.

If you've ever caught yourself reacting to a look or tone of voice, you can be pretty sure that some old inner wound is setting off that fear sequence. In seconds, our *I'm-not-loved* buttons are pushed, causing us to feel rejected, disrespected or judged. We defensively snap back, walk away or just stare at the person in shock. Because that experience raises cortisol levels and feels uncomfortable, we do not want to be around those people. These responses are safety mechanisms of the nervous system. They are effectively a form of body wisdom.

This dynamic also explains the breakdown of attraction in relationships. If our partner repetitively gives us a contemptuous look or speaks in a harsh tone, we begin to associate that person with the release of cortisol. Because the cortisol release feels uncomfortable, we begin to feel self-protective, defensive or on edge. Over time, attraction breaks down and we are left feeling resentment, bitterness or hatred toward that person, and ultimately repelled by them.

What often happens after this sequence of emotions is that we create a story about it. For example, we will decide, "He always disrespects me," "He hates me" or "She thinks I am worthless." Because we are stuck in our own emotional meltdown, we may not check to see what is actually happening for that person and how they feel. Our interpretation very often is incorrect. They are usually not disrespecting or judging us but are experiencing their own pain and rejection and simply revealing their own feelings via a harsh expression or tone. This leads to the sad miscommunication cycle couples often find themselves stuck in. Many relationships dissolve as the result of these old unconscious, reactive patterns.

When I look back at my emotional breakdown, which resulted in divorce, I see a similar pattern at work. My nervous system, influenced by unresolved inner wounds, developed a heightened sensitivity to my husband's tone. His harsh and abusive tone was actually an indication of his own fear and pain, but because I was so triggered and did not understand that at the time, all I heard was the abuse, and all I registered was how small it made me feel.

Personal transformation and self-empowerment can therefore be seen not only as a way to update our neural programming but also as a way to heal the ego: to clear the memory, remove the buttons, let go of pain, and let go of limiting beliefs. When we release our toxic beliefs, we completely reprogram the nervous system. We can let go of the false and disempowering reality created by our pain and evolve to our higher brain center, the neocortex, where we perceive the world through the lens of our essence, our higher intelligence.

Mindfulness is a great technique to help transform the way we respond to stress. We will delve deeper into how to practice mindfulness in the following section. For now, as we are in a self-reflective stage, we want to first gain awareness. Having greater self-awareness is essential because we must first be able to notice how our story of limitation and our fear pattern affects us before we can change.

The first step is to become aware of what triggers stress for you and how you express that stress. Here are two ways you can begin this process:

1. Spend a day reflecting on your thoughts, especially the stressful thoughts revealing your ego mindset. How do those thoughts make you feel? Begin to notice your feelings, and notice how your thoughts are giving rise to your feelings.

2. If you find it difficult to notice your thoughts, then another way to begin this process is by noticing your feelings. When you feel triggered or stressed, tune in to your feelings. Once you are aware of your feelings, notice what thoughts triggered them. What were you thinking just before you had those feelings?

CHAPTER 10

OUR RELATIONSHIPS WITH LOVE, MONEY AND HEALTH

"When the mind goes beyond the thought of 'the me,' the experiencer, the observer, the thinker, then there is a possibility of a happiness that is incorruptible."

Jiddu Krishnamurti

When we are lost in the ego-self, we are unaware of how it controls our moment-to-moment decisions. The trance-like state of the ego keeps us stuck in poor habits and situations that limit our potential. The influence of our *lower self* is clearly visible in three key areas: how we manage our relationships, our money and our health.

LOVE

"There's no better laboratory for self-study than through relationships . . . Relationships can introduce you to the parts of yourself that might otherwise remain hidden."

Caroline Myss

The Australian Bureau of Statistics reported that 46,604 divorces were granted in Australia in 2016. According to the American Psychological Association, about 40 to 50 percent of married couples in the United States apply for a divorce. According to the Office for National Statistics in the United Kingdom, there were 106,959 opposite-sex divorces in 2016. I believe that one of the reasons so many relationships end is because they are based in ego.

When I look back at my twenty-four-year-old self, I clearly see that yes, I loved Shaun when we met, but my childhood emotional wounds were wide open. At that age I was still processing the pain of my parents' divorce as well as the pain of high school judgement and rejection. The relationship dovetailed with my level of consciousness at that time, my belief systems, the pain I was experiencing, and what I expected life to deliver.

I needed to be loved, needed to prove myself, and was desperately trying to seek not only my father's approval but approval from every man I met. I needed to be loved to prove my worthiness. If I was loved, then I was good enough. If I was in a relationship, then I was worthy. The terms and conditions of my self-worth defined my choices.

I was also very idealistic about how love should be expressed. I needed romance and to feel as if I was being taken care of. I needed compliments, praise and validation to feel safe and happy. My sense of fulfillment in relationships was based on how well my partner fulfilled these expectations.

These requirements reveal an ego-based relationship where the hidden agenda motivating our choices and influencing our attraction is the belief that we are not good enough or worthy enough to be loved. As a result, we compromise ourselves, ignore intuition and make a safe choice. We choose the path that proves our (lack of) worth. We get so caught up in the emotional high of being needed that we fail to see that we actually *are* valuable and worthy. The pain of rejection and the fear of being alone override confidence and keep us locked in anxiety. Because we are fearful, and therefore activating our stress response, we are not able to be authentically open with others. Instead, we protect ourselves: we shield our hearts from pain and develop inappropriate expectations.

These relationships are therefore not based on truth. They are based on whatever society, religion and the media have conditioned us to believe, such as the belief that we need to be in a relationship to be whole and complete. If we are single, we feel unlovable, unattractive, lonely, isolated, and we wonder if there is something wrong with us.

The need for connection is certainly one of our greatest human needs. However, there is a difference between *needing* love and *wanting* love. There is a difference between ego-based love and soul-love.

Soul-love relationships, as opposed to ego-based relationships, are derived from self-love, from the belief that *we are the essence of love*. In soul-love our intention is *to be* love rather than to *need* love. We want to share our "whole" self, our healed self, with a partner. We don't need them to love us. We simply *want* them to be with us. These are two very different intentions. Ego-based relationships come from the mind. They make sense and fulfill our need for safety. And although these needs have to be met, when we are disconnected from the calling of our hearts, they eventually become a problem.

Couples I have worked with transform their relationships when they both individually work on themselves. When they heal their personal pain, they open their hearts to the other. Then they can love on a pure level. They become less codependent and needy and more interdependent and equal.

If we are disconnected from our inner essence and searching outside of ourselves, we develop a void. The ego is insatiable in its efforts to fill that void, and our urgency makes us needy and dependent. Nothing will ever be enough. No one will love us enough. There will always be someone letting us down. We will never really feel completely worthy or safe enough to completely open. We crave love and remain stuck in expectations:

- I need you to love me a certain way
- I need you to validate me
- I need you to put me first
- I need you to compliment me
- I need you to acknowledge me
- I need you to see me
- I need you to hear me
- I need you to support me
- I need you to build me up
- I need you to have my back
- I need you to stand by me
- I need you to protect me
- I need you to make me feel special
- I need you to respect me
- I need you to honor me
- I need you to nurture and pamper me
- I need you to provide for me
- I need you to mother me
- I need you to do things my way
- I need you to make me feel complete

When these expectations are unmet, our belief in our unworthiness is validated and we feel disappointed and unloved, which in turn makes us feel unsafe with others. Over time, this disappointment leads to a build-up of resentment, and our feelings of attraction diminish because on a deep level that person is not fulfilling our ego need to feel loved and good enough.

Even sex validates the ego's senses and expectations. Ego-sex is all about sexual gratification: the focus is on orgasm rather than mindful heart connection and sensual pleasure. The ego's need for worth is satisfied by the knowledge that we have provided pleasure for another person.

Here are a few indicators of how ego might be showing up in your relationships:

- We take comments and actions personally
- We become controlling or possessive
- We feel insecure, lack trust and can be jealous
- We find it hard to forgive
- We feel disappointment or resentment
- We feel our needs are not being met
- We turn to sex for connection, intimacy and personal gratification
- We fear abandonment
- Communication is antagonizing and defensive We lack compassion and are judgmental
- We get angry or frustrated easily
- We are dependent on the other person for our safety
- Physical attraction forms the basis of this kind of relationship
- We focus on or react to what other people think
- We keep score of wins and losses; we play "tit for tat"
- We fear rejection
- Relationships are based on financial security or status

I believe so many people today find themselves single because solitude offers time to heal and time for self-development. Ego drives are shifting on a planetary level, and fear no longer serves the journey of the soul. This is particularly true for the current spiritually awakening generation. The more we discover our essence, the more we discover our truth, and the less we are limited to an egoic existence.

Through the connection with our essence we transcend the ego's need for love. We let go of the inner child's pain and limiting belief system that keeps us stuck in a fear-based reality. We discover that loving ourselves is more empowering than needing to be loved. We enable ourselves to have a mature relationship based on pure love and spiritual awareness. Through the eyes of the essence, expectations turn into acceptance and fear becomes self-empowerment.

MONEY

"Abundance is not something we acquire. It is something we tune into."

Wayne Dyer

When I left my marriage over a decade ago, I walked out of a million-dollar home in the ideal location with five bedrooms and an indoor swimming pool. I had the *lot*. As I packed, I felt sick at the number of possessions crammed in our cupboards. All those post-argument shopping sprees when we thought that more possessions would somehow unite us! My eight boxes were all I really needed. I left my painful memories behind with the excess.

After a few months of separated life, I had another revelation. I was thousands of miles away from my opulent Bel-Air upbringing; I was "down under"—far away from the South African pretenses and estranged from all the stuff I had hoped would fill my emptiness. As I lay in my tiny apartment with only the essentials, I suddenly felt immense gratitude. Throughout my life, I always had moments of thankfulness, but this was different. My heart buzzed with an expansiveness I hadn't previously experienced. I was finally full.

It was as if I had to strip away all the clutter to have the space to see my life clearly. I now had the elbow room to see what really mattered. Not only did this new awareness help me reflect on my own money mindset, it also opened my eyes to how ego shows up in our relationship with money.

Our money mindset is influenced by our core beliefs. A healthy belief system generates feelings of worthiness, a natural comfort with prosperity, as well as healthy spending and saving habits. However, a limited belief system, stemming from our three toxic beliefs, reflects those distortions in emotional blocks toward money. Having money validates our self-worth, and a lack of it reveals the following limiting ego beliefs:

- I am only worthy and good enough if I earn an abundant income
- Success equals wealth
- I am a failure if I do not have money
- I am not worthy of abundance
- I need financial security to feel safe

- To succeed, I need a solid career
- Money is hard to earn or hard to maintain
- Money is the root of all evil
- People will accept me if I have money
- I will never earn enough
- You have to have money to make money
- I am not good with money
- People will respect me when I have money
- Money is the cause of stress
- Money is for greedy people
- Money is available to people who come from money
- Money is not spiritual
- Money will make me happy
- I don't know how to earn money
- Money will bring me status
- I need money to survive
- Money will offer me abundance
- Penny-wise and pound-foolish
- Money doesn't grow on trees
- Money reflects how good I am
- People will judge me if I make a lot of money
- People will use me if I have money

The ego-self confuses abundance with materialism and wealth with worthiness. The ego-self is based on a scarcity, fear-based mindset, and since the underlying emotion is fear, money and all the beliefs we hold around money cause us stress (because our nervous system gets trapped in our stress responses), and we get stuck in survival mode.

Worst of all, we get caught in the web of constantly having to prove ourselves—of constantly needing more money and more stuff to prove our worth. Once again the ego is insatiable: we will never have enough. Because the ego's beliefs are fear-based, the energy we hold around money is also fear-based. A fear-based mindset activates the following behaviors:

- We find it hard to acquire money
- We are controlling
- We are competitive
- We compare ourselves to others

- We have expectations around what we should have and should earn
- We need to look good and "keep up with the Joneses"
- We seek instant gratification
- We stress about bills and expenses
- We have a fear of missing out
- We constantly dream of having more
- We are future-focused, forever planning our next purchase
- We are stuck in the past, reminiscing about what we lost
- We are attached to possessions
- We are paycheck-driven and choose careers because of the living they earn us
- We complain that there is never enough

When we let go of our emotional attachment to money, money shifts from being something we need to accumulate to prove our worth to its original purpose as a neutral currency of exchange. When we realize that our energy determines the flow of our money, we are compelled to shift our fear-based beliefs and scarcity mindset to more empowering *money-attractive* beliefs.

Scarcity is merely the absence of abundance. As Tony Robbins says, "When we are grateful, fear disappears and abundance appears." When we are grateful, we know that *we* are enough, what we have is enough, and everything is in perfect order. Our fear-based scarcity beliefs transform into beliefs of abundance. Our motivations and decisions around money also change. With an abundant mindset we believe the following:

- We are alive for a purpose and want to share that purpose with the world
- We are fueled by enthusiasm
- We know we are enough and have enough, and that everything around us is serving our purpose
- We let go of material distractions and surround ourselves with the simple things we need
- Fewer and simpler possessions make us happy
- We let go of past attachments
- We let go of the need to survive and begin to thrive
- We become more generous

- We are less competitive as we know that our intention to serve will create opportunities
- We surround ourselves with beauty rather than excess
- We know that it is our birthright to have a full life. Prosperity follows this realization
- We drop our expectations and become more appreciative of what we have
- We stop chasing more for its own sake
- We stop focusing on the future and enjoy the moment

We are open to receiving goodness. An abundant mindset awakens when we let go of ego and embrace the essence of our true selves. Instead of controlling, competing, compromising and comparing, we flow with the natural abundance that is so prevalent in the world. We trust that our needs are always met, that we are always looked after. We begin to work *on purpose* rather than *for paycheck*, and pure intention instantly brings us feelings of wholeness and empowerment.

HEALTH

"The soul always knows what to do to heal itself.
The challenge is to silence the mind."

Caroline Myss

The ego's looping monologue, stuck on autoplay, has detrimental effects on three aspects of our health: our psychological/emotional health, our physical health and our energetic health. Although a few of these stress symptoms were mentioned in Chapter 9, let me elaborate.

Psychologically we get stuck in *busy mind syndrome*. "Monkey-mind" chatter creates turbulence and restlessness in the nervous system. We get stuck either ruminating on the past or anticipating the future. While thinking about the past and future are necessary cognitive functions, engaged in excessively they create anxiety. Thoughts such as these trigger a stress response:

- I can't do this
- I don't belong
- They don't accept me
- They are judging me
- Will my job be made redundant?
- Do they need me?
- Can I trust him/her?
- What if I fail?

The body is approximately 60 percent water. Positive, soothing thoughts are like a gentle breeze caressing a calm sea, but every time we have a stressful thought, a tsunami of waves floods the body's aquarium. This inner storm creates turmoil, leaving us feeling irritable, restless, nervous, angry, sad, anxious and frustrated.

Like a drug addict on a trip, stress hormones create hallucinations of reality. Adrenaline and cortisol kick in, distorting our perception. Instead of perceiving the truth about a situation, we arrive at inappropriate assumptions because we are looking through the lens of the ego's self-focus. *Ego-alert mode* perceives an intense stare from a person as judgement; we feel vulnerable when they look at us. This limited perspective does not consider the bigger picture. Instead of realizing that the other person might not be thinking about us at all or might be caught up in his or her own emotional stuff, we take their expression personally. Our protective mechanisms are triggered, and we defensively squawk, "What are you looking at?" As a result, we increase conflict in our relationships and that, in turn, increases our stress levels. Hormonal stress-addiction leads to addictive behaviors:

- Substance abuse
- Work addiction
- Perfectionism
- Addiction to self-defeating
- Overthinking
- Money addiction
- Love addiction
- Ego mindsets/emotions
- Competitiveness
- Drama and chaos
- Excessive spending

Physically, high levels of cortisol have been found to have dangerous effects on our health:

- Fatigue and tiredness upon waking
- Food cravings (especially sugary and salty foods)
- Alcohol cravings
- Weight gain (especially around the belly)
- Muscle pains or headaches
- Gut/digestive problems
- Inability to shake a cold
- Frequent illness
- Increase in insulin (which may increase chance of diabetes)
- Depression
- Compound stress may lead to adrenal fatigue or adrenal collapse/burnout

Physical stress plays a major role in the choices we make around food. Emotionally we get attached to food to make us feel better. Both sugar and alcohol can be seen as fuel for the ego, and they keep us stuck in and addicted to stress. We eat or drink to uplift ourselves, energize ourselves, numb ourselves, give us a sense of confidence, distract from boredom or loneliness, or because we want to connect socially with others.

While writing this chapter, a memory surfaced that generated a useful insight. Between the ages of seven and twelve I danced four times per week. I loved dancing. It was my therapy, my escape into a fluid world of creativity, and time with my best friend. Every Thursday evening after dance class, we would go to the food court in the Beverly Center and have chicken wings. I recall us devouring the chicken wings, building a plate of bones as high as my emotions! The emotion I feel when I tap into this memory is bliss—pure happiness. I feel loved and happy.

Like a well-trained Pavlovian dog, food became associated with belonging and blissful happiness. So whenever I felt empty and alone, I needed food to fill me up and make me happy. Over the years I have turned to food for emotional support, resulting in a debilitating food addiction.

Stress also impacts our *energetic health* and affects the natural balance of the body. Let's liken the busy thoughts and stress responses in the body to applications open on your smartphone. As they run in the background, they quickly drain your phone's battery. You periodically need to close those programs to prolong your battery's life. The thousands of thoughts and the physical responses that occur outside our conscious awareness drain our energy, leaving us feeling scattered and fatigued. All this background turbulence has serious effects on our energetic body. The more we gain awareness of dysfunctional and fearful thoughts, the more we clear our energy and manage it accordingly.

According to ancient Eastern medicine, the energetic body is made up of seven energy centers called chakras. Translated, the word *chakra* means "spinning wheel." Each energy center is a spinning vortex that our life force (*chi*) flows through. Healthy energy spins vibrantly and easily. Blocked energy will be more sluggish and heavy. Each chakra is placed over seven key areas in the body and governs surrounding organs and glands. In her book *Anatomy of the Spirit*, Caroline Myss explains how each chakra represents certain emotional lessons. Energy blockages in a specific chakra represent the emotional blockage and life lesson that relates to that chakra. For example, if we have an emotional block in our throat chakra, we will find it difficult to express ourselves clearly. We may not speak up for ourselves, or we may become aggressive or defensive.

Our thoughts determine the health or vibrancy of our chakras. Positive thoughts that generate positive emotions also generate a high frequency of energy. Negative thoughts generate negative feelings and a denser frequency of energy. We can easily feel the vibrations of those frequencies: when we are happy we feel uplifted and energetic, and when we are upset we feel drained and fatigued.

Here is a simple chart that outlines the seven energy centers to help you identify any possible emotional blocks caused by dysfunctional ego beliefs:

ENERGY CENTER/ CHAKRA	ASSOCIATED BODY PART	EMOTION/THOUGHTS ATTACHED	LIFE LESSON/ ASSOCIATED MEANINGS
Base (Root) Chakra Associated Color: Red	• Spine • Legs • Feet • Rectum • Immune system • Prostate • Bladder • Adrenal glands	**WHEN ENERGIZED:** • Feeling safe • Belonging • Grounded/relaxed • Secure • Material/financial safety • Present in the here and now **WHEN BLOCKED:** • Fatigue • Feeling unsafe • Insecure • Fear of not fitting it/ not being accepted • Rejection/ abandonment • Material instability and fear • Past/future • Restlessness	• Relating to our physical, material world. • Survival and safety • Ability to belong to one's "tribe" • Ability to manifest money • Connection to earth • Connection with family **POSITIVE THOUGHT PATTERNS:** • I am safe • I belong • I am accepted • I accept myself • I take responsibility for my life • I can manifest what I need • I am grounded

Sacral (Sexual) Chakra Associated Color: Orange	- Lower abdomen - Sexual organs - Large intestine - Pelvis - Hip area - Womb - Ovaries - Kidneys - Gallbladder - Adrenal glands - Gonads	**WHEN ENERGIZED:** - Healthy sexual energy - Charisma - Abundance - Creativity - Healthy relationships/ connection - Pleasure/sweetness of life - Maternal/paternal instinct **WHEN BLOCKED** - Guilt - Shame - Money issues (scarcity) - Risk averse - Sexual dysfunctions - Lower libido - Power and control issues - Addiction/ obsessions - Blocked creativity - Inability to be vulnerable	- Relating to sexuality - Relating to money and power - Healing relationships - Creative expression **POSITIVE THOUGHT PATTERNS:** - I express myself creatively - I accept my sexuality - I am sensual - I connect with others - I enjoy the pleasures of life - I am nurturing - I am abundant

ENERGY CENTER/ CHAKRA	ASSOCIATED BODY PART	EMOTION/THOUGHTS ATTACHED	LIFE LESSON/ ASSOCIATED MEANINGS
Solar Plexus Associated Color: Yellow	• Stomach • Liver • Pancreas • Spleen • Digestion • Middle spine • Adrenal glands	**WHEN ENERGIZED:** • Confidence • Belief • Healthy self-esteem • Empowerment • Care of self • Self-respect • Trust • Personal honor • Healthy boundaries • Self-care • Courage **WHEN BLOCKED:** • Shame • Blame • Submissive • Competitive • Aggressive • Loss of control • Sensitivity to criticism • No personal boundaries	Relating to how one sees oneself: fear, trust, confidence, empowerment, personality and self-esteem issues **POSITIVE THOUGHT PATTERNS:** • I am strong • I believe in myself • I can take care of myself • I can protect myself • I respect myself • I am disciplined

Heart Associated Color: Green	• Heart and circulatory system • Lungs • Shoulders and arms • Ribs/breasts • Diaphragm • Thymus gland	**WHEN ENERGIZED:** • Joy • Love • Acceptance • Connection • Forgiveness • Trust • Hope • Compassion • Unity • Gratitude • Peace • Openness **WHEN BLOCKED:** • Anger • Criticism/judgment • Resentment • Sadness • Grief • Loneliness • Hatred • Self-centeredness • Guarded/protected	Relating to love, forgiveness, compassion, joy **POSITIVE THOUGHT PATTERNS:** • I forgive and let go • I accept myself and others • I trust myself and the world • I am connected to everyone around me • I am grateful for everything in my life • I love myself and love others • I am peaceful • I am open and share myself with the world

ENERGY CENTER/ CHAKRA	ASSOCIATED BODY PART	EMOTION/ THOUGHTS ATTACHED	LIFE LESSON/ ASSOCIATED MEANINGS
Throat Associated Color: Blue	• Throat • Thyroid • Neck • Mouth • Teeth • Gums • Esophagus • Thyroid gland	**WHEN ENERGIZED:** • Clear expression • Good listening skills • Truthful • Creative expression • Willpower • Positive choices • Decisiveness **WHEN BLOCKED:** • Difficulty expressing self • Blocked creative expression • Excessive talking • Fear of speaking • Shyness • Too loud/too weak • Poor listening skills • Gossiping	Relating to will, self-expression/ communication, creative expression **POSITIVE THOUGHT PATTERNS:** • I speak my truth • I speak up for myself • I speak with integrity and purpose • I listen to understand • I am in control of myself and my choices • I articulate myself well • I choose my words wisely • What I have to say matters • I speak from my heart • I express my creativity with passion and purpose

Third Eye Associated Color: Indigo	• Brain • Nervous system • Eyes, ears • Nose • Hormonal issues • Pituitary gland	**WHEN ENERGIZED:** • Good imagination • Can read emotions of others • Truthful • Intelligent • Feelings of adequacy • Open-minded • Ability to learn from experiences • Intuitive • Insightful • Vision for life • Can see the big picture • Focused mind • Clarity **WHEN BLOCKED:** • Confusion • Stuck in the past • Delusions • Obsessions • Lack of spiritual awareness • Rigid thinking • Unimaginative • Cannot visualize future	• Relating to the mind, intuition, foresight, insight • Emotional intelligence (EQ), self-reflection • The ability to see beyond what the physical eyes can see • Psychic abilities **POSITIVE THOUGHT PATTERNS:** • I trust my intuition • I have everything I need within me • I listen to my inner wisdom • I understand that there is more to a person than meets the eye • I let go of perceived mistakes and trust I can create a successful future • I am clear • I use my imagination to empower my thoughts • I focus on the big picture

ENERGY CENTER/ CHAKRA	ASSOCIATED BODY PART	EMOTION/THOUGHTS ATTACHED	LIFE LESSON/ ASSOCIATED MEANINGS
Crown Associated Color: Violet	• Muscular system • Skeletal system • Skin • Cerebral cortex upper brain • Pineal gland	**WHEN ENERGIZED:** • Strong values • Strong ethics • Courage • Spiritual connection • Selflessness • Trust in life • Wisdom • Soul connection • Connection to cosmic energy • Experience of bliss • Faith mindset • Enlightenment **WHEN BLOCKED:** • Spiritual detachment/ spiritual addiction • Anxiety • "Busy mind syndrome"/over-thinking • Limiting beliefs • Materialism • Closed mind • Uncertainty • Limited body awareness (detached from feelings) • Learning difficulties	Relating to our spiritual connection and higher-self self-realization **POSITIVE THOUGHT PATTERNS:** • I am connected to my higher self • I listen to the wisdom of my soul • I trust the universe has my back • I have faith in my future • I am connected to everything around me • I can see the essence within each person • I am pure and free • I see the joy in every situation

Take a moment to tune into your body and notice where you feel tightness, tension or fatigue. Hold your attention on that part of your body and sense how your energy feels. Does it feel uplifted or drained? Drained energy signals an emotional block. Tune in to your emotions even more deeply and take note of your feelings and thoughts. What memories and limiting beliefs are "stuck" in your body, and what life lessons do they relate to?

CHAPTER 11

PERSONIFYING THE EGO-SELF: BEFRIENDING THE BEAST

"The greatest conflicts are not between two people but between one person and himself."

Garth Brooks

Meet Molly. Molly is my ego. Molly needs a lot of attention and, to be honest, only cares about herself and her ambitions. She's hungry—hungry for love, hungry for success and hungry to prove herself. She constantly seeks validation, is dependent on others, and makes choices based on her emotions. She is certainly not the finest version of myself. Her nickname is SP as she always defaults into her self-pity monologue:

I don't fit into society. I don't think I have the heart for this world. People don't really like me and certainly don't understand me. If only I had been born more beautiful, I would have achieved more in my life. And it's all because of my father. If he'd loved me more and done the right thing, I could have had more self-esteem and confidence. Imagine what I could have become if I'd had the right support!

Her insecurities cause social awkwardness. On a good day she can be confident—sometimes overconfident, even domineering. On her bad days she hides in the background and can't find anything to say.

She is a paradox, a perfectionist, a people-pleaser and a pest. Food, in particular, is a problem. Sugar is her vice. It's the main item on the menu at her pity party and feeds her emptiness. Food offers her the sweetness she craves. She has moments of clarity and moments of strength, but as soon as something challenging takes place that confirms her inner story, she retreats into her shell.

Melancholy and anxiety have owned her for many years. Constantly comparing herself to others exhausts her and holds her back from being all she can be. She is blind to her life purpose. She doesn't even realize that she has one. Her fear and self-doubt keep her stuck in low self-worth experiences. She has no idea what it would be like to be empowered. She assumes she's happy but knows something is missing; something is holding her back.

Now it's time for you to identify *your* ego-self, to personify your lower self in order to dissociate from it. Personification means we take the abstract and give it qualities that help us view it in a new light. Dissociation is a technique used to separate ourselves from difficult emotions. Once we properly identify the ego-self, we disrupt its control over us: we tear ourselves away from its controlling hand and begin to see who we truly are without the ego's conditioned awareness.

The following exercise is an intervention I have used with hundreds of clients to help them move beyond their ego and find their true essence. This exercise helps us play with the dark side of ourselves. By adding a bit of humor we can realize that the ego-self is not all of us; it is only a part of us—the pained parts that house all our fearful attitudes, beliefs and choices, and the decisions we made to "mindlessly believe." The ego is the adaptation of our true self, the person we believe we need to be to survive in the world. Just as the basilisk lizard can run along water for twenty meters before sinking, we are able to operate a false persona for a period of time, but ultimately it is unsustainable and "takes us under."

Ego personification allows you to objectify your fear and loosen your attachment to it. It helps you realize that YOU ARE NOT YOUR FEAR. It is not your identity. It is simply an emotion you have taken on because of a series of unconscious dysfunctional beliefs. Fear is your mask or shield protecting you from your most vulnerable insecurities.

INSTRUCTIONS:
- Think of a person or situation that usually triggers a fear/stress response.
- Notice all the emotions you feel and imagine catching them in a net, as if you are catching butterflies.
- Now imagine drawing those emotions out of your body. See them in front of you.
- Notice how you feel without that *E-GOO* inside you. Can you feel the space and expansiveness?

Now, let us create your ego profile.

1. What is the first image that comes to mind as you see all that emotion and negativity in front of you?

What does it look like? Some people see a big black bog, a black cloud, a scared child, a cartoon or movie character, or a little monster. (Try not to overthink this; have fun and notice the first image that comes to your mind.)

2. Give it a name.

(Fred, Jerry, Walter, Jacquie, Molly, Ginger, etc.) Again, trust whatever comes to mind first. The more fun you can have with this exercise, the better. Laughter lightens our emotions and dissolves the power we give to ego. It is the reason angels fly: because they take themselves so lightly.

3. Now think of all the behaviors that belong to ego.

These include your limiting beliefs, habits, thoughts, decisions, addictions, ego-values, needs and reactions. Tap into your ego's monologue and mindsets. Consider which of the four inner gremlins most frequently possesses you: Compete, Compare, Comprise or Control.

Include all the negative emotions those behaviors and beliefs create, such as anger, frustration, overwhelm, anxiety, depression, sadness, irritation, loneliness, guilt, shame, resentment, blame, exhaustion.
- What are your ego's beliefs?
- Which of your behaviors come from your ego?
- Which of your habits?
- What repetitive patterns do you observe?
- Which emotions are generated by your ego?

4. When you have identified your ego dynamic, consider how and when this personality was formed.

List any significant emotional events that come to mind. These are the moments when you felt trauma or pain as a child—the moments those key perceptions and decisions took place. Notice what beliefs and decisions you made because of these experiences.
- How do those emotions affect you physically?
- How do they affect you mentally?
- Observe which thoughts come from a fear-based mindset—your inner fear of not being good enough, not worthy or loved.
- How do you express your stress? (Fight, flight, freeze or a combination?)
- Observe your body language.
- Observe your emotions and feelings.

5. What reality are you creating for yourself?
- What decisions are you making for yourself and your life?
- What are the consequences of those decisions?
- What is this mindset costing you?
- What are you missing out on?
- What will you have in your life once you let go of this mindset?
- What opportunities open up for you?
- How does that make you feel?

HELPFUL QUESTIONS TO ASK
- Who am I if I am not my fear?
- When I remove the feeling of fear from my physical body, what is in its place?
- Who was I before I took on my limiting beliefs?
- When I let go of fear, who can I be?

HERE IS A CASE STUDY TO HELP YOU WITH THIS EXERCISE:

Janet was a forty-year-old client who came to see me because she had a problem with alcohol and desperately wanted to find a partner and have children. (She has given permission for me to share her experience in this book as she so perfectly depicted her ego-self.)

Janet named her ego-self "Jerry."

Jerry looked like a timid, sad and lonely girl. She stood in front of Janet with her head falling onto her chest and her shoulders sagging in surrender.

Jerry had just been slapped and yelled at by her father, who had told her that she was useless, was nothing like her sister, was ugly, and would never amount to anything. This was the memory attached to Janet's pain.

She knew she had good qualities, but her father's words had all but destroyed her and shut down any belief she had in herself. She realized that from that moment, she let go of any connection to her innocent inner child and developed hatred for her father, herself, and life itself. As she grew into her adult self, this hatred led her to sabotage every relationship that came her way. She drowned her sorrows with alcohol.

Janet went on to create a detailed list of who she is as Jerry and who she is when accessing her true self:

BELIEFS ABOUT HERSELF	ACTIONS/BEHAVIORS
- I am ugly	- Weak
- I am not as good as my sister	- Insecure
- My father hates me	- Needy
- My father thinks I am worthless	- Wants to be loved
- I am judged by everyone	- Scared to be alone
- Men don't love me	- Loves to drink
- I am boring without alcohol	- Needs to drink
- I need a drink to feel strong	- Needs a man
- I cannot be on my own	- Feels complete with a man
- Men don't like my body	- Hates her father
- I am worthless	- Allows herself to be abused
- I am unlovable	- Chooses the wrong men
- Only beautiful people have relationships	- Is very intense in a relationship
- I am scared of having children	- Loves to have sex
- I don't trust myself	- Loves to feel pretty
- I don't respect myself	- Wants to people-please and make everyone happy
- I am not proud of anything I have done	- Cannot communicate her true feelings well
	- Is ruining her chance to have children
	- Withdraws and sulks when upset
	- Judges herself and others

Perhaps you can see yourself through this raw and vulnerable case study, or perhaps your beliefs do not seem as severe. Whatever the case, who are you as an ego? Give the *ego personification exercise* a go.

Take a few days to reflect on your ego traits and contemplate the questions above. Keep a journal of your answers and insights. As you have a realization, write it down. If you struggle to answer the questions, ask friends to share their observations of you or work with a coach or therapist. We all have blind spots and can feel vulnerable facing up to them, so be gentle on yourself as you face your weaknesses. Remind yourself that this exercise is serving you and empowering you.

The ego personification exercise helps you recognize that those beliefs and behaviors are not your identity. They are the result of your fear story and the negative narration that has conditioned you over time.

This story is not the whole you. There is another part underneath the armor. There is another part buried deep within your core, dying to come out and be discovered. There is a core essence within you that is the whole, authentic and true, empowered you. This essence is calling you.

ARE YOU READY to discover your authentic essence?

For further assistance and insights, please refer to the Self-Discovery Hub on my website: www.cheryneblom.com

CHAPTER 12

A SUMMARY OF THE EGO-SELF

"There is no world apart from what you wish, and herein lies your ultimate release. Change but your mind on what you want to see, and all the world must change accordingly."

A Course in Miracles: Lesson 132

Here is a quick summary of the ego-self:

KEY FEATURES:
- The ego is the part of our brain that makes sense of the world around us.
- Like a computer's operating system, it operates by an algorithm (set of rules) that instructs us to think, feel and behave in the way that it believes will keep us safe.
- This coding is the result of every perception and decision made during the significant emotional events of our life. The ego, therefore, is our conditioned self.
- The ego separates us from others and makes us feel different and isolated.
- The ego is the lens through which we view the world around us.
- We are often unaware that there are other ways of viewing our world.
- The ego's mindset is one of fear because it has become separated from our authentic self.

EGO CORE FEARS/LIMITING BELIEFS:
- I am not loved
- I am not good enough
- I am not worthy

INTENTION/PURPOSE:
The ego aims to keep us safe and in the comfort zone of what we know.

Its key values are:
- Survival
- Self-protection
- Achievement

SIX CORE WOUNDS:
- Rejection
- Uncertainty/fear of change
- Abandonment
- Judgment/criticism/humiliation
- Betrayal
- Failure

FOUR CORE BEHAVIORS (GREMLINS) GENERATED BY A FEARFUL MINDSET:
- Compare
- Compete
- Compromise
- Control

TWELVE SELF-DEFEATING MINDSETS:
- Self-pity
- Self-loathing
- Self-harm
- Self-righteousness
- Self-doubt
- Self-sabotage
- Self-protection
- Self-sacrifice
- Self-absorption
- Self-indulgence

- Self-withdrawal
- Self-consciousness

PRESENTING EMOTIONS:

Anger, irritability, frustration, guilt, shame, embarrassment, resentment, disappointment, sadness, anxiety, restlessness, nervousness, worry, fear, confusion, and defensiveness.

PHYSICAL EFFECTS:

Survival mode: fight, flight or freeze

Anxiety, depression, mental illness, fatigue, increased heart rate and raised sugar levels.

"[W]e are, in our essential state, pure consciousness. Pure Consciousness is pure potentiality; it is the field of all possibilities and infinite creativity. Pure consciousness is our spiritual essence."

Deepak Chopra

PART TWO: SELF-DISCOVERY

On self-reflection we often discover toxicity clouding the clarity of our true self.

This is the tainted ego-self.

When we lift the clouds of doubt, we discover who we really are.

Self-discovery is a return to our essence.

It is knowing our authentic selves and what unique virtues we were born with.

Once we discover our individual virtues, we realize that we have a higher purpose.

We are here, in this lifetime, for a specific reason:

to contribute to and share our individual gifts with the world.

When we are connected to our essence we allow our purpose to speak louder than our fear.

We will light up the world in the best way we can.

We are left with a choice: to deliberately *choose* our thoughts and emotions—sadness or happiness, doubt or belief, fear or love.

We can be the old, safe version of ourselves, or we can be the purposeful version.

We can be the tainted ego-self or the authentic self; ego or essence . . .it is up to us to decide.

CHAPTER 13

THE COURAGE TO CHANGE

"God grant me the serenity to accept the things I cannot change; courage to change the things I can; and wisdom to know the difference."

Reinhold Niebuhr

I'm going to die here, I thought.

My extreme desire to transform myself and purify my thoughts and beliefs led me to the woods of an outer Melbourne suburb. I found myself a spiritual mentor named Eagle. I found his advertisement when flipping through one of those New Age magazines. The headline read, *Awaken the Shaman Within.* These words spoke to me. I felt not only interested in his course but *called* to participate. It was time to activate my soul's purpose and help people to heal. To do so I needed to be the best version of myself.

Almost a year had passed since I received what I now refer to as my "cosmic download." The insights I received about fear and ego had set me on a journey of self-inquiry to rid myself of the *toxins of fear*. These are the key statements that resonated the most:

> *This toxin takes over our perception of reality when we let it into our consciousness. We lose ourselves in this intoxicated state and forget who we truly are . . . As an agent of transformation, my role is to help people gain self-awareness and recognize the fear within them. Once they notice the effects of fear they can detach and purify themselves of this inner poison. And in this awakened state they will find their purpose and live courageous lives.*

In Part One we delved into the self-reflection stage. Although greater awareness is an important first step, it is not enough to be aware of the ego-self. I had done the work of identifying my ego-self. I knew which beliefs were limiting me. I was aware of all the decisions I had made in my defining moments. I was aware of how those decisions had imprinted me and scripted the terms and conditions of my self-worth. I knew which gremlins were at play. I understood my fear response and how I expressed my stress. I was aware of my self-doubt, my self-pity and my self-sabotage.

But this awareness wasn't enough. I wanted to understand who I am as an essence. Once I detach and purify myself of these inner poisons, then what? If I am not my fear, then who am I? How do I return to my true essence and allow this essence to become my new default mode?

Eagle's shaman training spoke to me. I felt it was going to take me on the next part of my journey, and indeed it did. Our first two sessions were so deep that I decided to surrender to the process and not question his guidance at all. When he asked me to wear a singlet top and light pants for our next spiritual mentoring session even though it was winter, I trusted him completely. I also knew that our work together would involve a type of vision quest.

A vision quest is a Native American ceremony, a rite of passage that helps a person through a life transition. Vision quests call their participants to escape the noise and clutter of day-to-day life, immerse themselves in nature, and retreat into silence. According to ancient wisdom, in this space of silence we can connect with our soul and hear our calling.

Eagle guided me on a gentle vision quest; the more intense journeys require three to four days of fasting and questing in nature on one's own. As I had two small children, I didn't have the freedom to do that. But I was also not ready for such intensity. I wanted to dip my toe into the water of the vision quest first. (It turned out that this was intense enough!)

So there I was, eyes closed, standing bare-footed in a "tree pose" with my spiritual mentor as he guided me into a meditative state. The evening fog felt like a vapor as it wrapped around my cold shoulders. Dew-damp ground held the imprints of my bare feet and the rustling leaves seemed to be cheering me on. Standing there, I realized how far I had come from what I thought was my broken self. I was worlds away from my stressful married life, from those nights where I lay in bed in despair.

But even though I could see the growth I had achieved and knew how much more of my limiting self I wanted to heal, I was breathless. I was having second thoughts. Fear had a tight grip on my brain and held me hostage to my story. My mind raced. I had flashes of myself collapsing, flashes of my body parts freezing. My inner drama queen could see the headline news: "Single mother of two found frozen to death in the southeastern suburbs of Melbourne. No one found her. She was left for dead."

What the fuck was I thinking agreeing to this quest! What is the purpose of all this? The adrenaline surging through my body was too much for me. I could not focus; I could not still my mind. My heart pounded. My breath was short, and my body was shaking.

"Cheryne, what did you ask me in our first session?" Eagle asked, breaking me out of my panic attack.

"I wanted to know how I could break free from the person I had become, the person who kept on sabotaging her own success, the person who kept avoiding taking responsibility for her own life and was stuck in childish ways. I wanted to break free from my fear. I wanted to change and understand how I can help my clients change. I wanted to stop the restlessness and rid myself of anxiety. I wanted to take off my mask. I was sick of being everything to everyone, sick of letting myself down, sick of letting my emotions get the better of me, sick of being scared to speak my truth and worrying what other people thought of me or fearing their rejection. I wanted to be my wise woman—the one whose voice was guiding me to my greatness. She is calm, centered, balanced. She is quiet. She is powerful yet loving. She is present and has a great presence. She is wise. She is soulful. She is mature. She is grace. I have stepped onto my soul path of purpose. And to honor my clients with integrity I need to move beyond my ego. If I can, so can they."

"Get out of your head," he guided. "Purify your mind so your heart can guide you. Pure thoughts will create a pure heart, and a pure heart will bring you peace and freedom." Then he whispered, "Travel 'under' your pain; a whole world awaits you."

I heard him walk away, leaving me baffled and frustrated. In pain. My eyes were still closed, feet shoulder width apart, my knees slightly bent, my hands outstretched in an arc in front of me as if I were hugging a tree. My arms and legs shook. It had been forty minutes now, and the lactic acid was building in my muscles.

I did as he instructed and focused on the pain in my body. Not only was I aware of the physical pain I felt then, I was also aware of old pain—stagnant pain. As I traveled with my mind deeper into my body, my pain felt endless. My entire physical body felt as if it were a massive iceberg of pain that blocked me from feeling more deeply into my body. There was no way through the pain, never mind a way under it. *What did that even mean?*

I remembered my meditation practice, which had become a large part of my healing process, and focused on my breath. Perhaps by "purify your mind" he meant for me to not let fear dominate. Trusting in this insight, I continued to bring my focus to my breath, allowing my mind to proceed with its tantrum but drawing my attention away from it repeatedly, and back to my breath. I stayed with the experience, my breath soothing and calming my trembling body until a delicate stillness settled upon and through me.

I began to imagine a golden sun above me, and inhaled the warmth of it into my body. I felt my iceberg slowly dissolve. I exhaled, using my breath to push the heaviness down my body and out through my feet. I fanned my breath through my body until the tightness melted into a clear and peaceful lake.

"Now you've gone fucking mad," I heard my ego say.

Breathe. Focus. Soften.

Breathe. Focus. Soften.

I imagined what Eagle would say: "Feel the warmth in your body. Find your wise woman. She is there. Hold her hand and walk with her."

I dived in deeper. Into the peaceful lake. Into the core of my body. "Under" my pain and into what felt like the vibrating cells of my bone marrow. This vibration felt like a current of electricity going through a light bulb—like orange beams of light pulsating in my cells. It felt powerful yet soothing, calm yet confident, masculine and feminine at the same time.

I followed the current of energy through a central column that stretched from the top of my head to the base of my feet. From there I felt roots growing out of me, connecting me to the ground. I followed the buzzing light as it flowed through the roots of my feet. Like a laser beam, the energy cut through multiple layers of earth. As the roots reached the nucleus of the Earth, the electric current poured into the bubbling volcanic center. A wave of magma erupted and sent a golden elixir back up my body and into my heart.

Based on my previous studies with Deepak Chopra and in Kabbalah and energy healing, I knew what I had tapped into, and I knew to trust in the connection I was feeling. This energy from the core of the Earth was the life force emanating from the heart and essence of Mother Earth.

Reflecting on my connection to Mother Earth, I saw her initials in my mind's eye: M.E. Oh, I loved that! It gave me a greater understanding about the power of this connection. As I connected with Mother Earth, I connected with **ME**. The light that was giving life to the Earth gave life to me. I was connected by an umbilical cord from her heart to mine. The nutrients of her essence nourished my own. Her pulsing life force breathed life into ME.

My mind suddenly felt still, and the shaking stopped. A euphoric feeling came over me. I felt as if I was home. I was whole. I was safe, complete and infinite. I knew what it was; I had found my essence under the heaviness of my pain. My wise woman was (is) the light buzzing through my body reminding me what is always within me: a powerful essence connected to the source of creation. As I opened my eyes I felt a new sense of peace, one that was mirrored in the lightness of dawn as it began to brighten the bush. Hours had passed. A new day had begun.

Every day for three months straight after that shamanistic experience, I practiced my ME morning meditation. I connected to my source of light and breathed it into my body, into my heart. I imagined that within my heart I had a dimmer switch and I could brighten the light and send it to every part of my body. I felt myself expand and I felt my essence pushing on my pain from the inside, as if it was slowly and thoroughly cleansing my pain body.

But on the Monday morning after my thirty-seventh birthday I found myself in the emergency room of my local hospital, doubled over in the most excruciating pain. Not the result I had expected after months of blissful meditation!

An ultrasound captured the image of a gallstone traveling toward my pancreas. Within hours the decision was made to remove my gallbladder, which I was told was filled with "sludge." As I lay in hospital, I began to reflect. I realized it was precisely ten years to the date that I woke up, eight months pregnant, with Bell's palsy. Ten years prior to that, at the age of seventeen, I was being treated for severe acne. Were these conditions somehow linked? And did they have anything to do with the chronic joint pain I experienced? What was my body trying to tell me?

I decided to pick up my daily go-to self-help book, *You Can Heal Your Life* by Louise Hay. In her book Louise lists many physical symptoms and illness and links them to related limiting beliefs and thought patterns. She offers an alternative positive affirmation to shift your thinking and heal your body. I had already witnessed the powerful effects of positive affirmations in myself and with clients, and was eager to discover the significance of this part of the body.

The gallbladder, I discovered, is linked to bitterness and hard thoughts. Bell's palsy revealed an extreme control of anger and an unwillingness to express feelings. Acne was the result of not accepting oneself or of disliking oneself. My joints, swollen with repressed anger and unexpressed words, were crying out for relief.

The vision quest with Eagle, as well as my morning meditation, had shaken things up and helped to bring the effects of my past to the surface. As I lay on the operating table, I breathed a silent prayer: *I release all anger and resentment and I forgive my past.* Guided by Louise Hay, I added her suggested affirmation: *There is joyous release of the past. Life is sweet and so am I.*

Three months after my gallbladder operation, I developed a severe case of rosacea, an inflammatory skin condition that affects the face causing redness, swelling, irritation and small pimples. It basically looks like you are constantly blushing, and the more excited or hot you get, the redder your face gets. Turning back to my guide, I read Louise's explanation that skin problems are the result of anxiety. *Fear. Old buried guck.* The effects of my emotional pain could no longer be suppressed. It was now "in my face." It was time to face up to what was truly needed for me to heal.

After months of going from doctor to doctor—from Western medicine to Chinese medicine to integrative medicine—I intuitively knew what was needed: I needed to cleanse and purify my body, physically, mentally and emotionally.

Over a two-year period I cut almost everything from my diet:

sugar, coffee, chocolate, dairy, processed foods, meat (for a short period), alcohol and most fruit. This process of elimination exposed profound revelations. I could clearly see my food addiction and how emotionally attached I was to food. I saw how reliant I was on alcohol to give me a sense of social confidence and take the edge off my anger or pain. Alcohol, sugar and coffee were ways in which I connected with friends. They were linked to my sense of belonging, to connection and having fun. What I realized most was how I lost myself to food and compromised myself. Intuitively, I always felt that certain food and alcohol disagreed with me. But I overrode my logic for the sake of connection or fun. From my ego Molly's perspective, who could say no to tequila shots—right?

My health cleanse included abstaining from sex and dating—what I referred to as "men-on-pause." I wanted no distractions. I was determined to break my codependency. Again I realized how often I put a man's needs above mine. It felt good to be selfish for a while.

I devised my own self-care plan that would help me stay connected to my core self and honor my core needs. My plan included meditation, Bikram yoga, beach walks, eating well, massage, a sound sleep routine, surrounding myself with positive people, music, enjoying fun times with my kids, and time alone.

On the weekends when my kids were with their dad, I retreated into nature in an attempt to continue my vision quest. This included walking, meditating, and mostly crying. My body had bucket loads of emotion to release. It was time to let go—and time to rise to my potential. On one of my days of deliberate solitude I was reminded of the words of my wise woman on the night prior to my cosmic download: "Love yourself more than your need to be loved." I was beginning to understand.

The lessons I present you with in the following chapters offer you the wisdom and tools I learned during this time. They will help to activate your process of self-discovery too. You will be able to move beyond your ego and discover who you truly are, what you ultimately need in order to be happy, and how you can activate your true purpose in the world.

Breathe. Focus. Soften.

CHAPTER 14

THE ART OF LETTING GO

"To forgive is to set a prisoner free and discover that the prisoner was you."

Lewis B. Smedes

After months of detox, I came to realize that this process was my body's way of letting go. I was not only letting go of the toxins caused by my emotional eating habits, but also releasing the emotions that kept me stuck in fear and the stories (beliefs) I was attached to—beliefs such as "Every man I have loved has hurt me," "I cannot trust men," "I will never be loved by a man," etc. I had avoided facing those fears because it meant letting those men, who I felt had hurt me, off the hook. There seemed to be an injustice in letting go. *They should pay for hurting me!* said my ego.

But the more I caught myself stuck in those outdated thought patterns, the more I realized they only held me back. I wanted to maintain the sense of empowerment and freedom and connection to Mother Earth and my true essence that I had experienced in my vision quest with Eagle. To do so, I had to let go of my past programming and clear myself of my fear mindset. I had to let go, not for them, but for me. I had to love myself more than I needed to be loved. Clearing my emotional body and upgrading my mind's coding into an empowering set of thoughts would generate a whole new perspective on life.

What I learned along the way is that there is an art to letting go. Letting go is a process, a life cycle, just like the transformation of the caterpillar into a butterfly. Instead of defaulting to our avoidance strategies of *distracting, reacting* or *contracting*, we can work through pain, face it, and clear ourselves of whatever the body and mind no longer need. Instead of staying stuck in survival mode, we can recondition ourselves to thrive.

In addition to my physical detox and meditation practice, I had to go through another process that I knew would set me free. This was the process of forgiveness. I had to forgive and let go. Four people immediately came to mind who needed my forgiveness: my dad, Shaun, Thor, and myself. I had to forgive in order to let go. I had to forgive in order to heal. And I had to forgive so that I could open myself up to a new life of ease. I wanted to feel peace within myself. I wanted to feel free. I wanted the life my heart knew I deserved.

All my research indicated that forgiveness was at the forefront of healing. Forgiveness is the "art of letting go." When we let go, we release the anger, resentment, hurt, frustration, disappointment and pain that keep us stuck in the past. We cannot be free in the present moment when we are stuck in the past. Not only does forgiveness rid us of a victim mindset, but we also cleanse the effects "un-forgiveness" has on the body. When we release these disabling emotions, we let go of toxicity in the body.

This letting go is a form of surrender. Not a surrender to the perpetrators but a surrender to the ego-mind that holds onto the negative story. We surrender not from a position of weakness, but from a position of courage and acceptance—the courage to change and acceptance of the perfection in the pain. As I moved through my cycle of forgiveness, I had two cathartic insights.

My first insight was about the men I felt were against me. These men who I thought had caused my pain were actually in pain themselves. They *needed me* to help them heal. My own neediness and codependency had not allowed me to realize I had that purpose. I took their words and actions personally, and resigned myself to anger and self-pity. They had not intended to hurt me. *Their* actions were a cry for help, a projection of their own fear of not being worthy, loved or good enough. *Only hurt people hurt people.*

When I finally stopped taking their behavior personally and let go of my anger, I found compassion. I saw them as wounded warriors with broken hearts and tainted egos. Compassion gave me the clarity to see through the filter of my fear and transform that illusion into love.

My second insight was the realization that the events I perceived as painful were not happening *to* me; they were happening *for* me. As I relinquished self-pity, I saw that each experience enabled my growth and acted as a catalyst for transformation. Instead of asking, "Why is this happening to me?" in a victim's whine, I asked that exact question with courage and curiosity. With an open mind and heart I was able to see that every person, every challenge, comes with a message, a lesson. And when we are open to receiving each message, we crack open our pain and let go of the past. As Rumi says, "The wound is the place where the Light enters you."

I spent approximately six months working through my forgiveness process. At the beginning of 2012 I made a trip home to South Africa. I spent three weeks with my extended family in Wilderness, a majestic beach town along the Western Cape coast. Known as the nature-lover's utopia, this healing retreat is hugged by the Indian Ocean. Each morning I walked along our secluded beach in solitude, enveloped by the healing vapor of the salt spray. I felt my body absorbing the minerals and trusted the negative ions to aid in my purification.

How comforting to know that I was being cleansed by such a great body of water. Sanskrit teachers refer to the Indian Ocean, whose vastness covers a fifth of the Earth's surface, as a "mine of gems." As I inhaled her healing energy, I let my tears flow. Releasing them, I felt my thoughts and emotions being purified. I began to see the perfection in my pain. I understood Rumi's words: "You are not a drop in the ocean. You are the ocean in a drop." We are all connected, bound by sacred contracts to help each other heal. We help each other clear out the impurities of our fear so that we can return to the natural state of our essence. Our greatest teachers are the ones who challenge us the most, as they force us to question, which enables our growth.

I suddenly felt at peace with my past and had love for the men I thought had hurt me. I mentally sent waves of grateful love from my heart and imagined each man basking in their light. I forgave. I let go. I was free. One month after my return to Australia, my skin cleared up.

I share with you now a breakdown of my process of forgiveness to ignite *your* healing journey:

1. Forgiveness Visualization Exercise

Begin by imagining that you are sitting in the audience of a theater looking at a dark stage. There is a single spotlight in the middle of the stage. Place the person you are forgiving under that spotlight. You can see him, but he cannot see you. Observe that person as if he were a stranger, not the person you know. As an outsider, what do you observe about him? What does his body language tell you? What do his eyes communicate? If you could look deeper into him, what is in his heart and what is in his pain?

This detached perspective allows you to see the other person dissociated from *your* pain. It allows you to observe the person compassionately. Write down everything you observe, and notice how viewing this person compassionately allows you to have a different perspective.

When I completed this exercise with my father, I realized that he harbored pain from his own upbringing. I clearly saw the cloud of fear tainting his ego and causing him to need to prove himself and seek his own father's approval. I was able to view him as a man, a wounded man, and not only as my father. I was able to step back from what I needed him to be as a father, and understand (and accept) what he was capable of giving. Compassion melted the self-protective wall I'd built around my heart. I let go of anger and disappointment. I let go of the expectations and needs I had for him and accepted him for who he is.

2. The Release Letters

Once you are able to be more detached and compassionate, you can begin to release the emotions you are holding in your body. I recommend writing three letters: the Purge, the Lessons, and the Gratitude Letter.

THE PURGE LETTER

This is a letter that you do not show anyone, especially the person you are forgiving. The point of this letter is not to try and change them, make a point or seek justice, but to clear the toxic emotions from within *you*. Having a conversation with the person you are addressing will only increase conflict and reignite the negative feelings within you. This is a way for you to purge the emotion by expressing it. Let all those emotions out instead of repressing them.

In this letter, as the name suggests, you express all of your pain, anger, disappointment, frustration, shock and disgust. You write out, in as much detail as you can, everything you feel that person has done to you. Do not hold back on your hurt and self-pity. Clear that old story out of your body. Let your victim-self have its moment.

When you have finished writing the Purge Letter, tear it up and burn it. A burning ceremony symbolizes letting go. As you watch the paper burn, imagine the ashes releasing the past out into the universe and dissolving your pain forever.

THE LESSONS LETTER

Once we have expressed what we need to say in our Purge Letter and we have completed our own mini "fire ceremony," we begin to write a new letter. This letter is aimed at generating a new perspective on the past and helping us let go of the meanings we make. Creating a new meaning, or gaining a new perspective, is called *reframing*. Once you change your meaning about something, you never see it in the same light.

This Lessons Letter is about creating an empowering reframing by focusing on all the lessons you learned from the person, situation or the pain itself. For example, in the Lessons Letter I wrote to my dad, I said I now realized that he had taught me to be independent and to trust myself. I realized that I needed self-love and I needed to believe in myself, and I had gained those abilities in the process of dealing with what I perceived to be his rejection of me. I learned that I no longer needed his approval or validation as I could meet those needs for myself. I took responsibility for fulfilling myself—I let go of the dependent child and began to make more mature decisions regarding what I needed.

THE GRATITUDE LETTER

Once we are aware of the lessons gained, and we see the perfection in the pain, we can appreciate the experience. Without those events, we would never have learned our lessons.

Gratitude is an antidote to anger. When we feel gratitude, we produce a hormone called oxytocin in the body. This is known as the feel-good hormone and balances out the stress hormones produced by our negative emotions. Oxytocin allows us to see the world through rose-colored glasses rather than through our fear filter. Gratitude instantly opens our heart and allows us to see the world with our essence-awareness. In this final letter, write about everything you feel grateful for. Notice how the feelings of gratitude soften your emotions. Set your prisoner free and let love guide you forward.

SELF-FORGIVENESS

My process of self-forgiveness took a slightly different format.

I visualized myself standing on stage and gazed at myself, but I imagined I was looking at a stranger. I searched within my eyes to notice what story they told. I witnessed the rawness of my vulnerability. I easily saw the cloud of fear hanging over me, and the toxicity of my belief that I was not worthy or lovable. It was like a thread weaving an intoxicating story throughout my consciousness.

As I journeyed into my memories, I met the eyes of my five-year-old self. She stared back at me. Her eyes took me to my first day of kindergarten. I was reminded of my shock and disappointment over being teased for my funny accent and frizzy hair. I then met the eyes of my nine-year-old self. She was lost in her sadness: she felt abandoned by her father. My mental movie leapt to an image of my fourteen-year-old self, who felt that boys only wanted her for sex. In each memory my eyes told the same story: they spoke of a little girl who was lost. She had forgotten who she truly was.

I imagined standing with my five-year-old self. I took her hand and asked her to walk with me. I imagined the two of us watching a memory of my three-year-old self at play. I asked her to remember who she was back then. Who was she before that limiting belief about herself was formed?

There was my blissful three-year-old self, back home in South Africa playing in my garden. I was carefree, creative and full of life. I asked my five-year-old self to notice the qualities in my three-year-old self. What gifts did she encompass? Together we noticed her sense of fun, love and belief. She did not know to doubt herself; she only knew how *to be* herself.

I asked my five-year-old consciousness to remember those gifts, to awaken to those gifts. As she absorbed that message, I saw her light up and expand. I passed on the message to my nine-year-old self and I saw her rise with confidence. Together, they passed that feeling of value to my fourteen-year-old self, who could then decide to be true to herself and hold to her morals. As I observed the pureness of my essence, I saw the love that was within me.

I forgave myself because I understood that my decisions had been made by a tainted ego-self that had forgotten who she really was and what was within her. From this awakened perspective, I saw the perfection and the lessons learned in each experience. Each defining moment helped me turn back to the space of love. A deep sense of gratitude followed for each experience and for the pain I had been through. I felt awash with gratitude that I was reconnecting with the love I had within.

I felt a huge release within myself as a result of reframing my beliefs. I felt awake, whole, expanded, free and at peace.

This process of forgiveness allowed me to cleanse my ego-self of the toxins that kept me stuck. My neural coding was upgraded, and I was able to filter the world with expanded awareness. A new story scripted my thoughts. In the absence of my fear filter, I began to perceive the world through the lens of my essence, my higher mind that first experienced life with wisdom instead of fear. Every new challenge I now faced had a different purpose that I could approach with the same openness and curiosity. Without the rigidity of my fixed mindset, I could be more flexible and discerning. I could now navigate my awareness through life with a *growth mindset*.

CHAPTER 15

THREE RULES FOR A GROWTH MINDSET

"Only as you discover your own unreality—wrong conclusions, pseudo-solutions, evasions—will you reach the core of your being. Slowly but surely you will begin to act and react from your core, rather than from the erroneous and distorted superimpositions."

Eva Pierrakos, Pathwork Guide Lecture No. 95, 1962

Before we dive into discovering our essence, we need to ensure that we are traveling forward with the correct mindset. We cannot make changes to ourselves while we think the same thoughts and attitudes that created our ego-self. We have to shift our thinking and motivation in order to transform our experience of life.

Imagine holding a rock. Feel the weight of the rock and pass it from hand to hand. Now imagine trying to break the rock, or to turn it into something else. You can't, right? That is because it is rigid, hard and fixed. Unless you smash it to the ground or use the appropriate machinery, you have little chance of changing it.

Now imagine holding a ball of play dough, just like you might have done as a child. Feel the weight of the play dough and pass it from hand to hand. Imagine playing with it and turning it into something else. It's easy, right? It bends, adapts, is flexible and molds into whatever shape you desire it to be. It is light and facilitates playfulness. It opens your imagination to a multitude of possibilities.

The rock and the play dough demonstrate the difference between a *rigid* or *fixed mindset* and a *flexible* or *growth mindset*. With a fixed mindset we remain stuck in our conditioned egoic ways and believe that we are who we are and cannot change. With a fixed mindset, we regard the ego-self as our identity and we have little belief in any possibility of change. Carol Dweck, a renowned professor of psychology at Stanford University, is known for her work on mindset. She explains the fixed mindset as belonging to those who believe they have fixed traits. These people tend to avoid challenges so as not to fail. A growth mindset, on the other hand, is when a person believes that with hard work, persistence and the right knowledge, he or she can develop the traits necessary to succeed.

This is relevant to personal transformation because if we are not open to growth and change, and remain rigid and fixed in our conditioned ways, than we remain *uncoachable*. Like the rock, we cannot do much with that attitude. Alternatively, when we are open to breaking past patterns of thought and behavior we become malleable. Like the play dough, we can transform into whatever our imagination desires. A growth mindset shatters the ego's self-fulfilling prophecy. It smashes through the glass ceiling of limiting beliefs. It will allow you to journey into the depth of your unconscious mind, into your pain, into your coding, so you can notice what needs to change.

A growth mindset has three distinct qualities: curiosity, humility and vulnerability. Curiosity enables us to explore the world with a childlike enthusiasm and wonder. Humility enables us to realize that we do not know it all, that we are human, and both failure and success are part of learning. And vulnerability enables us to have the courage to drop our guard, to prioritize being authentic over wearing a protective mask. This means stepping into the rawness of your truth and seeing vulnerability as a strength rather than as a weakness.

In my last session with my spiritual mentor, Eagle, he offered me three rules to live by, three rules to ensure that I would disrupt my ego's coding and continue to grow into my ideal self.

"With these rules, you will stay connected to your essence," he said.

Since then I have made these rules my personal guidebook, and I offer them to each client I work with. I have created various steps for each rule to help us embrace personal transformation with a growth mindset. As we journey into the realm of self-discovery, to identify who we truly are, these three rules help us expand our awareness and celebrate what awaits us on the flipside of fear.

RULE #1: FROM PAIN COMES GROWTH

"The thing about pain . . . it demands to be felt."

John Green, *The Fault In Our Stars*

Embracing the rule "From pain comes growth" means that you no longer avoid pain, you embrace it.

- You no longer *distract* yourself with wasteful vices (such as alcohol, drugs, sex, shopping, social media or other numbing habits).
- You no longer *react* and give into your emotions (such as anger, sadness or worry).
- You no longer *contract* into the safety of withdrawal (discussed in Chapter 3).

By stepping into the pain, you step into the e-goo. You face the ego-self, you feel the effects of its toxicity, and you listen to its pain. Pain tells a story. It signals to us that something is wrong, that something is out of alignment. Listening to the messages of pain is the first step in growing.

The acronym to help you implement this rule is **CORE:**

COURAGE
OPTIMISM
RESILIENCE
ENERGY

Many of the dance teachers I had in my youth guided me to "embrace my core" to help with balance, control my movements, and support my back. So, as we journey into the turbulent rapids of our emotions, it is wise to face our healing journey with a *core*-ageous mindset. Unlike the caterpillar, which probably does not know that its "death" is a precursor to a greater life as a butterfly, we can embrace the uncertainty of change with a sense of adventure, knowing that whatever pain we experience will lead to growth and joy and our flight of freedom.

Courage

The ability to let go and break the mindset and behaviors fueled by fear requires immense courage. In her book, *Daring Greatly*, Brene Brown reminds us of the inspiring words spoken by Theodore

Roosevelt: "The credit belongs to the man who is actually in the arena, whose face is marred by dust and sweat and blood; who strives valiantly, who errs, who comes short again and again." She elaborates further by saying, "Our willingness to own and engage with our vulnerability determines the depth of our courage."

Your willingness to feel your vulnerable emotions opens you up to healing. Your ability to face your ego-self with curiosity, humility and vulnerability is a demonstration of courage. Courageousness allows you to activate your core, clear out the cloud of fear with tenacity and determination, and hold yourself together while your emotions erupt.

Optimism

Positive psychologists speak of *learned optimism*. This means that positive emotions like optimism and courage can be learned with the right focus, the right processes, and the desire to change. With an optimistic mindset, we see pain as an opportunity to grow. Optimism empowers us to conquer any challenge and face adversity with an unstoppable attitude. The perspective that optimism provides is that failure, mistakes or problems are merely obstacles that *can* be overcome. Instead of resorting to our pessimistic and self-defeating mindsets, such us self-pity or withdrawal, we focus on the positive. Finding one piece of joy or gaining a new insight or recognizing an opportunity in a difficult situation opens our eyes to seeing the bigger picture. Optimism allows us to remain focused on our greater goal and creates a future-pull momentum.

Resilience

There is a remarkable phenomenon to be discovered when we hit what we think is rock bottom. In that moment, when our knees hit the floor, we realize that although fear said we would sink, we don't. We discover that we bounce! In that moment, as we are catapulted back into life, we discover what we are truly made of.

Jess Van Zeil is a dear friend who I coached for a short period after she went through a great adversity. At the age of twenty-one she was diagnosed with a rare form of cancer called conjunctival ocular melanoma. A year after her diagnosis, Jess was told she had to have her left eye removed to ensure her survival. Jess allowed herself to sink into her emotions for a short period of time. In her words, she gave herself a day. She then discovered how she could reframe her situation and focus on a positive solution. Instead of giving in to her grief, Jess decided to be the hottest, most inspiring *pirate*. She searched Etsy and other online stores for gorgeous eye patches. She wore her beaded, feathered and brightly-colored patches bravely, and is now thriving as a motivational coach and speaker guiding people to be *powerfully positive and ridiculously resilient*.

Jess's story not only demonstrates the power of the human spirit; it demonstrates the power of resilience and our ability to reinvent ourselves whenever we are faced with a significant life transition. We can get back up, dust ourselves off, and "thrive forward" with greater purpose, passion and optimism.

Energy

Where our focus goes, our energy flows. When we embrace transformation with courage, optimism and resilience, our energy expands rather than contracts. Instead of shutting down in fear, which causes us to feel energetically blocked, heavy and depressed, we "lift up" and feel lighter, freer and more enthused. We have the energy to "keep on keeping on"—with empowerment, endurance and enthusiasm.

Embracing the mindset "From pain comes growth" allows you to use these CORE resources to help you feel your feelings and connect with your pain. We will discuss that process further in the self-mastery section of this book.

RULE #2: DO NOT TAKE ANYTHING PERSONALLY

> *"There is a huge amount of freedom that comes when you take nothing personally."*
>
> Don Miguel Ruiz, *The Four Agreements*

Taking things personally is the default mode of the ego-self. After all, its motivation is survival, and its focus is "What's in it for me?" From the lens of the tainted ego, we think people are against us, judging us, trying to bring us down or hurt us. This limited perspective does not allow us to see into *their* true intent or into their pain. We take it personally rather than exploring what motivates their behavior.

People usually project their beliefs and pain onto each other. The

Jewish proverb "We do not see things as *they* are, we see things as *we* are" means that we judge events through the filter of our values and beliefs. As we have discussed, each perceptual lens is uniquely coded by a person's beliefs and decisions. Therefore, others' comments or reactions to our behavior are based on their limiting beliefs, which they project onto us. When we step back from a conflict and observe the other person with this in mind, we notice what is actually occurring with a higher intelligence rather than from our limiting, reactive "default" mode.

The acronym to help you implement this rule is **CALM**:

COMPASSION
ACCEPTANCE
LOVE
MINDFULNESS

CALM is the opposite of stressed. When we are calm, the nervous system is in neutral rather than in fight, flight or freeze mode. With CALM, we can observe situations with far more clarity.

Instead of saying to yourself, "Don't take it personally," you can now take a deep breath and say, "Be calm," as you activate the following internal resources:

Compassion

Similarly to gratitude, compassion acts as another antidote to anger. Where anger is an emotion driven by the fearful mind, compassion is driven by the heart, which has the ability to see into the essence of another person. I am passionate about compassion as I truly believe it will bring peace into our world. Compassion has the power to moderate judgment, transform fear and dispel ethnocentricity.

I define compassion as "a detached understanding of another person." I use the word *detached* because, unlike empathy, we do not need to *feel* another person's pain. We can simply understand it. Sympathy and empathy help us achieve compassion; however, they are different. With sympathy we feel sorry for another person. With empathy we try to relate to what they are going through by putting ourselves in their shoes. With compassion, we observe and allow, in an attitude of no judgment. This applies to us as well as to others. When activating self-compassion, we rein in the inner critic and accept ourselves with the same kindness and openness.

By being compassionate instead of taking things personally, we can step back and think about what might be going on for that person. "Listen to understand, not respond," as the late Steven Covey taught. The other person's words, that we might be reacting to, are not an attack on us but insight into their own projected beliefs. Compassionate awareness softens us, soothes us, and allows us to stay calm amid the chaos of conflict.

Acceptance

Acceptance expands on the virtue of compassion. Once we have a detached understanding of another person, we can accept him for who he is and accept what he believes. We can accept that each one of us has some degree of fear and limitation. All egos are tainted in a unique way due to individual neural coding. Everyone has pain buttons that trigger an emotional reaction. What others say is true from *their* perspective, from their unique map of the world; it is not necessarily the correct perspective *for us*.

Acceptance allows us to be less defensive, less critical and less righteous in our ways. It therefore enhances harmonious communication. Acceptance can also be seen as the opposite to having expectations. Instead of expecting others to behave in the way we want or need them to behave, we accept their truth and their perspective. We accept their opinions in a responsive rather than in a reactive way.

Love

Compassion and acceptance enable us *to be* love, unconditionally. Unconditional love is the quintessential nature of the essence. Where fear judges, love allows. Where fear erupts, love is gentle. Where fear lashes out, love is kind. Love has no need to control a person or situation. Love does not need to be right—it has nothing to prove. Love wants to create an open space for a person to communicate her truth. Love listens. Love knows that we have the power to help a person grow, and that instead of making others wrong or justifying ourselves, we can influence them to recognize and own their projections.

So, instead of reacting with defensiveness or anger or hurt, with love we step back, take a deep breath—or two, or three . . . or six—and we ask a question to clarify *their* map.

Let's imagine a person snaps at us and says, "You are doing that all wrong! How stupid." Our initial default mode might be to snap back in defense. Instead, imagine embracing Rule #2: *Do not take anything personally. BE CALM.* With love and this rule in mind, you can respond by asking something along the lines of, "How, from your perspective, is it supposed to be?"

This instantly allows the conversation to take a less intense turn and be more productive instead of conflictual. Only the ego-self, whose pain button says, "So you think I'm not good enough?" reacts. The essence has no pain buttons, so nothing can be triggered. The essence is aware that those who call someone else stupid fear they are stupid themselves. That comment is their own projection, so we move on with compassion, acceptance and love.

Mindfulness

I like to think of *mindfulness* as a mindset (a set of attitudes, giving rise to a state of being). The *mindful mindset* explains our essence perfectly. With a fearful ego mindset we are reactive and make critical judgments. With a mindful mindset, we remain responsive and function as the observer, not the judge. We take personal responsibility for the way we respond, which enables us to respond to our world effectively, in a calm way rather than in a fearful way.

Mindfulness allows us to remain engaged in the present moment rather than react to any unfinished business, which is effectively baggage lying dormant in our unconscious caves. We respond from our higher, *essence-based* intelligence, which usually represents the best version of who we are.

Mindfulness allows us to float above the event. This helps us to dissociate and detach from our emotional reactions and be a third-party observer instead of the victim, and to respond in the way love responds.

RULE # 3: DETACH FROM DRAMA

> *"Maturity is what happens when we learn to only give a f*ck about what's truly f*ckworthy."*
>
> Mark Manson, *The Subtle Art of Not Giving a F*ck*

When Eagle mentioned Rule #3 to me, I was reminded of the movie *Changing Lanes*, which stars Samuel L. Jackson. His character, a recovering alcoholic, quotes his AA sponsor: "We are a society addicted to chaos."

This comment and this rule resonated the most with me as I realized how much drama and chaos I created in my life. As I reflected on my limiting beliefs, I found the belief *Nothing works out anyway*. This belief had been embedded in my ego-consciousness as a result of leaving the country of my roots, losing the family structure I knew, losing my family home, losing the childhood I knew and then leaving South Africa again at the age of twenty-one to come to Australia. According to my life pattern, there was comfort and predictability in chaos. I would almost anticipate drama; I saw it as a way of coping, of preparing me for life. It created a set of expectations, and so, unbeknownst to my conscious awareness, I developed an addiction to chaos in order to validate my fear.

Not only do such limiting beliefs generate stress and fear within us, they also produce adrenaline and cortisol. As we discussed in Chapter 9, the body becomes addicted to these stress hormones and we subconsciously set up dramas in order to feed our addiction. When life feels boring or stagnant we get a restless urge to shake things up. By deliberately detaching from drama, we break this old fear cycle, and our thoughts and desires become more conscious and intentional.

The acronym I offer to help you implement this rule is **WISE**:
WISE
INSPIRED-ACTION
SOUL-CENTERED
EXPRESSION

Like an owl, which has a 360-degree view of its environment, we too can see beyond the limited sight of the tainted ego.

Wisdom

With wise awareness we can, as Oprah Winfrey says, *turn our wounds into wisdom*. Where fear is disabling, wisdom is discerning. Where fear is stupid, wisdom is sage. Where fear is fueled by drama, wisdom is fueled by knowledge. Wisdom has the grace and humility to know that we are always growing and always learning. Wisdom is able to purify the ego's fear with its higher intelligence—it shines light onto darkness. When I connect with the voice of my wise woman, she guides me to be less reactive and calmer. Instead of seeking drama, I navigate uncertainty through the virtues of my essence.

Inspired Action

When we are stuck in our fear-based patterns we react to our world with desperation—desperation to be safe, heard, validated, worthy, accepted and loved. But when we are committed to our growth, we respond with *inspired action*.

Desperation makes us more impulsive, emotional, reactive and drama-hungry. Inspired action is connected to our intuition, which understands beyond what our limited personality can perceive. Inspired action feels purposeful and inspiring. We are left feeling proud rather than ashamed.

Inspired action gives us personal integrity rather than dissonance as we are aligned with a pure intention. Instead of resorting to our conditioned egoic ways, we unlearn the patterns that no longer serve us or that bring us shame. We recondition the ego to behave in ways that foster self-respect and confidence.

Soul-Centered

Where the ego-self needs drama, the soul (the essence) wants peace. Being soul-centered means we are connected to a higher purpose and desire to serve. The soul sees purpose and meaning in every opportunity. The soul has an inner knowledge, an inner knowing, and does not lower itself with worrisome thoughts. The soul holds the scriptures of wisdom, and when we are wise and follow inspired action, we express the soul.

Expression

Expressing the wisdom of our soul means following the guidance of our intuition. It means expressing ourselves with strength and grace, gentleness and assertiveness. This means impeccable speech and communications. Give up gossip! Give up blaming! Giving up complaining! Leave all of that with your drama queen and her victim story.

Wise expression knows what is right for you and knows how to create necessary boundaries. And, more precisely, wise expression knows the power of silence, stillness and surrender. Allow these three rules to open your consciousness to a growth mindset as we now explore the anatomy of the essence.

CHAPTER 16

THE ANATOMY OF THE ESSENCE

As I began to love myself I freed myself of anything that is no good for my health – food, people, things, situations, and everything that drew me down and away from myself. At first I called this attitude a healthy egoism. Today I know it is LOVE OF ONESELF.

As I began to love myself I quit trying to always be right, and ever since, I was wrong less of the time. Today I discovered that is MODESTY.

As I began to love myself I refused to go on living in the past and worrying about the future. Now I only live for the moment, where everything is happening. Today I live each day, day by day, and I call it FULFILLMENT.

As I began to love myself I recognized that my mind can disturb me and it can make me sick. But as I connected it to my heart, my mind became a valuable ally. Today I call this connection WISDOM OF THE HEART.

We no longer need to fear arguments, confrontations or any kind of problems with ourselves or others. Even stars collide, and out of their crashing, new worlds are born. Today I know THAT IS LIFE.

Charlie Chaplin, excerpt from "As I Began to Love Myself"

Now that we have identified how to soften the rigidity of the ego-self with a growth mindset, we can explore the anatomy of the essence. We can use the three rules—"From pain comes growth," "Do not take anything personally" and "Detach from drama"—as a code of conduct to break the disempowering patterns of the ego-self.

True empowerment and personal transformation take place when we know who we are in our essential nature. Not only do we learn how to disrupt our relationship with fear, we specifically "meet" our authentic self.

We discover a greater sense of self, a self that has more depth, more meaning and a clear purpose. Within your essence, there is no fear because you are connected to universal energy (Mother Earth), a source of power conceiving everything in the universe; the same source that gives life to all of nature gives life to us. This source is made of pure energy and unconditional love. As we tune into the life force vibrating through us, we feel our essence. Like a speck of diamond dust, we are born with full potential to shine brightly. This pure potential and unconditional love is the molecular basis of our essential nature.

The essence perceives the world through a lens of love. And so the essence, in its purest form of self, is love. This is self-love. Self-love is the complete unconditional acceptance of who we are with absolutely no judgement. We do not question our worth or compare ourselves. We know that not only are we enough but also who we are is how nature intended us to be.

When we have a mindset of self-love, we express the energy of love within the self. The concept of self-love I offer here is not a conceited or narcissistic love for oneself—that form of self-love stems from the ego-self trying to prove itself or place itself above others. Self-love means a pure expression of love: self-acceptance, respect, kindness and love for others. Self-love can therefore be seen as the opposite state to the ego-self. Another way to understand this is to think of fear and self-love as energy vibrations. You either vibrate in a frequency of fear or a frequency of love. The first will weigh you down, as it is dense energy, and the latter will uplift you, as it is pure light energy.

Where the ego-self shuts down and wraps itself in layers of protection like an onion, self-love wants to expand and share itself. Like the petals of the lily opening to light, self-love opens us to all the opportunities life has to offer. Our life purpose is to not only actualize the pure potential within, but to share the essence of our self-love with the world around us.

Where the core fears of the ego-self are *I am not loved, I am not worthy, I am not good enough*, self-love has a different perspective. Self-love has three distinct qualities: *trust, belief* and *faith*. These three qualities act as three pillars for emotional well-being. They can be seen as a foundation for spiritual intelligence. I use spirituality synonymously with self-development because the development of ourselves, the discovering of our true essence and its full potential, is a spiritual journey. *We are not human beings having a spiritual experience; we are spiritual beings having a human experience.*

Trust, belief and faith are a powerful trinity. Throughout history the triangle has had mystical meaning relating to strength and balance due to the fact that it can withstand whatever weight is placed upon it. Trust and belief form the base foundation, and together they give us faith. Trust and belief can be seen as the left and right sides of the body, moving us through life with fortitude, and faith can be seen as our heart center, housing the wisdom of our soul. With trust, belief and faith we can manage whatever life throws at us, even if it has been thrown with the utmost strength.

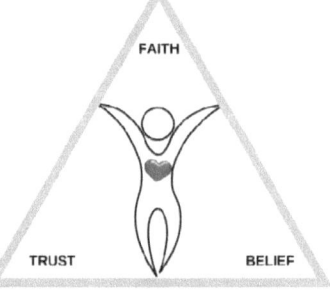

A few years after I opened my life-coaching business I was offered the opportunity to buy into a wellness center. Every cell in my body wanted to embrace this opportunity. I wanted a center that offered people a safe place to heal and work on their well-being—a space for them to evolve into the best version of themselves. In my inspired state, I used what was left of my divorce settlement to purchase this business.

At first, the lack of financial security threw my ego-self into a whirlwind of panic. Interestingly, this is when rosacea broke out. My nervous system flipped into survival mode and I experienced moments of anxiety and uncertainty.

As I commenced my healing journey and physical detox, I felt as if I had been backed into a corner. My ego-self told me to give up and get a job where I could receive the security of a paycheck. My self-pity told me that, based on society's rules, I was a failure. If I had no money in the bank, then I was a nobody. Yet my essence knew better. My essence was committed to my purpose of helping people heal and transform. Was I going to give in to my fear and my ego-self, or was I going to surrender to my essence?

I had jumped, but I had no safety net. However, when I tuned into the voice of my essence, my intuition told me everything would be all right. I made a commitment to the universe that I would "be" my purpose wholeheartedly. I knew I would always be looked after—all I had to do was trust and believe and take a leap of faith. The triangular faith-trust-belief model that I developed arose out of experiences like this, and was reinforced by the wisdom of my teachers.

Instead of ruminating on my fear and scarcity mindset, I focused my mind and my energy. I woke every morning to a powerful mantra: *I am here to serve in the best way I can, so please bring me today's miracles. I expect a miracle because I have trust, belief and faith.*

To date, my daily miracles continue to show up. When expenses such as insurance premiums or school fees piled up, more clients would book in. I would receive emails and gifts of gratitude from them, thanking me for helping them, some even going as far as to say I saved them from suicide. In the silence of my heart I say, *Namaste; thank you, in turn, for being today's miracle.*

TRUST

> *"Go confidently in the direction of your dreams.*
> *Live the life you have imagined."*
>
> Henry David Thoreau

Think of a tree trunk that grows bigger and stronger over hundreds of years. It stands tall, deeply rooted and connected to Mother Earth. It grows confidently.

Trust offers us the same foundation of well-being. Instead of feeling anxious or disabled by our fear, trust offers us resilience through life's trials. Trust is like bamboo. Although rigid, bamboo is agile. It bends and flows with nature, but it does not break. One only needs to visit a building site in China and witness bamboo being used as scaffolding to understand its strength.

Take a moment and imagine a central column running through your body. Imagine this column to be a stalk of bamboo and feel its strength through your spinal column and body. This sense of strength and power offers us a foundation for being more agile and adaptable. Instead of feeling weakened by our fear and contracting within ourselves, trust helps us to expand. We go with the flow and continue to grow, with our roots deeply connected to our source. Trust meets us once we *flip* our fear.

Imagine standing on the shore at the ocean and getting into a small canoe. You have no map, but you sail off into the horizon on an adventure. If you are filled with fear, you will most likely panic and anticipate all the disasters that may lie ahead of you. In addition, you may ruminate on past memories where you have failed or experienced trauma. Bottom line, you would not be present. Your energy would be scattered, and you would feel as if you were paddling upstream against a tough current. With this fear mindset, chances are you would exhaust yourself quickly.

Now imagine flipping your fear into trust. Stand on that shore and change the lens or the filter through which you perceive the event. Trust allows you to embrace uncertainty with a calm and focused mindset. When we are problem-focused, the problems persist; when we are solution-focused, solutions exist. We find our way. We flow forward with presence, certainty, determination, lightness and a sense of fun. We experience the joy in the present moment, and we know that we are always safe.

Fear needs to control; trust likes to flow.
Fear likes drama; trust is effortless.
Fear resists; trust persists.
Fear contracts; trust expands.
Fear creates expectations; trust accepts.
Fear judges; trust observes.
Fear is angry; trust is compassionate.
Fear looks outside for answers; trust searches within.

Trust can be broken down into the following five components:

Timing

With trust we hold the knowledge that everything happens at the right time. Trust has patience and moves organically. Like a 300-year-old tree that slowly grows and weathers any storm, trust knows that everything works out at the right time. Trust knows that everything works out at the end of the day; if things have not worked out, it must not be the end.

Resources

With trust we know that everything we need is within us. We have been given the internal resources to cope with adversity. And when we focus on our inner resources, we find them. This means tuning into your body, listening to your feelings and following the guidance of your intuition. With trust we can lean in and embrace life.

Understanding

With trust we understand that the universe, source, God, or whatever we believe is controlling our destiny is always conspiring for our success. Life happens *for* us, not *to* us. We accept our experiences, both good and bad. We remember that from pain comes growth, and even in moments of adversity we trust that everything is happening to enable that growth. We accept this challenge as our life purpose.

Surrender

Trust actively surrenders. This means we do not passively submit to situations; active surrender means we let go and wait patiently without any expectations or need to control outcomes. We detach and trust everything will work out for our good.

Teach

Trust is a reminder that every person, situation or challenge is a teacher. With trust we know that every person is teaching us a lesson, especially the ones who challenge us the most. Instead of resorting to anger or victimhood, trust searches for the lessons of growth. Instead of focusing on our *stressings,* with trust we focus on our *blessings.*

STEPS TO CULTIVATE TRUST:

1. Use daily affirmations or personal mantras to direct your focus toward trust. For example, as you wake up, say the following positive statement: *I trust that whatever is happening right now is for my greater good. I know I will be able to handle whatever comes my way.*
2. Use creative visualization to imagine trusting yourself in moments that challenge you. As you focus on this internal image, notice

what you are doing and what internal resources you are utilizing.
3. Practice feeling trust, even if you have to fake it until you make it. Imagine the feeling of being bamboo—feel the strength in your body as you imagine yourself trusting life. (These first three points help program your senses to elicit the desired emotion of trust in your body.)
4. Ask yourself a powerful self-coaching question, such as *What internal resources do I have within me that can help me handle this challenging situation?* Questions activate thought patterns, so as you ask yourself a question focusing on self-trust, you will direct your focus. Trust and act on the answers you receive!
5. Look back, logically, on past memories where you were worried about a situation not working out, and with hindsight, notice how everything happened in perfect order—exactly as it needed to happen and for your benefit. As the fourteenth Dalai Lama says, "Remember that sometimes not getting what you want is a wonderful stroke of luck."
6. Practice critical thinking. This means you observe the situation using logic to notice what is real and what is false, what is reasonable and what is orchestrated by your internal drama queen. Once we detach from drama, we can let go of excess worries and trust in the wisdom we receive. We practice trusting our intuition to be our compass.
7. Follow through on your first thoughts. I love this exercise. For one day, before your mind steps in, determine to act on the first thought you have. For example, you may have a thought to contact a particular person. Follow through on that thought immediately before you are derailed by thoughts such as, *I'll do that later*, or *I don't want to interrupt them*, or *I feel too shy/embarrassed/awkward to make contact right now*.
8. Flip your focus. As you notice yourself slipping into fearful thoughts, flip your fear into trust as quickly and easily as if you are flipping a coin. Notice how differently the situation appears through a lens of trust.
9. Practice mindfulness. Bring your focus into the present moment by letting go of thoughts that either focus on the past or anticipate or predict your future. Explore what opportunities are present in the here and now.

10. Practice self-trust as often as you can. Trust is a muscle, and the more we flex it, the stronger it gets.

SELF-BELIEF

"I am not what has happened to me. I am what I choose to become."

Carl Jung

Sarah Findlay is a dear client of mine who epitomizes the power of self-belief. Six months before her wedding day her fiancé called off their wedding. Sarah was devastated. The life she had worked toward, the life she dreamed about, collapsed in a heartbeat. Homeless and heartbroken, Sarah had to piece her life back together. She honored her feelings and grieved for a period of time. She did her work to heal and built a strong foundation of self-love. As a result of listening and trusting in her intuition, Sarah made a bold decision to follow her dream and move from Melbourne, Australia, to Los Angeles. Less than two years after her breakup, Sarah rebuilt her life and is now thriving in California as a publicist and writing a book about her journey. She is also the host of a successful podcast that discusses modern issues on dating and romance. Sarah did not let life knock her down—she believed in herself, believed in her dreams. She let her essence be her compass. She trusted in the perfection of her pain and created a life for herself beyond her wildest imagination.

Self-doubt creeps in when we let the opinions of others influence our beliefs and cloud our clarity. Self-belief is demonstrated when we listen to our intuition. Belief gives us the conviction to follow through on whatever it is that we trust in; it enables us to follow through on inspired ideas. Not only do we trust that we have everything within us to handle challenges, but we also believe in and have confidence in our abilities.

Almost every family member told Sarah she was crazy for wanting to move away from

home, but Sarah stuck to her guns and chose to honor herself and have confidence in what she believed in. As a result of believing in herself, Sarah discovered her soul's purpose.

Self-belief is cultivated as we develop the ability to be discerning with our thoughts. Once we know which beliefs and behaviors belong to the ego-self, we can choose to reframe them with empowering thoughts guided by our essence. Reframing is a mindset tool used to create new perspectives and therefore change the meaning we hold. This means changing our internal story. The more we reframe disempowering egoic thoughts, the more we build constructive beliefs.

There are five clear steps to developing confident self-belief:

1. Integrity means being true to yourself, honoring your word, and following through on what you say you are going to do. It means breaking the pattern of people-pleasing and putting ourselves first. When we breach personal integrity, we let ourselves down and end up feeling ashamed. This leaves us feeling disempowered. On the other hand, every time we honor ourselves, we build our self-confidence and respect our choices.

2. Respect is what we feel every time we honor ourselves, whereas we feel guilty when we dishonor ourselves. Integrity breeds self-respect and pride. These feelings build our self-worth.

3. Self-worth evolves from respect and integrity. The more we respect ourselves, the greater sense of self-worth we have. This helps us rewrite the terms and conditions of our self-worth. Instead of needing to be accepted or loved or to fit in, the love and respect we have for ourselves champions our self-worth. Knowing our own self-worth gives us clarity.

4. Clarity gives us power. With integrity, respect and self-worth, we know who we are and what we want. This inner knowing gives us the confidence to be our true selves.

5. Certainty of self is confidence—it is self-belief. We honor what we know is right for us and what we believe in. We make confident "I am" statements. For example, with certainty we say, "I am a good person. I am a loving person. I am a powerful person." Our unconscious mind believes whatever we say after the words *I am*. Statements such as: "I am hopeless," "I am pathetic," "I am a loser," "I am not worthy" or "I am ugly" unleash fear. Placing a positive statement after the words *I am* refocuses the mind and builds healthy beliefs.

HERE IS AN EXERCISE TO FOSTER SELF-BELIEF:

Take a piece of paper and draw a line down the middle. On the left side list all the limiting beliefs and behaviors you identified in your ego-personification exercise. On the right side of the page, reframe your limiting beliefs into empowering beliefs. Here is an example:

LIMITING BELIEFS AND BEHAVIORS	EMPOWERING BELIEFS (SELF-BELIEF)
<ul><li>I am weak and give in to people</li><li>I am stupid and always fail</li><li>I do not know how to succeed</li><li>Bad things always seem to happen</li><li>I am scared of change and always feel alone</li></ul>	<ul><li>I am strong</li><li>I am capable</li><li>I am able to do whatever I put my mind to</li><li>I am resilient and always land on my feet</li><li>I am safe and will always have the right people in my life</li></ul>

FAITH

> *"To trust in the force that moves the universe is faith. Faith isn't blind, it's visionary."*
>
> Marianne Williamson

Once we have cleared the cloud of fear from our consciousness, we can perceive our world with a faith mindset. Faith is the act of trusting and believing; with trust and belief we can take a leap of faith. It is a deep inner knowing that a life force greater than us is in control of our destiny—an omnipresent force that always conspires for our success and growth. When we are connected to this energy we can feel its power within our essence. Faith is an expression of the essence of self-love.

Fear is the expression of the tainted ego-self. And because there is an inner duality between the ego-self and the essence, what this really boils down to is choosing between fear and faith. Fear is a choice made by the ego-self. Faith is a choice made by the essence (self-love). One decision keeps us stuck in our old habitual ways; the other enables us to consciously evolve. The cross can be seen as a symbol of these two choices. When we act from fear we move "horizontally." This means we continue to develop our personality as it is without challenging it or changing. When we act from faith, we grow "vertically." We grow more and more into our higher selves, our soul-self. In every challenging moment, we come upon this crossroad: a path of fear or faith? Ego or essence?

The inner resource to help develop greater faith is acceptance. Faith is acceptance and acceptance is faith. When we surrender with trust and we have confident belief, we can accept that everything happens as it needs to. We accept our painful paths because they helped us grow. We accept difficult people because they teach us great lessons. We accept ourselves because we know that we were born whole and complete with the exact strengths we need to actualize our unique purpose.

Acceptance also helps us release the attachments the ego-self holds onto. These are all the expectations we have for people and situations in our lives. When we attach, we need people to be a certain way and we need to achieve various outcomes. This attitude leads us to be controlling and demanding instead of compassionate. Acceptance helps us let go and detach.

The forgiveness exercise offered in Chapter 14 is designed to help you foster acceptance. As you reflect on your three letters and the conversation you had with your inner child, what can you now accept? As we accept, we let go even more. As we accept, we experience greater peace. And as we accept, we grow into our lessons. We evolve.

Think about the expectations you have for yourself and others that dictate the terms and conditions of your self worth (Chapter 6). How can you turn those expectations into acceptance? Here is an example:

TERMS AND CONDITIONS OF SELF-WORTH	WHAT I ACCEPT WITHIN MYSELF/ WHAT I HAVE FAITH IN
• I need to be successful • I should be financially secure and have money • I must be wealthy to be worthy • **EXPECTATIONS OF OTHERS** My children: • I need them to achieve and do well • My partner: • I need you to support me and always be there for me	• I accept that being my purpose in an authentic way makes me successful • I accept that I will always have what I need and will be looked after • My self-worth is based on who I truly am and what I offer people, not what is in my bank account • I accept their unique gifts and know they have their own lessons to learn in life • I accept that I am self-sufficient and love myself more than I need to be loved. I therefore do not *need* you, but *want* to share life with you.

To embrace trust, belief and faith we need to know the steps to connect with our essence. Let's explore the pathway to the essence in the next chapter.

CHAPTER 17

THE PATHWAY TO THE ESSENCE

"Your vision will become clear only when you look into your heart. Who looks outside, dreams; who looks inside, awakens."

Carl Jung

Just as the ego-self expresses itself through four self-limiting behaviors—compete, compare, compromise, and control—there are four behaviors that express the essence. The four behaviors of the essence are different in that they do not occur in isolation, separate from one another, but rather one after the other. They can therefore be seen more as a *pathway* to the essence, or as four steps to discovering your essence.

These four steps are *connection, calm, clarity* and *confident courage*. They offer a way to break through the conditioning of the mind and clear the cloud of fear from the tainted ego. As we purify our thoughts and let go of the emotional pain buried within our bodies, we discover what awaits us beneath our pain body. Instead of perceiving the world through a fear filter, we see the world through the clarity of trust, belief and faith. We enter the "galaxy of the essence."

CONNECTION > CALM > CLARITY > CONFIDENT COURAGE

The Pathway to Essence

STEP ONE: CONNECTION TO SELF

The pathway to the essence begins with connection. Three parts consolidate this connection:

1) Connection to ourselves: Being connected to this internal energy allows us to feel the energy of love within us and to perceive the world through a lens of trust, belief and faith. In this space of connection we can hear the voice of our intuition guiding us with her wisdom, and we express self-love instead of fear. In this state we feel the vibration of our essence flowing through the body.

2) Connection to a higher source: This means we are connected to the "ground force" of Mother Earth. (As I connect with Mother Earth, I connect with ME.) We are grounded and connected to the same frequency that moves through the cosmos.

3) Connection between the mind and heart: This means that instead of the mind and heart working in discord, where the heart says one thing and the mind says another, they work together in harmony. The mind is led by the heart. Or, more specifically, the ego-mind is led by the essence. We know who we are and what we want, and there are no limiting beliefs or dysfunctional behaviors in our way.

Before we explore the pathway to connection, let us first fully understand what is meant by *dis*connection and how we can differentiate between the two. When we are disconnected we experience the following traits:

- We are stuck in our thoughts and keep ruminating over the past or anticipating our future. As a result, we are filled with mental clutter and not fully engaged in the present moment.
- We have no body awareness. We are "talking heads" separated from our bodies. We are also numb to our emotions, which means we do not notice how our thoughts affect our feelings. We get the sense that we are simply going through the motions of life. We are not fully present, and are possibly even in a trance-like state.
- Having no body awareness also means that we push ourselves beyond our threshold as we are not tuned into our body's

warning signals of fatigue. Illness or burnout may force us to stop and take a break.
- We feel disconnected from our soul. This means we do not know what it means to be heart-centered. We do not know who we really are or what we ultimately want. We prioritize our survival habits or safety habits and continue to mold ourselves into the person we believe our environment needs us to be.
- We feel fear, isolation and loneliness. We are ungrounded, scattered, restless, anxious and depressed.
- The nervous system is in fight, flight or freeze mode, making us reactive and emotional.
- The mind is judging, criticizing or worrying.
- We cannot hear the voice of our intuition or do not know how to recognize it. We need some form of drama to make us stop and listen.
- We are stuck in a control pattern, often without recognizing we are being controlling. For example, we want our partner or children to behave a certain way, we want things to go our way, and we have strict rules and unrealistic expectations.
- We continuously compromise ourselves by people-pleasing. When we are disconnected from ourselves we have no personal boundaries and tend to self-sacrifice instead of putting ourselves first.
- We search for connection outside of ourselves. This means our relationships remain codependent: we need the other person in order to feel complete. Our inner separation makes us feel desperate to belong and fit in. This inner separation creates an internal void that we try to fill via unresourceful habits, which often turn into addictive behaviors. (Drinking, smoking, taking drugs, sex addiction, retail therapy, comfort eating, gossiping, complaining and negative thinking are a few examples.)
- We do not realize how our actions impact others. When we lack self-worth and are disconnected from self-love, we do not think we matter enough to have an effect on others. This means we do not feel we have a purpose. We do not feel that we contribute anything valuable/worthwhile.

I like to think of self-connection as similar to a WIFI connection. When we are connected to WIFI we have access to the worldwide web wirelessly, wherever we are; anything we need is only a click away. When we are connected to ourselves and our internal source of power, it is as if we are plugged into an endless supply of energy, power and knowledge.

We therefore need an effective connection to give us full power. This is achieved by developing *habits of connection*: daily rituals, habits and routines that connect us to our essence. Instead of our safety habits being our top priority—things like getting to work on time, making sure all bills are paid promptly, or doing what society feels is acceptable—we begin to put our happiness habits first. This is achieved by practicing self-care.

Self-care is the art of self-connection. It is the practice of taking responsibility for our own well-being and happiness. This means connecting to our internal source power and "filling ourselves up" before we do anything else. If we are unplugged, exhausted or distracted, we cannot be guided by our essence. As a result, the ego-self takes over our awareness.

There are many forms of self-care. To discover which is right for you, all you need to do is tune into your feelings and notice what uplifts your energy. It may be exercise, yoga, walking in nature, qi gong, surfing, swimming, being with good friends, music, having a massage, dancing, singing, horse riding, or anything else, including whatever you may have done as a child to feel happy.

My favorite self-care ritual, and one I am passionate about teaching, is meditation. Meditation is the supreme pathway to self-connection because it helps us move through the layers of egoic thoughts and tune into the voice in our heart. When the mind goes quiet, we can hear our soul speaking. It guides us to hear/tune into our intuition.

Meditation practice, such as *mindfulness meditation*, is the act of plugging in and connecting to our essential energy. Meditation slows down the mind and in turn slows down every system in the body. As our brain waves slow down, our heartbeat slows down, our musculoskeletal system softens, and our nervous system is less stimulated. And, most importantly, meditation connects us to our breath, the body's self-regulation tool.

The breath can be seen as the medium that unites the mind and the body. As we focus our mind on our breathing, we can direct our breath to clear out the toxins created by impure (fearful) thoughts. We can release the damaging effects that stress has on the body, such as high levels of cortisol and inflammation. As we inhale fresh oxygen, we take in the cosmic life force. As we exhale, we let go of carbon dioxide and release whatever the body no longer needs. As we clear out the effects of fear from the body, we begin to feel more space and lightness; we can feel our essence vibrating deep within the bubbling core of our inner landscape. We discover the wondrous world existing just beneath our pain. This powerful connection to our breath and our life force results in a grounded sense of calm because we are fully engaged in the present moment.

STEP TWO: CALM

Once we are connected to our essence, we feel a sense of calm. We feel safe and know that everything will be all right. There is much empirical evidence for the calming benefits of self-connection through meditation.

As discussed in Chapter 9, there are two parts to our nervous system: the sympathetic nervous system and the parasympathetic nervous system. We have already explored how the sympathetic nervous system is triggered by fearful thoughts that result in our survival mode and safety habits. When we connect with our breath and to our core-self, we activate our parasympathetic nervous system. The sympathetic nervous system revs up the body, just like the accelerator of a car. The parasympathetic nervous system slows it down, just like the brakes. The parasympathetic nervous system activates the *relaxation response*. This is the opposite reaction to our fight, flight or freeze mode. Dr. Herbert Benson defined the relaxation response as our personal ability to help the body release chemicals that slow down our muscles and organs and increase blood flow and oxygen to the brain. Meditation produces the relaxation response. "We claim no innovation but simply a scientific validation of age-old wisdom," Dr. Benson says regarding the calming effect of meditation on the nervous system.

Modern neuroscientists have found that meditation strengthens the relaxation response by activating the prefrontal cortex. In one study, MRI brain scans of people who had completed an eight-week meditation course revealed a significant shrinkage of the amygdalae and a thickening of the prefrontal cortex. The prefrontal cortex (PFC) is situated at the top of the brain, as if it is literally our higher self. The

PFC is responsible for executive functioning, such as the following:
- Differentiating between conflicting thoughts
- Recognizing what we value as right or wrong, same or different, good or bad
- Being able to notice the consequence of a situation or predict outcomes
- Effective problem solving
- Goal setting
- Willpower
- Short-term memory
- Impulse control
- Discernment and forethought

Similar to positive emotions such as optimism and resilience, relaxation is a learned behavior. We need to practice calmness by breaking our relationship with fear. As we navigate our awareness through our fear and under our painful emotions, and connect with our core essence, we return to calmness. We train the brain to stop, breathe and think about what is going on around us. Instead of mindlessly reacting to life, we develop mindful responses such as the *powerful pause.*

Pausing causes the breath to interrupt the neurological patterning of the conditioned self. As we stop our negative and limiting thinking, we prevent the brain from resorting to its habitual reactions. With this level of awareness and self-control, we can discover our calm, more empowered self.

Pause for a moment and visualize the difference between your reactive, emotional self (ego-self) and your calm, mindful self (authentic self). Notice the steps you are taking to be calm. Become aware of how being your calm self makes you feel. Notice the connection with your essence, and allow trust, belief and faith to navigate your actions and responses now.

Our calm self can therefore be seen as the best version of us. And once we are connected and feel calm, we have clarity.

STEP THREE: CLARITY

Clarity allows us to lift the veil of fear and see what is going on. Instead of taking things personally, attaching to drama or fearfully avoiding pain, we can perceive a situation through the senses of our higher intelligence. Clarity gives us a sense of personal power by providing us the feeling of being in control. Instead of feeling out of control, we experience ourselves as being in control of our thoughts, emotions and choices. We have no need to desperately control situations, because we are calmly *in control.*

Instead of the mind and heart being in discord, with clarity the mind and heart work in harmony. We can experience life through the wisdom of our heart rather than through a limiting belief system. When we are connected to our heart center, we can see into the heart of another. We therefore have more compassion, tolerance, intelligence, grace and peace. In this state of mind we are able to recognize the pain and suffering in another person. Instead of reacting or shutting down in fear, we can now relax, expand and proceed with confident courage.

STEP FOUR: CONFIDENT COURAGE

Confident courage allows us to express our authentic self courageously. This means we allow ourselves to express our essence instead of our ego-self. Because the ego-self is our conditioned mode, we default to this position initially. Once we connect, feel an inner calm and activate our higher clarity, we can break our patterning and go forward with confident courage.

Confident courage enables us to make bold decisions with strength, purpose, conviction, commitment, inner peace and freedom. We have the courage to be our true selves. We have the courage to choose happiness over safety and love over fear. We have the self-belief, trust and faith to break our self-defeating mindsets and develop a healthy mindset based on our inner virtues.

Following these four steps will help you access your authenticity and express the twelve self-empowering mindsets that are outlined in the following chapter.

CHAPTER 18

TWELVE SELF-EMPOWERING MINDSETS

"Let choice whisper in your ear and love murmur in your heart. Be ready. Here comes life."

Maya Angelou

The twelve self-defeating mindsets of our ego-self act as our Achilles heel and rob us of personal power. In contrast to this, the twelve self-empowering mindsets of the essence act as superpowers—like Zeus and his thunderbolt. These superpowers are as follows:

1. **Self-awareness**
   - We are aware of limiting beliefs as well as our authentic self
   - "I am," "I feel," "I believe"
   - We are the mindful observer of self
   - We have the ability to manage our moment-to-moment choices
   - We are connected to ourselves

2. **Self-acceptance**
   - We rein in the inner critic and accept ourselves fully
   - "I accept myself," "Who I am is enough," "I am perfectly imperfect"

- We let go of unrealistic expectations of ourselves without dropping our standards
- We let go perfectionism, procrastination, self-pity, self-doubt, self-righteousness and the need to be validated
- We acknowledge our unique strengths that help actualize our life purpose

3. Self-belief
- We listen to the internal voice of our intuition and what we know is right for us
- "I believe I can do whatever I put my mind to"
- We believe in our capabilities, our ideas and creativity
- We have self-belief and self-acceptance and love ourselves unconditionally

4. Self-respect
- We honor ourselves and our needs
- "I respect my mind and my body"
- We have the ability to make healthy choices for ourselves
- We honor our sensitivity and surround ourselves with positive people and positive energy
- We have healthy personal boundaries
- We put ourselves first instead of people-pleasing
- This mindset is the antithesis to self-sabotage

5. Self-trust
- We have the ability to embrace uncertainty or challenge with a strong mindset, trusting that everything we need is within us
- "I go with the flow of life"
- We know that everything will work out in the exact way it needs to
- We have the ability to make courageous heart-centered choices

6. Self-esteem
- We value our worth
- "I value myself"
- Our choices we make regarding what we allow into our lives, whether relationships, employment or friends, are a direct

reflection of how much we value who we are
- We consciously create happiness, positivity and a strong support base around us
- In addition to what we attract, self-esteem allows us to recognize our significance and how we can contribute to our world

7. Self-worth
- Similar to self-esteem, self-worth stems from a deep knowing and belief in our personal value
- "I am worthy," "I am significant and have a powerful purpose to contribute"
- We have nothing to prove
- We are worthy because we are unique and have the ability to make an impact on the world in whatever shape or form
- Reflect on the list you wrote in Chapter 15 regarding what you accept within yourself and notice how worthy you feel

8. Self-confidence
- We have certainty and clarity
- "I know who I am and what I stand for"
- We have self-awareness and personal integrity
- We make decisions that honor our truth and therefore feel proud of ourselves
- We eliminate the shadow of shame and guilt that otherwise cloud our clarity and leave us confused and disempowered
- These are often not easy decisions to make
- We honor our essence and choose to be truthful over and above being fearful

9. Self-sufficiency
- We trust in our ability to manifest what we need, be it financially or emotionally
- "I can take care of myself"
- We break the pattern of codependency
- We take responsibility for both our happiness and our success
- Instead of needing others to love us, we tap into our internal fountain of self-love and fill ourselves up
- Instead of giving our power away, we cultivate, conserve and

channel our energy toward our inner resources to help us feel independent and free

10. Self-care
- We commit to our habits of connection that help us connect with our essence because we know that to live "courageously happy" requires energy
- "I nurture myself"
- We put ourselves first and refuel our energy without the fear of being selfish
- We plug into an infinite power supply
- We light up our souls so that we can shine

11. Self-management
- We tune into our thoughts and emotions and manage our responses
- "I manage myself, my thoughts and emotions"
- Instead of resorting to our habitual, knee-jerk reactions, we can pause, reflect and choose how we want to respond. Instead of fearing, we manage ourselves in difficult situations or around people who may have previously intimidated us
- We have the ability to manage our time, money and energy because we are connected, calm, clear and confident

12. Self-love
- We love ourselves rather than *needing* to be loved, feel worthy, or feel good enough
- "I love and accept myself unconditionally," "I express the love within me"
- We uplift our energy with mindful thoughts and action
- We eliminate negative self-talk because we know that the quality of our happiness is determined by the quality of our thoughts
- We let go of *distraction habits* that keep us trapped in our pain and fear
- Instead of hiding in our comfort zones playing small, we choose to expand and share our essence
- We empower ourselves by making choices with self-love

These twelve mindsets can be seen as "muscles" of the essence. As we focus on these mindsets, we breathe life into them and allow them to grow. Use these twelve mindsets as antidotes to the twelve self-defeating ego behaviors. Trash self-doubt and cultivate self-belief! Burn self-sabotage and fire up self-respect! Reverse self-withdrawal and generate self-trust! As you flip your focus, you flip your fear and switch from ego to essence.

Every one of us was born with unique virtues—inner resources that help us manage our lives and grow into our greatness. We will explore these virtues in the next chapter. They define the *essence of you.*

CHAPTER 19

THE ESSENCE OF YOU: WHO YOU ARE AND WHAT YOU VALUE

> *"I am brave, I am bruised*
> *I am who I'm meant to be, this is me*
> *Look out 'cause here I come*
> *And I'm marching on to the beat I drum*
> *I'm not scared to be seen*
> *I make no apologies, this is me"*
>
> Lyrics from "This is Me," *The Greatest Showman*

Throughout this book, you have learned that the ego-self is your conditioned-self that comprises all your perceptions and all the decisions you've made through your life experience to date. Your ego-self is your "I"-dentity, though it is masked by the various roles you play in life: parent, boss, employee, sibling, friend or frenemy. Your ego-self encapsulates your beliefs. Although your beliefs are *your* truth, they are not always *the* truth. They may define the way you see reality, but they do not define who you are. Therefore, the ego-self is not your authentic self and definitely not the best version of you.

Taming the ego-self and breaking our conditioned ways calls for a shift in our belief system. Every time we challenge and change a limiting belief and reframe it into a more empowering thought, we grow and align ourselves with our truth. This means moving away from a belief-based system, whereby our beliefs rule our perceptions and decisions, and moving toward a virtues-and-values-based system, whereby our virtues and values shape our focus.

As I worked through this model with clients, many asked, "Well, if I am not my ego-self, who am I? What motivates me now if I am not driven by my fear?" These are brilliant questions because our ultimate goal is to break our relationship with fear and unlearn the adaptations we made to our essential nature. We want to tear up the contract we wrote with ourselves, and rescript our terms and conditions. We want to break our safety habits and embrace our happiness habits—*to stop surviving and begin thriving*. We want to flip our focus from a fear to a faith mindset.

The reality is that our beliefs are not set in stone. They can easily change. They do not have to define us, as *we are not our thoughts*. When we peel through the layers of our emotional onion, and as we tune into our feelings and travel through our pain, we stumble upon these limiting beliefs and the adaptations we have made. We can trace the development of our fear and how it began to pollute the effervescent bubble of our essence.

In facing our defining decisions, letting them go and forgiving, we are able to reframe our beliefs and subsequently shift our mindset. Letting go of pain and clearing cellular memory enables us to shed the layers of the ego-self. As a snake sheds its skin, we transform and move closer toward a sensitive core-self who has patiently waited for us all along—a flame of possibility that was suffocated by a cloud of doubt. This is the essence of you.

The essence can be seen as the innermost core of our self—our speck of life. It has a physical presence too; it is the little beating dot that is visible on our first pregnancy ultrasound: our heartbeat. That little dot, our heart, represents our aliveness. Within that tiny area, that measures only a few millimeters across, lies the mapping of our true self: the seed of Mother Earth, planted in the soil of a mother's womb. Within that speck of life lie not only the universal qualities of nature, but also our unique

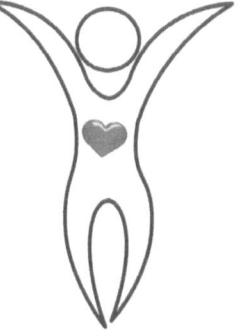

blueprint. This blueprint is expressed through our individual virtues, values and the daily habits, thoughts and actions we take.

VIRTUES

Our virtues are our character strengths, our natural gifts. They offer us the potential to realize optimal levels of thinking and behaving so that we can achieve our most inspired goals. Our virtues represent the resources we have within us. They are the tools we use to navigate through life. They are our superpowers, and hold the key to us actualizing our full potential.

We were each given unique qualities that will enable us to master our life's mission. Some people are brilliant at mathematics because they will need that skill to realize their contribution to society. Others may have great empathy: they understand people's deeper needs and are able to work with them. Instead of comparing ourselves to others and thinking that who we are is not enough, we can embrace *our* virtues. Instead of trying to adapt ourselves to fit in, we can recognize that *our* virtues are our greatest strengths. They enable us to make a difference—to stand out and make a significant contribution to society.

Our virtues are actually what come most easily to us, yet we often disregard them and don't even recognize them as strengths. We take our virtues for granted and think we need to be something other than who we are to succeed. It is our life's purpose to master our virtues and share them with the world.

The virtues of our essence can be likened to essential oils. An essential oil is a pure extract of a plant such as lavender or tea tree. You could say that our essence contains various "extracts," which are the individual parts of our authentic self and represent the opposite mindset to fear. Our virtues represent our resourceful behavioral patterns and positive mindset. Where beliefs are our subjective experience of reality, our virtues act as a moral compass, keeping us aligned with our truth and greatness. And as we prioritize honoring our virtues instead of obeying the ego-mind, they help us achieve ultimate states of being. These ideal positive emotions are our authentic values.

VALUES

Our values are what is most important to us and represent what we consistently prefer to feel. They are organized in a hierarchy from most to least important, and reveal a key component of what motivates our decision-making process. Each significant emotional experience impacts what we choose to value. As we grow and begin to see the world differently, our values change. When we are disconnected from our essence, in an egoic trance-like state, we value what the ego-self desires and needs. We place value on our safety and what will prove our worth over and above what brings us authentic happiness. We satisfy the hedonistic needs of the ego-self because we are unaware of our virtues.

This disconnected state creates a clash between our authentic values and our limiting beliefs—a split between the mind and the heart. The heart wants to follow the wisdom of the essence as its inner compass, while the mind, influenced by our limiting beliefs, wants to keep us safe. When we act on our limiting beliefs, we sabotage ourselves. The body goes into stress because it is out of alignment. Pain, fear, stress, frustration, guilt, shame and anxiety can be seen as warning signals that let us know we are out of alignment with our values.

Incongruence is what we experience when there is a clash between our inner egoic needs and the values of our essence. For example, we may value freedom and have "a free spirit" as a core virtue. However, our need for emotional or financial security may sabotage our quest for freedom. Instead of making choices that enhance our sense of freedom, we make choices that enhance safety. A person deciding to stay in or leave a relationship might feel split: her intuition (the voice of the essence) may guide her to leave a difficult relationship, but the ego-self, which needs to know it is loved and safe, may decide to stay. The key here is to honor both the mind and the heart, the ego-self and the essence, to find a compromise that makes sense to the mind and feels good to the heart.

Congruence is achieved when we honor our authentic values. Our authentic values are the ideal emotional states we can experience when we prioritize "being" our virtues. As opposed to feeling incongruent, this state of alignment helps us achieve the positive feelings and outcomes we desire (such as peace, freedom or happiness). Knowing what we authentically value and honoring that enables us to experience what matters most.

Our virtues describe who and what we are being (how we conduct ourselves). Our values describe what we truly desire. Our daily habits, thoughts and actions define what we do and the choices we make. For example, when we are being calm (a virtue), we experience inner peace (a value). When we prioritize our value of inner peace, we reprioritize the hierarchy of our values, which in turn shapes our future choices and behaviors. We will prioritize being calm over stressed, and as a result may choose to have greater work-life balance above overachieving.

Our virtues and values help us notice where we are reacting to life from fear instead of faith, which makes them an effective decision-making tool. When we dishonor our values and our virtues, we veer off path and feel uncomfortable. For example, when I take something personally, and react emotionally, I dishonor my value of compassion. Instead of feeling empowered because I have been compassionate, I am more likely to feel shame and regret.

Our values can also be seen as the vertebrae that unite the mind and the heart. When they are aligned, the virtues of our heart can easily direct the mind. We feel congruent because our virtues are evident in our actions and we can feel we are expressing our highest values. However, when we dishonor our virtues, we are incongruent with our values. There is a blockage in our "vertebrae" that disturbs this flow. Just as you may visit a chiropractor to realign your spine, making your virtues your values keeps you connected, fully energized and aligned with your life purpose. You will know you are honoring your virtues because you feel more energized and uplifted—you feel connected, calm, clear and experience confident courage.

Because our fear responses are based on imprinted decisions that have become conditioned, we default to them. We therefore need to know our virtues

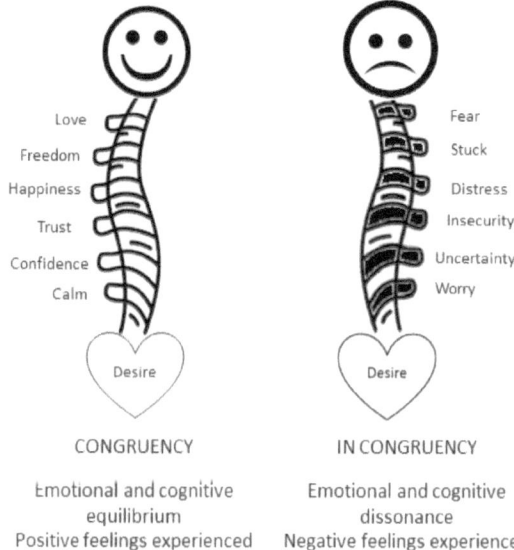

well and develop the daily habits that fully express them. In doing so, we will make them our top values. When we understand that fear is just a mindset, it has less power over us because we know that with enough practice, repetition and focus, we can change. As we learned, the onion and lily come from the same family, but where the lily opens itself to the light, the onion forms hard, self-protective layers. Shedding the layers of our "emotional onion" allows us to transform into a beautiful flower that wants to open and reveal itself.

DISCOVERING YOUR VIRTUES AND VALUES

In Chapter 11 I offered you an exercise to personify your ego-self—to bring your ego-self to life and recognize clearly what fearful beliefs and actions you have developed. I introduced you to Molly, my ego-personification, and explained how she led me to make poor decisions for myself. These fear-based decisions led me astray from my soul's calling. My need to be loved led me to compromise my core values. Once I connected with my virtues, they began to act as my GPS, helping me to navigate my life through the consciousness of my essence, my true and authentic self, with trust, belief and faith.

So, here is an exercise to help you elicit and implement your core virtues and values so that you can discover how to be the best version of yourself. This exercise is divided into two parts. In the first part we are going to elicit and define your virtues, and in the second part we are going to outline how you make these virtues your values (your primary focus) by implementing them in your daily thoughts and habits. We are going to define who you *really are* and how you can then *be* your authentic purpose. (For further assistance, please refer to the virtues elicitation and implementation example at the end of this chapter.)

PART 1: VIRTUES ELICITATION

1. Go through the following list of virtues and select the ten traits that resonate with you the most. You will most likely want to select them all! However, you will notice that certain words stand out from the others. Trust in your intuition and select these. (Try not to overthink this; tune into your feelings.)

Ask yourself the following questions to identify your core virtues:

- When I let go of fear and self-doubt and think of the best version of myself, who am I?
- What are my qualities?
- What are my unique character strengths?
- What behaviors (traits) make me feel most proud of myself?
- How would the people who love me the most describe me?
- What character traits do I want to be known for?

2. Once you have selected your top ten, define each one. Aim to define them positively by describing what they *are* rather than what they are not. For example, I define *compassionate* as having a detached understanding and acceptance of myself and others. It shows up as me not taking anything personally. As you can see, I am not only specifying what I must not do, I am directing my mind toward how I can *be* compassionate. (That definition therefore becomes my rules/guidelines to being compassionate). When I take things personally, judge another person, criticize or gossip about them, I dishonor my greatest virtue of being compassionate.

3. Now give each virtue a rating (0 to 10). This is a rating of how aligned you are to each virtue at this moment in time. Zero would signal that you are completely incongruent with your virtue and 10 would highlight complete congruency. Be honest. Your rating may differ in different situations. You may be portraying your virtues at work, yet sabotaging your virtues in relationships. Give yourself an overall rating.

4. Observe your rating and list the sabotaging behavior and beliefs disrupting your alignment. Where are you incongruent with your virtues? To make this easy, notice where you may be competing, comparing, compromising and controlling. Notice where and how your fear of not feeling loved, worthy or good enough is showing up in your life. Reflect on the areas of your life where you feel most stressed, anxious or disempowered, and notice how you are being your fear instead of your virtues. Notice the thoughts and behaviors that drain your superpowers, and where your virtues and values clash with your needs.

Here's an example of an internal clash between our virtues, values and sabotaging patterns:

VIRTUE	VALUE	SABOTAGING PATTERNS
Adaptability Definition: Being flexible with my thoughts and behaviors and adapting to people's needs as well as to changes in my life.	**Inner peace** When I am being adaptable I experience a feeling of inner peace, which allows me to stop controlling and go with the flow of life.	**Fears** that stem from my belief that I am not good enough to be loved: I need to avoid rejection and ensure that I am not abandoned by others. **Incongruent behavior:** When I feel scared that someone may reject or abandon me I experience inner conflict. I then begin to control others and want things to go my way. By controlling others, I minimize the risk of getting hurt.

A LIST OF OUR VIRTUES, THE "EXTRACTS" OF OUR ESSENCE—OUR CHARACTER STRENGTHS:

Able	Forgiving	Open-minded
Accepting	Forthright	Passionate
Accountable	Free	Patient
Adventurous	Friendly	Peaceful
Ambitious	Fun	Perceptive
Articulate	Generous	Persistent
Assertive	Gentle	Persuasive
Appreciative	Graceful	Playful
Authentic	Grateful	Practical
Aware	Growing	Proactive
Balanced	Happy	Pure
Beautiful	Healthy	Purposeful
Capable	Helpful	Relaxed
Calm	Honest	Reliable
Caring	Honorable	Resilient
Certain	Humble	Resourceful
Charismatic	Imaginative	Respectful
Clean	Independent	Responsible
Committed	Innovative	Responsive
Compassionate	Insightful	Reverent
Confident	Inspiring	Self-directed
Considerate	Intuitive	Self-discipline
Content	Integrity	Serene
Cooperative	Intelligence	Sensitive
Courageous	Joyful	Service-oriented
Courteous	Just	Sincere
Creative	Kind	Sociable
Curious	Loving	Steadfast
Decisive	Loyal	Strong
Detached	Mature	Stable
Determined	Meticulous	Spiritual
Devoted	Merciful	Systematic
Disciplined	Mindful	Tactful
Dignified	Moderate	Thankful

Diligent	Modest	Tolerant
Empathetic	Nurturing	Trustful
Energetic	Nobile	Trustworthy
Enthusiastic	Obedient	Truthful
Committed to excellence	Objective	Understanding
Expressive	Organized	Valuable
Fair	Orderly	Whole
Flexible	Open-hearted	Wise

PART 2: VIRTUES AND VALUES IMPLEMENTATION

The "BE-DO-HAVE coaching model" is one of my favorite tools for implementing change. This model asks three key questions:

1. Who/what do I need to BE to honor my virtues?

This question helps us break through old conditioning by focusing on the present moment. Specifically, it asks which of the virtues we want to express in a given moment in time. It is designed to remind us to connect and focus on our virtues instead of our default reactions. Focusing on who/what we are *being* activates our essence awareness, and we are able to consciously create our authentic self in that moment. (Who do I need to be, right now, in this very moment?)

In addition, by asking ourselves this empowering question we highlight and reveal *the intention* behind our behavior or what is *motivating* our behavior. If we act on our fear and express a stress response, we are being fearful. Our behavior is being driven by or motivated by fear. The expression of fear has a negative consequence that returns to us. For example, if someone criticizes us and we take it personally, we may react with defensiveness and justify our behavior. We may also criticize the other person to make us feel better. This behavior will most likely enhance conflict and create negative feelings of shame, anger or guilt.

2. What do I need to DO to honor my virtues?

This question helps you focus on the habits, daily rituals and routines you need to implement in order to honor your virtues. This question therefore directs your moment-to-moment choices and ensures all of your actions and goals are congruent with your virtues.

3. What will I <u>HAVE</u> in my life when I honor my virtues?

This key question helps you identify the positive, constructive feelings you will experience on a daily basis as a result of expressing your authentic self. These positive emotions are your authentic values (what you ultimately want to experience every day). In addition, think about the goals or accomplishments you will achieve when you live those values. Steven Covey, in his book *The Seven Habits of Highly Effective People*, guides us to "start with the end in mind." When we are aware of the outcomes we want to achieve, we have absolute clarity around which direction we want to take and how we are going to get there.

To answer this question, look at the following list of values and identify the emotion each virtue will help you feel. Go through the list of your top ten virtues. What will you experience within yourself as a result of "being" this virtue? In addition, list what will be present in your relationships, career, health, finances and personal development as a result of living in congruence with your virtues.

Values List: What you value most; what you ultimately desire to feel and how you desire to behave each day.

Abundance	Fairness	Passion
Acceptance	Faith	Patience
Accountability	Fame	Peace
Achievement	Family	Perception
Adventure	Flexibility	Perseverance
Affection	Forgiveness	Perspective
Ambition	Forthrightness	Persistence
Appearance (Physical)	Freedom	Persuasiveness
Articulate	Friendship	Playfulness
Assertiveness	Fulfilment	Pleasure
Authenticity	Fun	Power
Awareness	Generosity	Practicality
Balance	Gentleness	Proactivity
Beauty	Grace	Purity
Belief	Gratitude	Purpose
Belonging	Growth	Recognition
Capability	Happiness	Relaxation
Calmness	Harmony	Reliability
Certainty	Healthy	Resilience
Charisma	Helpful	Resourcefulness
Choice	Honesty	Respect
Cleanliness	Honor	Responsibility
Clarity	Humility	Responsiveness
Commitment	Imagination	Reverence
Compassion	Independence	Safety
Confidence	Innovation	Security
Connection	Insight	Self-worth
Consideration	Inspiration	Serenity
Contentment	Intuition	Service
Cooperation	Integrity	Sincerity
Courage	Intelligence	Socialness
Courtesy	Involvement	Solitude
Creativity	Joy	Strength
Curiosity	Justice	Spirituality
Decisiveness	Kindness	Temperance

Detachment	Love	Thankfulness
Determination	Loyalty	Tolerance
Devotion	Maturity	Trust
Dignity	Mindfulness	Truthfulness
Diligence	Moderation	Understanding
Empathy	Modesty	Unity
Endurance	Nurture	Vitality
Energy	Nobility	Wealth
Enthusiasm	Obedience	Wholeness
Excellence	Objectivity	Wisdom
Expression	Organization	Wonder

VIRTUES ELICITATION AND IMPLEMENTATION EXAMPLE:

The example below is a condensed version of a virtues and values elicitation and implementation exercise. I recommend doing this exercise every six to twelve months to notice how you are improving. A higher rating will reveal greater congruency with your virtues and values.

Part 1: Virtues Elicitation

PART 1: VIRTUES ELICITATION	DEFINITION	RATING (0-10)	SABOTAGING PATTERNS (BELIEFS AND BEHAVIORS KEEPING US STUCK) *(CONDENSED VERSION)
Compassionate	• I do not take anything personally. • I have a detached understanding and am accepting of others as well as myself.	7	**Behaviors:** • I take things personally. • I am oversensitive. • I am judgmental. • I expect people to behave a certain way. • I judge myself. • I let my inner critic take over my thinking, which causes me to need things to be perfect. • I procrastinate. • I feel sorry for myself. • I feel like I am the victim. **Limiting Beliefs:** • Everyone sees the world as I do. • I need to be right. • I am not good enough. • People will judge me. • I need to be a certain way for people to accept me. • I don't belong anywhere and desperately want to fit in. • I am ugly. • I am stupid. • I am overweight. • I am weak.

Wise	• I detach from drama and let my higher self direct my choices.	6	**Behaviors:** • I attach to other people's drama and take on their energy. • I am overly empathetic and take on other people's problems. • I try to fix people. • I compromise my own personal values and boundaries. **Limiting Beliefs:** • If I help others, they will love me. • My life is full of dramas and I need them to prove that I can overcome anything.
Courageous	• I embrace challenges with my core strength. • I listen and act on my intuition	4	**Behaviors:** • I avoid pain and play safe. • I ignore my inner guidance. • I listen to other people's opinions over my own **Limiting Beliefs:** • I must avoid pain at all costs. • I cannot handle rejection. • Other people know better.

Accepting	• I have faith that everything is happening for my greatest good.	4	**Behaviors:** • I try to control the outcomes to situations. • I control others. • I have high (sometimes unrealistic) expectations of myself and others. • I get stuck in anticipatory thinking as I desperately try to anticipate and predict the future. • I hold onto the past and replay scenarios and conversations where I have let myself down or when others have hurt me. • I am unforgiving. **Limiting Beliefs:** • I have failed and will always fail. • I cannot trust people. • Bad things will always happen, and I have to be ready.

Playful	• I am light-hearted and use my creativity and humor.	2	**Behaviors:** • I take things too seriously. • I get stuck in self-loathing (negative self-talk). • I am constantly in a fight/flight response. • I am emotionally reactive and take things personally. • I get trapped in rigid thinking and focus on the problems. • I get stuck in routine and forget to take time to laugh and have fun. • I don't look for (or see) the joy or humor in a situation. • I compare myself to others. • I am overly competitive. **Limiting Beliefs:** • Life is hard. • Other people have more fun. • Other people get more. • Nothing works out for me (so I feel sorry for myself).

Part 2: Virtues and Values Implementation

BE MY VIRTUES:	DO (WHAT ARE MY PERSONAL RULES, RITUALS, AND ACTION STEPS) (CONDENSED VERSION)	HAVE MY CORE VALUES:
Compassionate	• Do not take it personally. • Pause and think about what is going on within others: • What are their beliefs? • What are their struggles? • Notice what buttons are being pushed within me and manage my inner fear. Be in the present moment. • Do not judge or criticize others. • Keep quiet until I have processed my thoughts. • Soothe my own emotions. • Ensure I am not reacting emotionally; stay calm and present. • Unfold what is really going on—do not assume I understand and do not make up my own story. • Clarify by asking questions.	**Peace** • I feel peace within me and as a result I experience peace in my life. • My relationships are peaceful, and I am able to be loving and present.
Wise	• Detach from drama. • Do not take on other people's emotions. • Breathe and connect with my essence—listen to the voice of my higher self: What would my soul tell me to do? • Visualize my wise woman and allow her consciousness to dominate my thinking and awareness.	**Wisdom** I feel my wise woman guiding me, and ensure that all of my thoughts and actions are aligned with my higher self.

Courageous	• Remember that from pain comes growth. • Embrace challenges, knowing that they will be hard and things may not go the way I want to, but it will be easier if I focus on the lessons and growth along the way. • Listen to my intuition. • Act on inspired thoughts. • Be brave and get out of my comfort zone. Challenge myself. • Speak up for myself with calm assertiveness.	**Strength** I feel strong, like bamboo, and I make courageous decisions that take me out of my comfort zone.
Accepting	• Accept my virtues as my greatest strengths and ensure I am developing them—it is my life's purpose to master these muscles so I must embrace and use them. • Accept others and look for their virtues. • Have faith in all situations and wake up every morning expecting miracles.	**Self-acceptance** I accept who I am and share my virtues in my daily interactions with others.
Playful	• Play with my kids and find joy in all moments. • Look for the humor in situations—let my quirky sense of humor be my greatest asset in becoming resilient. • Make sure to have fun and laugh every day and not take myself or others too seriously.	**Fun** I feel light and playful and use my sense of humor to laugh and not take things too seriously.

The hardest part of this work is *remembering to remember* breaking our conditioned reactions and default mode. Here are some tips to a successful transformation:

- Create a vision board. This brings your deepest desires to life and acts as a daily tool to keep you focused and inspired.
- Print out your worksheets and read them daily as they can function as a manifesto for how to be your authentic self.
- Write your own book on how to be you.
- Keep these supportive reminders on your phone/iPad or screen saver.
- Create a daily mantra incorporating your virtues.
- Visualize yourself *being* your virtues as you wake up in the morning so that you activate them from the beginning of the day.
- Pick one to begin with and focus on mastering that one before moving on to the next.
- Purchase a piece of jewelry or design a tattoo to remind you to be your virtues.
- In moments that challenge you, ask yourself the following question: What virtues do I need to *be* right now, and what do I have to *do* to *have* what I want to have?
- Keep on practicing and affirming—do this work continuously. As you gain new levels of self-awareness, add new behaviors, beliefs or tools to your lists.
- If you feel unsure or blocked, work with a coach.

CHAPTER 20

LIVING WITH PURPOSE AND PASSION

"He who has a 'why' to live for can bear almost any 'how.'"

Friedrich Nietzsche

In addition to the question, "Who am I?" many soul-seekers ask, "Why am I here?" *and* "What is the purpose of my life?" When we are disconnected from our essence and lost in an egoic mindset, our purpose is to achieve safety, stability, security and worthiness. And although these are basic survival needs, they do not offer us deep meaning. Without a clear purpose, the uncertainties of life feel scary, empty, directionless and meaningless.

One of my favorite theories in psychology is existentialism, a personality theory that describes us as spiritual beings with freedom and responsibility. Viktor Frankl, one of the most well-known existentialists and author of *Man's Search for Meaning*, developed his theories while observing human nature within the atrocities of a holocaust camp. Frankl noticed that "everything can be taken from a man but one thing: the last of the human freedoms—to choose one's attitude in any given set of circumstances, to choose one's own way." In every given moment, especially the ones that challenge us the most, there is meaning and a purpose. And when we master the ability to find an empowering purpose in every moment, we master our life purpose. Our ability to consciously choose our response raises us as human beings; it gives us dignity and power. Our personality is in a constant "process of becoming" because we are presented with new choices in every moment. Our decisions determine what we become.

When we connect with our essence and are aware that our essential nature is love and self-love, our purpose is clear. As our virtues are the extracts of our essence, our purpose is to understand, express and master our personal virtues in every opportunity.

Our spiritual evolution echoes our life purpose. We are here to learn the lessons that will facilitate our growth. With this growth mindset, we can overcome (and, with faith, accept) any challenge. In each experience where we flex our "virtue muscles," we "sculpt our greatness." And the more we master this skill of *being* our virtues, the easier and more pleasurable life becomes.

Many people believe that their purpose lies in the career path they choose. If they become a teacher, a scientist, a coach, an entrepreneur, a business owner, an artist, musician, a writer, or fitness professional, then they have accomplished their life's purpose. However the role we decide to play is not our ultimate purpose; that is merely the shopfront we choose to display our passion to the world, and our passion can change and evolve: a teacher can become a writer, an artist can become a teacher, a scientist can become a coach. What remains constant is who we are *being* and what intention we inject into our actions. It is our purpose to express our essence not only in the work we choose to do but in every encounter with others—and especially in challenging moments.

When we are intentionally being our virtues and our values, we implant the essence of love into what we do. When we follow our ego-drives—starting a business because it will give us financial status and prove our worth, for example—our intention can be more fear-based. This is because it possibly stems from a fear of not being good enough and a belief, based on the terms and conditions of our self-worth, that money will make us worthy. Here we are working for a paycheck rather than working on purpose.

Instead of thinking that your purpose is a career path, think of your purpose as the ability to be your virtues and values in every moment. This means that if you travel on a bus and have a conversation with a stranger, by taking the time to share yourself openly and make that person feel good, you live your life purpose. In that moment, which may seem insignificant to the ego-self, you are being your highest purpose.

Whenever we express and share our essential self (by being our virtues), we express self-love and we leave the other person feeling inspired, uplifted, empowered—and in his or her own "love state." On the other hand, when we take things personally and shut down, we lose the opportunity to be compassionate. When we play small and avoid risk, we lose the opportunity to be courageous. When we seek employment just because it earns us money, we lose the opportunity to be passionate. Life is empty and meaningless because we are disconnected from our purpose.

Being our virtues means we offer the world the greatest gift: the gift of truth and loving expression. Our virtues are our calling—they drive us to achieve our destiny. We become "love leaders," sharing our light with the world. The ability to lead with love is our greatest purpose of all. Imagine our world when we all work to achieve the same goal of being love!

In his book *A Leader Without a Title*, Robin Sharma explains that being a leader has nothing to do with what title we have or the view from our office. Being a leader means being the best version of us and expressing our greatness with passion. This means we tap into our creativity and can be more innovative. It means we do not play small or keep our opinions to ourselves. It means we make a difference to our own teams, communities and families by utilizing our unique strengths. These behavioral choices give each and every one of us the opportunity to be a global leader, significantly contributing to and changing our world.

Therefore, our intention to *be* our virtues reveals our purposeful *why*—our "why we are here." The path we choose in order to express our purpose reveals *what* we are here to do, and our virtues reveal *why* we are here to do it. When we activate our purpose in every moment, we give our lives meaning.

With this in mind we can script ourselves a powerful mission statement, or what I like to call a *personal purpose proposition* (PPP). This is a contract we commit to achieving in our life—it is the way we actualize our highest purpose and calling. Our PPP replaces the Ts and Cs we wrote for ourselves as scared and insecure children. Instead of our terms and conditions of self-worth, which stipulate our expectations and needs, our PPP is a personal commitment to *being our virtues*.

The following exercise offers you a template for creating a personal purpose proposition.

Complete the following sentences:

1. I am here to master my virtues of being (List your top ten virtues).
2. I will do this by (List the main action steps you noted while completing the BE-DO-HAVE exercise).
3. This will give me (List your values here).
4. I am passionate about (List your passion here) and will significantly contribute to the world and make a difference by (List the work/mission you commit to doing here).

HERE IS AN EXAMPLE:

My Personal Purpose Proposition:

I will be compassionate by always seeking to understand a person's inner struggle and beliefs.
I will be wise by always connecting to my inner wise woman (intuition) for guidance.
I will be courageous by allowing every challenge to facilitate my growth.
I will be gracious by being kind and caring to myself and others.
I will be serene by staying calm and connected to my breath and inner essence.
I will be accepting by having faith and trust that everything is working in perfect order.
I will be aware by practicing mindfulness and being engaged in the present moment.
I will be playful by always looking for the humor and joy in a situation.
I will be grateful by being thankful for all the blessings in my life, and I will always expect miracles.
I will be free-spirited by authentically speaking my truth and expressing my creativity with passion.

These virtues help me achieve my values of Peace, Wisdom, Love, Calm, Self-Acceptance, Mindfulness, Fun, Wholeness and Freedom. My values help shape my every decision.

I am passionate about <u>empowering people and helping them discover their true essence.</u> I will significantly contribute to the world and make a difference in my work <u>as a therapist, writer, and speaker.</u> <u>This includes my interactions with my children, partner, family members, friends, colleagues, and strangers, and particularly with the people who challenge me the most.</u> Every person or situation that challenges me gives me an opportunity to activate my purpose.

Handy tips to working with your personal purpose proposition:
- Write your personal mission statement on one page and view it daily.
- As you master certain action steps and virtues, adjust them accordingly.
- Use your personal purpose proposition as a mantra to remind you to always activate your purpose.
- Be consistent and patient with yourself.

The more we connect with our essence, the more we activate our purpose. This connection enables us to remain calm instead of becoming stressed. We can experience clarity instead of confusion. We can have confident courage instead of fear. And in each challenging moment, we know how to engage our faith mindset. There is a science to remaining calm and powerful, and simple steps we can take to master this inner greatness. Let us explore the "science of calm" in the next chapter.

CHAPTER 21

THE SCIENCE OF CALM: TRAIN YOUR BRAIN TO PERFORM AT ITS BEST

"If one thinks of oneself as free, one is free, and if one thinks of oneself as bound, one is bound. Here this saying is true:
'As one thinks, so one becomes.'"

Ashtavakra Gita

In Chapter 17 I discussed the benefits of meditation as a *habit of connection*—a daily ritual to help us connect with our inner self and activate our relaxation response. When we are calm, we know our nervous system is in "safe mode." This means we feel safe—we are managing fear successfully and are in a state of mindfulness. We are being mindful when we are fully present in the here and now. It is a state of self-awareness, self-connection and self-regulation. With a *mindful mindset* we manage the mind (our thoughts) as well as our emotions (our reactions). We act as the observer of ourselves and take responsibility for whom we choose to be—ego or essence.

Meditation can be seen as the "inner exercise program" that builds the muscles of our virtues and enables us to master our greatness. I am passionate about teaching meditation, not only as a habit of connection, but also as an essential mindset tool to train the brain to perform at its best and focus on the positive. By being positive I do not mean a euphoric feeling of happiness where we dream about sunshine and lollipops. *Positive focus* means the ability to direct your thoughts, your mind, toward the emotions you want to feel. Think of the BE-DO-HAVE model. If you want to have strength (your desired positive emotion), who do you need to *be* and what do you need to *do* to *have* strength? This mind hack trains the brain to focus on what we want rather than what we do not want, and allows us greater clarity.

In addition to positive thinking and the benefits of meditation, another important point is the biochemistry of meditation. Instead of producing toxic hormones such as cortisol and adrenaline, which are the result of fearful thinking, when we meditate and focus our mind in a positive direction, healthy hormones and neurotransmitters are produced.

Some of the essential neurochemicals that increase in the body when we meditate are listed below:

- **Oxytocin,** which is known as the "love (or bonding) hormone." Oxytocin is released during childbirth, breast-feeding, orgasm, and when we meditate. It helps us feel more connected and loving toward others. We see the world through rose-colored glasses.
- **Serotonin**, which is known as the "happy hormone." When we meditate, our levels of serotonin increase, which lifts our mood and builds our sense of well-being. Serotonin is also thought to be a key neurotransmitter for sending messages from one part of the brain to another.
- Endorphins, which are the "natural high hormone." The quartet of oxytocin, dopamine, serotonin and opiate endorphins help enhance our mood and manage pain. Meditation can offer us an elevated state of bliss and joy. This is a similar experience to what is known as the "jogger's high," the elevated feelings we experience after exercise.
- **DHEA,** dehydroepiandrosterone, which is the "longevity hormone." Some scientists have described meditation as the fountain of youth because it increases this essential hormone that is thought to help us to live longer.
- **GABA,** gamma-aminobutyric acid, which is also known as the "calm chemical." Interestingly, addictive behavior such as alcoholism has been linked to low levels of GABA. This neurotransmitter helps reduce stress levels and increases feelings of calm.

- **Melatonin,** which is known as "the sleep molecule." This hormone helps improve the quality of sleep and is boosted during meditation. Practicing meditation before bed can therefore help us achieve a deeper, more restful sleep.

It's clear that developing the habit of meditation can not only improve our health but also train us to be the "emotional alchemist" of our body. Just as an alchemist turns base metal into gold, so, too, can we transform our negative emotions and their toxic effects into positive, "golden" feelings.

The style of meditation that has been beneficial to myself and many of my clients is what I refer to as *mind focus meditation*. The goal is to use the power of our focus to intentionally create a desired emotional state. We empower ourselves by taking control of our thoughts and training ourselves to come into the present moment. The outcome is that our brain focuses and performs more effectively.

We take in information from the world around us through our senses of sight, sound, touch, taste and smell. Focusing on each of those senses one at a time, in an intentional way, elicits a calming response. It's equally effective to visualize a calming image, repeat a positive statement, and focus on our breath

DIRECTING OUR SENSES OF SIGHT, SOUND AND FEELING

- **Sight:** Visualization uses our imagination in an intentional way to create a desired emotional state and simultaneously reprogram the nervous system. Visualize an image that you associate with relaxation, such as a still lake, and notice how it effortlessly makes you feel calm. It's also effective, of course, to look at pictures or the real thing!
- **Sound:** Focusing our self-talk in an intentional manner by using a mantra or a positive statement is another way of using sound to reprogram our nervous system for greater relaxation. As you visualize your symbol of calmness, add a positive statement such as *I am calm, I am relaxed or I am in the present moment. Listening to soothing music will also generate a greater sense of calm.*

- **Feelings:** Connecting to the sensations in your body, and in particular to the flow of your breath, guides you to slow down and relax. So, along with picturing a calm scene, and telling yourself you are calm (inner narrative), focus on your breath. Feel your breath expanding into your body, melting your stress away and creating a sense of lightness. The breath is a powerful tool for self-regulation that can very quickly and effectively produce calmness in our bodies by slowing down our brain waves and heartbeat. It softens the musculoskeletal system and allows the immune system time to recharge.

TIPS FOR EFFECTIVE MEDITATION PRACTICE:
- As you wake up and before you reach for your phone or jump up and onto your to-do list, take a few minutes to connect with your breath and your body and consciously choose your mindset for the day. You do not even need to get out of bed. If you have time and are not likely to be interrupted, take longer than a few minutes. Twenty minutes is considered to be a very effective and centering period of time to spend in meditation, but even two intentional minutes is better than nothing. If you have the space, create a nurturing meditation environment with candles, music, and meditation cushions, or find a lovely spot in your garden. Alternately, a local park or beachfront can provide a beautiful environment for a morning meditation.
- Shorter, more frequent bursts of meditation are most effective. You do not need an hour to meditate—that can be counterproductive and actually create stress. Best practice is five to fifteen minutes, three times per day.
- Use your breath to create a pause any time you feel your emotions erupting. This can be as simple as stopping and taking three to six slow breaths. The pause is also a good time to return to the intention or mindset you established in your morning meditation.
- Add essential oils such as lavender to stimulate your sense of smell. This in turn can activate the memory center of the brain and assist in slowing down a busy mind and an overstimulated nervous system.
- Practice, practice and practice. It takes time to build new

habits, and the mind learns through repetition. The more consistent you are, the more competent you will become. The more competent you become, the more confidence you will have in your practice. In time you will notice that you are able to drop into a deep meditative state quickly, and will feel calmer and clearer when challenged.

There is no right or wrong way to meditate. Because our imagination and essence are unique to us, it is important to find our own groove and what works for us.

CHAPTER 22

EMBODYING THE ESSENCE

*"The ego urges you to accomplish,
while the soul merely asks you to enjoy the process."*

Doreen Virtue

The ego personification exercise we explored helped us draw our ego-self outside of our body and observe it objectively. With the ego-self outside of the feeling body, we have an empty void and can replace it with our essence. This means we are not only thinking of what our essence is, but we are actually feeling it in the body. The exercise I offer in this chapter helps us embody the essence and enhance the feeling experience within the body.

To *be* our essence, we cannot only think about it, as that is merely intellectual knowledge. To be our essence, we need to *feel* it, to *experience* it. To think is to know; to feel is to embody. We all have an understanding of what calmness is. To feel calm is to actually *be* calm. Likewise, we understand the concept of unconditional love. To feel unconditional love is to be it. Embodying our essence helps us *be* our virtues. It is not enough to intellectually know our virtues and intellectually understand the value they offer us; we have to feel them and know them authentically. Being able to feel the presence of your essence within your body enables the development and expression of wisdom because confident self-knowledge gives rise to good judgement.

As meditation helps us connect with our feeling body, it is an essential tool for embodying the essence. The more mindful we are about what we are feeling, the more we can attend to our fearful emotions and maintain a *faith mindset*. This means bringing our awareness out of the thinking mind (out of our thoughts) and into the feeling body to ensure that the essence is in charge of our consciousness. When in charge, the essence can navigate our choices. To begin this process, we have to tune into the feeling body. We do this by focusing on our *emotional centerline*.

The ancient practice of Tai Chi and Qi Gong describe the emotional centerline as the innermost core of the feeling body where our emotions are felt and stored. Like yoga, Tai Chi and Qi Gong aim to unite us with our essential life force, known as *qi* in China and *prana* in India.

The centerline is an illuminated column or laneway that runs through the center of our body and channels cosmic energy. It extends up into the "Heavens" to connect us with universal energy, and extends down into the ground to connect us with Mother Earth. Imagine the carousel ride at a theme park: the centerline is like the golden pole that runs through the center of the horses and moves them up and down. It can be visualized as a pillar or beam of light running through the core of our body and connecting us to the universe.

Every emotional experience is stored along our emotional centerline. It is where we store our emotional wounds as well as our pure emotions. When our centerline becomes clogged with emotional pain, the natural flow of our essential energy is disturbed. The pain clouds its purity. Think of a pure river flowing with ease. Emotional pain is like boulders that get stuck in the river and disrupt the water's flow, forcing it to slow down, detour or be stopped altogether. Our emotional reactions are like boulders of stored pain being pushed through our emotional body. It can feel like an inner storm erupting along our centerline.

In their book *Meditation, An In-Depth Guide*, co-authors Ian Gawler and Paul Benson note that the emotional centerline is home to our inner child. They explain: "The inner child is a metaphor for your vulnerability, your sensitivity, your fears and your needs. The inner child, which is experienced in your center, also carries the residual energies of your childhood wounds." When we avoid our feelings by *distracting, contracting or reacting*, it is as if we abandon our own scared inner child who, as a result, fearfully perceives him or herself to be unloved, unworthy or not good enough.

By mindfully focusing on our centerline, we attend to our inner child and help her/him feel safe. As we soothe our inner child's emotions, we return to a sense of calm. We attend to our inner child with the help of our breath. Our breath acts like loving parental hands caressing a scared child. As we "hug" our fearful child with our breath, negative emotions begin to settle. The essence acts like our own inner sage, holding the ego-self while whispering, "Remember: those negative thoughts are an illusion—false evidence appearing real. Remember your core virtues. Remember who you are. Be calm and see clearly what is happening around you." As we embody our essence by giving its spirit a tangible form, we connect with cosmic wisdom. As a result, we are able to remain more calm, clear and confident when challenged.

ESSENCE EMBODIMENT

Here is a *meditation technique* to cleanse your emotional centerline and embody your essence. Use this exercise to attend to negative emotions when they arise. This exercise is also a way to build a connection with your essence and feel its presence within the body. By maintaining a connection with your essence, you will be able to stay connected with your authentic self and override the conditioning of the ego-self. This means you stop reacting from your fight, flight or freeze mode and respond in a more empowered and mindful way. Every time you respond with essence-awareness, you strengthen the muscles of your virtues and take another step forward in realizing your life purpose.

The Steps to Embodying Your Essence
- Close your eyes and begin to focus inside your body. Connect with the flow of your breath and feel your breath moving up and down your body. Visualize your centerline in the center of your body. See it as a beam of light that may appear white or golden in color. It is as if you are shining a spotlight into the core of your body.
- Extend your centerline above you, into the cosmos as far as your imagination allows. Extend the centerline down into the ground and connect it with Mother Earth. Feel the cosmic energy flowing through you.
- As you focus on your illuminated centerline, observe your negative or distressed emotions. What do they feel like? What

color are they? What thoughts do they stem from? What memories within your inner child are they attached to?
- Direct your breath toward your centerline. Imagine your breath as your essence. Feel the presence of your essence like the warm hands of a parent soothing your inner child. Take in a nice big breath, and as you exhale, allow your out-breath to melt any anxiety. Feel your emotions and tension softening. Release your negative emotions as per the exercise in the previous chapter.
- Imagine your essence to be the voice of your inner wisdom—an inner master or sage that guides you. Think of your virtues, think of your personal purpose proposition, and allow your positive focus to empower your emotions. Do this by focusing on your "I am" statements. (For example: I am compassionate, I am love, I am calm, or I am wise.)
- As you repeat your "I am" statements, feel your virtues. (Feel the compassion, feel the love, feel the wisdom.) Draw those feelings into your body. Notice where in your body you feel them. (They are usually felt within the chest or stomach area.) Focus on your virtues by drawing your breath into those areas. As you breathe the life force of your essence into those positive feelings, notice how they expand. Imagine your breath to be a gentle light that moves those feelings around your body. Feel the warmth of that light. Feel your breath working in synchronicity with the light. Use your breath to fill your body with those feelings—breathe them into every cell and crevice of your body. Feel them expand, as if your breath is blowing up a giant inflatable. Feel them settle into your body, and hold your focus on them for a few moments. You are teaching your body to feel these ideal feelings and anchor them into place.
- You are now embodying your essence. This connection will generate a calm centeredness. You will then have the clarity to proceed in a calm manner with confident courage.

Your ability to embody your essence and flip your focus from fear to faith in challenging moments will help you master your emotions. As you clear out emotional pain that may be lying dormant in your centerline, you allow self-love to flow effortlessly through you. This means the tainted ego-mind no longer has control of your emotions. It means you no longer react to others and life events from a place of pain. You can now master yourself and express your greatness. Self-mastery is therefore the ability to let your essence lead—to allow your heart-wisdom to direct your mind.

In Part Three we will discuss, in greater detail, how to effortlessly achieve this process of self-mastery.

CHAPTER 23

A SUMMARY OF THE ESSENCE

"The most important kind of freedom is to be what you really are."

Jim Morrison

Here is a quick summary of the essence:

KEY FEATURES:
- The essence is the heart and soul of who we are.
- It expresses our authentic nature.
- It can be seen in our childlike enthusiasm and curiosity for life.
- The essence represents the best version of who we are—the person we are without the presence of fear.
- It is made up of our virtues, values and personal purpose.
- The essential nature of our essence is love—self-love. (This is the opposite state to the ego-self.)

ESSENCE IS GROUNDED IN THE FOLLOWING WISE PRACTICES:
- Trust in ourselves and in universal order
- Belief in our unique nature, strengths and capabilities
- Faith that each life experience is there to enable our growth
- Personal virtues that offer us internal resources for realizing our potential

- Personal values that offer us the positive emotions and outcomes that matter most to us
- A personal purpose proposition—our own mission statement for contributing to our world in a significant way

INTENTION/PURPOSE

The essence has a growth mindset. Its purpose is to help the ego-self discover who it truly is and actualize its highest potential.

In practical terms, this means to discover our virtues, define our values, and know what daily habits and action steps will keep us aligned with our truth.

THREE RULES ENABLE A GROWTH MINDSET:

1. From pain comes growth: Embrace your **CORE** strength
Courage
Optimism
Resilience
Energy

2. Do not take anything personally: Stay **CALM**
Compassion
Acceptance
Love
Mindfulness

3. Detach from Drama: Be **WISE**
Wisdom
Inspired Action
Soul Centered
Expression

FOUR BEHAVIORS THAT LEAD US TO THE ESSENCE:

Connection
Calmness
Clarity
Confident Courage

TWELVE SELF-EMPOWERING MINDSETS:

- Self-awareness
- Self-acceptance
- Self-belief
- Self-respect
- Self-trust
- Self-esteem
- Self-worth
- Self-confidence
- Self-sufficiency
- Self-care
- Self-management
- Self-love

EMOTIONS FREQUENTLY EXPRESSED:

Joy, freedom, happiness, bliss, expansion, love, truth, alignment, peace, courage, empowerment, vitality.

It is important to remember that your personal values indicate which positive feelings you want to create. Therefore, as you implement your BE-DO-HAVE plan, you are embodying your essence.

PHYSICAL EFFECTS:

Relaxation response: calm feelings that trigger executive brain functioning and thus assist with problem solving, articulate communication and general well-being.

"When the voice and the vision on the inside is more profound, and more clear and loud than all opinions on the outside, you've begun to master your life."

Dr. John Demartini

PART THREE: SELF-MASTERY

Self-mastery is the ability to recognize the core fears of your ego-self, know the character strengths of your essence, and be able to express these virtues in every moment.

Self-mastery is having the ability to forgive and let go— to ensure you are not replaying the past nor anticipating the future, but you are calm, connected and engaged in the present moment, acting on trust, belief and faith.

Self-mastery means knowing how to soothe turbulent emotions when they erupt so that you can manage your reactions as well as your self-talk. You no longer crave acceptance or have anything to prove. You courageously choose to be authentic even if that means being vulnerable, because being authentic means you are living your truth.

Self-mastery is therefore the mastery of your inner virtues, which enables you to express the best version of yourself. This ability to flip your fear into self-love opens you both to greater opportunities and to greater levels of personal freedom and happiness.

CHAPTER 24

A DELICATE BALANCE

"The cave you fear to enter holds the treasure you seek."
Joseph Campbell

"What do I need to be truly happy?"
"What is my heart asking for?"

As I stood on the edge of the cliff at Uluwatu Temple, I asked myself these questions. I was in Bali facilitating a wellness retreat with a company called Loving You. I was honored to be a part of this retreat as it was aligned with the intention of my last few years of healing: "Love yourself more than the need to be loved."

These two questions were the basis of the workshop I had presented to the beautiful women attending the retreat. On this particular day, we had a day off for sightseeing. This offered me some personal time to connect with the golden energy of Bali. I had a strong calling to visit Uluwatu Temple, and I had learned not to ignore nudges like this.

Built on a steep cliff seventy meters above sea level, Uluwatu Temple offers breathtaking views. In the fifteenth century, Hindu priest Dhang Hyang Dwijendra lived in this temple. It is believed that within this temple he experienced an elevated state of consciousness called *moksha*, the highest level of liberation and self-realization. *I am ready to experience my own personal freedom*, I thought as I breathed in the force of the Indian Ocean.

A year had passed since I visited Wilderness in South Africa. After that trip I returned to Australia a different person, with a desire to maintain my new feelings of self-connection and calm. I wanted to feel consistently aligned with my virtues and behave in congruence with what I believed was my truth. I thought having a grounded centeredness meant that I would experience a new life of peace. However, I was quickly reminded that achieving bliss on a mountaintop is a very different situation to achieving bliss in daily life as a mother, business leader, counselor, cook, housekeeper, and more. I returned home to face one of the most difficult years of my life, a year that forced me to stop, listen and balance all areas of my life.

The healing process and rest I experienced during my trip home prepared me to face a new set of challenges. My next cycle of growth was now on my doorstep because mastery is *not* about not experiencing stress at all; it is about how we navigate our way *through* stress.

Upon our return from South Africa, my daughter and her father had a falling-out and Ashleigh came to live with me full time. She was emotionally broken and needed my love and support. It is one thing to go through one's own suffering, but when a mother watches her children suffer, the pain feels much greater. We know what despair feels like, and when it is mirrored back to us, all our pain buttons are pushed. All we wish for as mothers is the well-being and happiness of our children, and when we cannot control that, we feel helpless.

My daughter's mental state became my top priority, and running my wellness center and coaching business in conjunction with supporting her really tested my skills and ability to juggle many responsibilities. As the year unfolded, I prayed for balance and stability in order to manage this intense set of responsibilities. The opportunity to assist with the retreat in Bali offered me respite from an emotional year and time to get silent, reconnect with my essence, and listen to her guidance. And so I found myself at the top of this majestic cliff, wrapped in the vapor of the Indian Ocean once again and breathing in the healing energy. Reconnecting with **M.E.**

Sitting alone in the silent temple I prayed to my wise woman: *What do I need to be truly happy? What is my heart asking for? Please help me find my balance.*

I sat in meditation, waiting for her answers. Then I heard her voice.

Your happiest moments are when you are being a mother. The past seven years since your divorce have offered you the time to re-establish yourself and be the mother you want to be without any interference. Your children's early childhood was robbed by your emotional distress at the time. Your heart is yearning to simply be "the mother" without all the stress and chaos you have experienced. The balance you are searching for is to be more engaged and present as a mother and be a therapist. You want a loving home again with a kind man who understands you and accepts your authentic self. The achievement of this balance will give you authentic happiness.

And then she said something that truly came as a shock: *You will have another baby.*

On that note, I opened my eyes. Wow. I stood for a moment and let those words settle into my body. The busyness of life had prevented me from hearing my deepest desires. Having this time to pause and listen let me tune into my heart and hear my wise woman. She spoke from the depth of my truth. The thought of another child sent a surge of happiness through my body. I felt an expansiveness in my chest and a sense of excitement. *Okay, Universe*, I thought. *Let's see where this goes!*

I returned home to the usual end-of-year busyness. The guidance I received in Bali settled into the background but continued to subtly guide me. A month after returning from Bali I went on a date with a man I had briefly met a few months prior.

Jorian and I met on a night out with mutual friends. Similar upbringings and philosophies of life instantly drew us together. We had attended the same high school in South Africa, and although I only vaguely remembered him, he clearly remembered me—and my shaved hair! As a young child, Jorian, like myself, had experienced the pain of his parents' divorce. Similar life experiences offered us a shared story of not belonging or fitting in anywhere. It felt as if we were two lost souls who had finally found someone who would truly understand! His kindness and understanding spoke to the core of my pain. For the first time in the history of my relationships, I experienced what it was like to be the authentic version of me. It was not as if I was intentionally being inauthentic in my past relationships; I had just never fully understood the power of vulnerability until I met Jorian. He offered me an unfamiliar sense of safety and stability.

Within a few months of dating we decided to move into a house together. A few weeks later, I fell pregnant. As I was in my forties and Jorian had been convinced that he was incapable of impregnating a woman, we were at first both in shock. We were still only getting to know each other, and Jorian, having no previous children of his own, was still adjusting to his new role as stepparent.

The onset of morning sickness forced me to stay in bed and, lying there in stillness, I was reminded of the message I received at Uluwatu Temple: *You will have another baby.* The swiftness of Jorian's and my connection felt like it had been orchestrated by the little soul growing within me.

Although slightly concerned by how a third child would impact all of us, I was overjoyed. As my due date drew closer, I made the decision to leave the wellness center. This was a difficult decision as the center felt like my home. The clients I worked with and the therapists who were part of the team reflected the success of my mission. But I knew that I needed a quieter, calmer life in order to nurture this new soul. This soul who was making me nauseous was also miraculously bringing me what my heart truly wanted: the happiness and the balance I had asked for in the temple in Bali.

During my pregnancy I stumbled across "Empowering Birth" classes. I wanted my labor to be an expression of everything I had learned over the years. I envisioned this birth to be a representation of my finest, wisest self. I did not want this baby to be born into the energy of fear. I felt his essence guiding me. I did not want this birth to be medicalized. I wanted to use the muscles of my virtues to birth this baby. My meditation practice had strengthened my mind, and I knew with the right mindset I could achieve whatever I wanted. My mantra throughout my pregnancy was "I have everything within me to birth this baby easily."

Throughout the last month of my pregnancy, whenever fear allowed its tentacles to creep into my consciousness, I focused on my mantra. I would visualize my labor day and see myself birthing this baby with ease. I felt the empowerment I needed in my mind and the strength I needed in my body to make this happen. All my senses were focused on a natural and easy birth process.

My waters broke three days past my due date, at 10 p.m. It was showtime. I lay on the couch and watched a movie to distract myself from the discomfort. Two and a half hours later contractions commenced. In no time at all they were a few minutes apart. At 1:30 a.m. I was on the birthing table and the midwife who was examining me was saying, "You are eight centimeters dilated, Cheryne. No time for drugs." *Of course*, I thought. Just as I had intended. "You ready, Cheryne?" she asked. She was beaming—in love with the whole miracle of birth. "Yes," I replied. *I. Am. Ready.*

As I closed my eyes, I saw an image of a bear birthing her cub in the woods. I imagined myself as the bear. I felt her natural instinct to birth in the wild, with Mother Nature as her only support. "I have everything within me to birth this baby," I repeated. I roared a mighty grizzly roar. For a while I lost track of time and space as I rolled with the rhythm of the birthing stages. I was brought back to my awareness as I felt the midwife tapping me on my leg. "Open your eyes, Cheryne, here comes your baby." And then, at 2:06 a.m., there was Jai.

The first few months were a challenge: sleepless nights, adjusting to the demands of a blended family, and learning to understand and co-parent with a man who was still, effectively, a stranger. Yet Jai brought balance into my life. I moved my life-coaching practice home and worked around the hours he slept. For a few months I experienced an empowered emotional state, the same state I had brought home from Bali. But as time progressed and sleep deprivation set in, I noticed behavior patterns that I thought I had dissolved returning. I began to feel the heaviness of depression. Feelings I had not felt since a teenager were stirring. Darkness weighed upon me and negative thoughts returned. Old patterns such as people-pleasing re-emerged. My fear of rejection shifted my consciousness from creativity to reactivity.

When Jorian and I argued, or if I felt he was judging me, I felt the wounds of rejection and my fear of abandonment returning. The physical depletion caused by pregnancy, birth, breast-feeding and sleep-deprivation lowered my level of awareness and reawakened ego patterns. I lost track of my self-care routine and began to re-experience the same melancholic emotions I felt in my previous relationship—the very emotions that had led to my emotional breakdown.

Luckily, I had done enough work to recognize the signs. I had grown too much to submit to my fear.

I focused on coaching myself back to empowerment. This became a crucial time for me to reflect and discover my next growth opportunity.

I realized that Jai's birth offered me more than work-life balance. This was a time to balance my ego-self and my essence and express my true authenticity. Instead of working with contrast (bouncing between happiness and unhappiness), I began to understand how I could now work in harmony and unity (a centered state where I didn't resist difficulties but flowed with them). I began to recognize how my essence could guide my ego-self.

The name Jai, in Sanskrit, means "victory." Victory for me meant self-mastery: the ability to transform my fear into my greatest strengths. This was the time to utilize the tools I had learned and activate my purpose. The first step I took was to write my ego-self a letter:

> Dear Molly,
> I no longer have room for you in my life. You are disturbing my balance and I will not let you take over my consciousness again. I thank you for your past services, but you no longer serve me. I no longer need your protection nor your conditioned ways. I know what my strengths and inner resources are and so I am good to proceed from here. The balance I have been yearning for is this state where my mind and heart are at peace and my thoughts and behavior reflect the intentions of my heart. I must now be my virtues in every moment. From this moment, my virtues will guide me. You no longer have control of my mind because I don't need the old forms of protection any more. Now my essence is lighting the way for me. You can continue to protect me in useful ways but not in the old reactive fearful way. We have everything we need within us to be happy.
> Love,
> Cheryne, The Wise Woman

My next step involved bringing my practice of meditation back into my day as well as all the other habits of connection I needed to return to. During my morning walks I began to reflect on how I could maintain this empowered state of balance within myself. It was during one of those walks that I consolidated all the pieces of my coaching model. I saw how I could quickly recognize ego patterns when I felt triggered, and instead of acting on them, activate my virtues instead. I wanted to share these insights with others, and the concept for a book took shape as I walked.

To assist the process of mastering ego patterns, I formulated four self-coaching questions. The goal was to help myself recognize when I was in a state of fear, disturb my habitual reactions, and navigate through my fear toward my core virtues. This new intervention allowed me to connect with my essence. I could now see the perfection in the pain I was experiencing. My relationship, my children, and any challenges I faced were helping me grow into the best version of myself. These moments of stress were opportunities for me to express my virtues.

I began to offer my clients the tool of these four questions and witnessed them, in turn, achieve and maintain a similar empowered balance. The four questions acted as a tool to break unresourceful patterns of fear stemming from the ego-self and reprogram my focus toward my essence. The four questions enabled what I began to call the self-mastery stage of our coaching sessions.

And so I offer you the **HAPPINESS FORMULA:** four easy and effective questions you can ask yourself to flip your fear into a faith mindset and express your best self. These four questions integrate all the tools I offer you in this book and present them in an easy format so you can coach yourself toward your own version of authentic happiness.

CHAPTER 25

THE HAPPINESS FORMULA

> *"The happiness of your life depends upon the quality of your thoughts: therefore guard accordingly, and take care that you entertain no notions unsuitable to virtue and reasonable nature."*
>
> Marcus Aurelius

Emotional management is the key to self-mastery. When we are in charge of our emotions, we ensure we do not react to life but respond in a calm and intentional manner. So, how do we learn to stay calm and connected instead of emotionally reactive? How can we break our conditioning, detach from our disempowering egoic stories and activate our virtues (our higher purpose) in every moment? How can our fearful emotions and pain be a catalyst for our greatest growth?

The Happiness Formula is a series of four questions you can ask yourself to challenge your thinking, regulate your emotions and respond to stress in an empowering way. These questions enable you to be your own life coach—to train yourself to disengage from your "fear self," utilize your virtues, and embrace your authentic essence. You will not only tame your ego-self, but transcend the self that no longer serves you—and in the process, you will realize your life purpose.

The four questions of the Happiness Formula are:

WHAT AM I FEELING?
WHY AM I FEELING THIS?
WHAT IS THIS REALLY ABOUT?

WHAT ARE MY LESSONS?

To disrupt the path of the ego-self, we need to change our thinking. Instead of mindlessly ruminating on the past or projecting into the future, we actively and mindfully challenge and manage our thoughts and emotions so that we can be fully present in each moment. We let our essence lead the way to our greatness!

The Happiness Formula is based on the premise that the external stressor is not the cause of our stress; it is just the button that triggers our *I'm-not-good-enough/worthy/loveable* story. By now you know that our emotional reactions do not represent what we are truly feeling. You know that fear lies at the core of your reactions and has created emotional wounds that are easily reopened. *It is not necessarily the current issue that is the problem; the old beliefs that issue triggers within you are the real problem.*

When we take things personally, we usually respond defensively, perhaps by snapping or by shutting down. Either way, those reactive behaviors represent a fear response and increase conflict in our relationships. They also promote our own suffering and keep us stuck in a limiting story that enhances anger, frustration, disappointment, shame, and blame.

Every time you break your habitual reactions, you heal more of your pain. *Heal* is related to the word *whole*. Through the healing process we become more whole, and instead of our wounds being triggered unconsciously, we become more present to how we manage our internal state. As our wounds were imprinted when we were young and impressionable, we will default to them first. Our outcome in healing is not to eliminate buttons altogether, a self-defeating goal, but to continually learn from our reactions and evolve our responses so that we master our emotions, which will result in a greater sense of well-being.

Happiness, therefore, is a choice. It is a decision. It is the meaning *you* create. You can have a happiness mindset or an unhappiness mindset. This starts with a decision to let go of the past and stop anticipating your future so that you can be immersed in the here and now. The four questions of the Happiness Formula offer you a way of becoming more conscious of what you are feeling so that you can deliberately choose how you want to feel. That is mastery.

The Happiness Formula guides you through four key stages of emotional self-mastery:
- Self-awareness
- Self-regulation
- Self-comfort
- Self-management

SELF-AWARENESS

Self-awareness is the ability to be aware of our thoughts and feelings—to recognize egoic behavior and know where it stems from. Without such awareness, we continue to run on autopilot rather than being in control of our emotions. Without self-control we take things personally. We let adversity bring us down; we remain stuck in a mindset of self-pity, self-loathing or self-sabotage where the ego-self indulges in limiting thinking.

Self-awareness is the first step to personal growth and change. It also allows us to maintain a connection with our essence. It helps us become more resilient, engaged and empowered—to know we can manage any situation. It allows us to commit to our life purpose of growing from each experience.

There are two significant processes that help us increase our self-awareness:

1. Metacognition: the ability to be aware of our thoughts. To be able to think about how we think and observe the *quality of our thoughts.*

2. *Mindfulness: the awareness of how our thoughts make us feel, and the capacity to bring our focus to the present moment.*

SELF-REGULATION

With increased self-awareness, you can regulate your emotions and therefore monitor your emotional reactions. By continuing to let your emotions get the better of you, you remain stuck as the victim of your circumstances. Being aware of your emotions and regulating your responses makes you the victor of your challenges instead. You remember that from pain comes growth, and you allow every difficult person or challenging situation to bring out the best in you.

Here, you embrace your power to choose. Every positive choice is an act of self-regulation. Ego-self or essence? Fear or love? Old conditioned patterns or updated character strengths? Depression, anxiety and stress, or calm, confident courage?

SELF-COMFORT

Maintaining a connection with your breath and mindfully creating your focus helps you soothe your emotions and stay calm. Using your breath to regulate your emotions will instantly make you calmer. Your calm self in turn activates your best self. By self-comforting, you take responsibility for yourself. This means you have the ability to respond effectively, knowing who you need *to be and what you have to do in order to have your desired result. You then become the manager of your emotions and the manager of the meanings you create in every moment.*

SELF-MANAGEMENT

Self-management is the ultimate expression of self-mastery. You become the manager of your life, the captain of your ship, the designer of your destiny—the architect and the engineer. You achieve self-empowerment and personal freedom because you have broken free from the chains of your fear and have mastered your moment-to-moment choices. You begin to navigate your life with trust, belief and faith because you have the strength, the knowing, and the ability to handle anything that life throws at you. You are aligned with your core virtues and values, and this builds your self-confidence and self-belief. You know you have everything within you.

These four stages help you connect with your essence and achieve self-mastery. All you need to do is **STOP**:

<u>Sto</u>p your negative thoughts and connect within.

<u>Think</u> about what is happening within you—what emotions are arising and what pain buttons are being pushed.

<u>O</u>bserve an internal sense of calm and think about what virtue (internal resource) you have within. Soothe your emotion with your breath and positive focus. Be calm.

<u>Proceed </u>with a clear mind and a sense of purpose. Experience confident courage.

THE HAPPINESS FORMULA CAN BE SUMMARIZED AS FOLLOWS:

STOP Stop your negative thoughts and become aware of how they are making you feel.	**QUESTION 1: WHAT AM I FEELING?**
THINK Notice what you are feeling and explore why. What limiting beliefs are being triggered? How can you recognize ego traits?	**QUESTION 2: WHY AM I FEELING THIS?**
OBSERVE AND BREATHE Recognize how your story of limitation is being triggered. Become aware of which wounds are being triggered. Focus on letting go of your pain and negativity. Soothe your emotions by using your breath to calm the emotion in your body.	**QUESTION 3: WHAT IS THIS REALLY ABOUT?**
PROCEED Which virtue is needed in this moment? Which one of your character strengths are you incongruent with and how can you activate the muscles of those core virtues? How might they guide you? (Refer to the list of your core virtues to answer this question.)	**QUESTION 4: WHAT IS MY LESSON HERE?**

Over the next few chapters we will work through each of the four questions. Spend some time understanding the nature of each question and mastering the steps before proceeding to the next question.

CHAPTER 26

QUESTION 1: WHAT AM I FEELING?

"The body is your friend; it is not your enemy.
Listen to its language, decode its language, and by and by,
as you enter into the book of the body and turn its pages,
you will become aware of the whole mystery of life."

Osho

The first question of the Happiness Formula is *What am I feeling?* This question is designed to help you get out of your head, out of your thoughts, and into your body so that you can manage your emotions. In turn this question offers you a pause between a stressful trigger and your reaction. This "powerful pause" enables you to disrupt your conditioned reactions. With awareness you have a greater chance of choosing to respond in a different, more empowering manner.

I began using these questions in my second marriage when Jorian and I were arguing. I did not want to submit to the communication patterns I had in past relationships. My default patterns disempowered me and increased conflict and disconnection. I wanted to let the virtues of my essence navigate me through my relationship with the knowledge that in doing so, we would maintain and sustain the purity of our connection. When my partner was angry about something, I let him speak and then asked him for some time to process my thoughts and feelings. On the days I could, I would walk up to a local park with my journal and work through the questions. I took responsibility for soothing my emotions instead of arguing back. I was able to recognize what his words triggered in me, release them and lean into my virtue of compassion rather than taking what he said personally. This allowed me to see his point of view more clearly and calmly. Each time I displayed compassion toward him, he would offer it back, and we were able to negotiate our differences effectively.

The ability to tune into your emotions, and feel them, will ultimately lead to your ability to heal them. As you "feel and heal," you become whole again, clear out negative energy and purify the toxic effects that emotions such as fear, anger, resentment, sadness and shame have on the body. We hold onto the resourceful ego beliefs that help to build us, and review the limiting beliefs hindering our growth. Clearing the clouds of self-doubt allows the light of our essence to expand.

Emotions are energy—a neat summary is "Energy-in-motion." Energy cannot be stagnant as nothing in nature stands still: weather patterns change in seconds; our physical body is in a continual state of cell and tissue breakdown and renewal; likewise, emotions are impermanent. If you sit with an emotion for long enough, it transforms—just as clouds clear to allow the sun to shine. It is worthwhile testing this for yourself; next time you feel a strong emotion, instead of resisting it, allow it to be there and observe it. You'll find that it soon changes its state into another, possibly similar emotion, but the transformation process will keep going until you are several emotions away from where you began.

IMPORTANT POINTS TO RECALL FOR QUESTION 1:
- When we are caught up in our thoughts, they rule our focus and keep us stuck in an outdated coding system. As previously mentioned, every thought instructs the body to feel something. Our negative thoughts keep us stuck in disempowering stories, creating a delusional reality (false evidence appearing real). These stories keep us trapped in ego consciousness—we are imprisoned by fear.
- The more we repeat our stories of limitation, the more we perpetuate feelings of depression, anxiety, stress, loneliness, worry, anger, sadness or resentment. The more we feel those

negative emotions, the longer the body stays stuck in pain and suffering. The wounds remain, and difficult people and challenging situations continue to trigger us. The only pathway to essence is through our pain, so instead of avoiding it, advance into it. Pain is simply a messenger.

- Mindfulness is an excellent technique to connect with and tune into our feelings. Observing mindfully means we do not directly experience the feeling. Instead, we observe our emotion and notice what we feel without judgment or submitting to our stories. We also do not seek reassurance or help from an external source. Rather than searching outside of ourselves for answers, we turn the lens inward, knowing that as we work through our pain body and focus on our core virtues, we are growing. *From pain comes growth. The more we challenge our thoughts and clear their negative effects, the more we master our life lessons and build the muscles of our virtues. With this mindset, we let our essence lead.*
- Focusing on our feelings also helps us to develop greater body awareness, which is an essential skill for achieving self- as well as stress-management. Being able to (a) recognize when we have been triggered and (b) recognize our stress response will help us S.T.O.P. the process and return to calmness. Reread the stress symptoms that were discussed in Chapter 8 and notice what symptoms you experience when you are triggered. Noticing these symptoms will confirm that you are emotionally reacting; you can then employ the Happiness Formula.

Make sure you create a *reflective space* to work through the steps of the Happiness Formula. I don't mean a physical space, as in your meditation location, but a powerful "pause" during which you allow your emotion to subside. Specifically this means remaining silent when someone criticizes or challenges you. Disengaging from challenging situations or conversations will feel difficult as we all have a natural tendency to want to defend or justify ourselves. But as you give yourself breathing space and time to work through your emotions, you will be able to respond to situations in an empowering and calm manner. This in turn helps you resolve conflict and enhance the quality of your relationships.

You can also use the Happiness Formula when you feel fearful about an event in your future or when you are replaying a past experience or when you have to make a decision, since the process gives you the time and space to work through your emotions.

STEPS FOR WORKING THROUGH QUESTION 1:

1. **The first step is to STOP your emotional reaction.** Stop your thoughts. Visualize a stop sign, say the word *STOP* to yourself or snap your fingers. As you break your state of thinking, you break the habitual emotional response. You may also like to imagine using a remote control to pause the "scene" you are in.

2. **Recognize that you have been triggered.** Note and observe your stress response. Acknowledge that you are currently in a state of fear. Remember that this process is a way for you to tame your ego-self and break your habitual ways so that you can engage the essence of you instead.

3. Instead of snapping at the other person, **give yourself reflection time.** Leave a conversation and come back to it when you are calm. If you anticipate or ruminate over an event, stop your thoughts and tune into your feelings.

4. **Breathe into your body and notice your bodily sensations.** Bring your awareness to the top of your head and scan through your emotional centerline to notice two things:
   - Any tightness, tension or heaviness in the body
   - Where in your body you are feeling those sensations

5. **Tune into your feelings.** Focus intently on your feelings as if you were looking through a kaleidoscope or magnifying glass. Simply notice these feelings, without attaching any meaning or judgment. Train the mind to focus on your feelings instead of your thoughts.

6. Now ask yourself the first question: **What am I feeling?** (Refer to the Feelings List below to help you articulate your feelings.)

7. **Notice the first feeling and label it.** For example, "I am feeling angry."

8. **Now ask yourself what else** you are feeling. For example, "I am feeling judged."

9. Repeat this process until you have about six to ten layers of emotion.
10. As you acknowledge your emotions, you may find yourself going more deeply into your pain. It is perfectly all right to cry. Just as we sweat when we exercise, crying is a way for the body to release emotion.

With every emotional layer you release, you shed unnecessary layers of protection—the self-protective layers that were knee-jerk reactions to pain. Instead, the self-acceptance and self-love you demonstrate in the process of stopping your automatic reaction and tuning in creates new, healthier forms of protection.

Once you are aware of your feelings, proceed to Question 2.

HERE ARE A FEW SCENARIOS OF THE HAPPINESS FORMULA IN ACTION:

SCENARIO 1 BACKGROUND INFORMATION:	SCENARIO 2 BACKGROUND INFORMATION:	SCENARIO 3 BACKGROUND INFORMATION:
Sally and her husband are having an argument. "You never support me. You are always thinking of yourself—you are so selfish!" he yells at her.	Paul has been asked to speak in front of his colleagues at their upcoming conference. Although public speaking is his greatest fear, it is also a secret passion of his.	Marnie is scrolling through her Facebook feed and notices a picture of her friends at a party. She was not invited to the party.
DEFAULT EMOTIONAL REACTION:	**DEFAULT EMOTIONAL REACTION:**	**DEFAULT EMOTIONAL REACTION:**
Immediately, Sally feels a knot in her stomach and her throat closing up. Tears are building and she wants to snap at her husband and defend herself.	Paul feels his heart pounding at the thought. His body feels hot and he begins to perspire. His mind races as he anticipates the possibility of failure and judgment from his peers.	Marnie feels her chest tighten and a restlessness in her stomach. Her face feels hot. Tears begin to well up and her throat constricts. She is confused.
CREATING A PAUSE:	**CREATING A PAUSE:**	**CREATING A PAUSE:**
Sally breathes into her body to soothe her emotions as she actively listens to understand her husband. She asks her husband for some time to reflect on what he has said before she comments.	Paul breathes into his body to calm himself and slow down his heartbeat. He accepts the offer and decides to work through his feelings when he gets home that evening.	Marnie tunes into her thoughts and notices the question "Why was I left out?" She breathes into her body to soothe her emotions. She allows herself to have a cry and feels her body soften.

USING THE HAPPINESS FORMULA: QUESTION 1:	USING THE HAPPINESS FORMULA: QUESTION 1:	USING THE HAPPINESS FORMULA: QUESTION 1:
Sally takes herself to a quiet and private spot and has a bit of a cry to release the emotional build-up of her emotions. She then tunes into her body and asks herself what she is feeling. These are the feelings she notes: • I feel hurt • I feel enraged • I feel judged • I feel worried • I feel inadequate • I feel misunderstood • I feel alone • I feel unloved	Paul takes out a journal and begins to ask himself what he is feeling: • I feel panic • I feel confused • I feel insecure • I feel anxious • I feel threatened • I feel embarrassed • I feel fearful • I feel like a fraud and I am scared they will see through me. • I feel like I do not know enough, or am not as good as some of my colleagues.	Marnie spends some time noticing her feelings, takes out her journal and writes them down: • I feel shocked • I feel alienated • I feel hurt • I feel insecure • I feel abandoned • I feel jealous • I feel rejected • I feel worthless

ANGRY							
Let down	Humiliated	Bitter	Mad	Aggressive	Frustrated	Distant	Critical
Betrayed Resentful	Disrespected Ridiculed	Indignant Violated	Furious Jealous	Provoked Hostile	Infuriated Annoyed	Withdrawn Numb	Skeptical Dismissive

HAPPY							
Playful	Content	Interested	Proud	Accepted	Powerful	Peaceful	Optimistic
Aroused Cheeky	Free Joyful	Curious Inquisitive	Successful Confident	Respected Valued	Courageous Creative	Loving Thankful	Hopeful Inspired

FEARFUL					
Scared	Anxious	Insecure	Weak	Rejected	Threatened
Helpless Frightened	Overwhelmed Worried	Inadequate Inferior	Worthless Insignifacnt	Excluded Persecuted	Nervous Exposed

SAD					
Lonely	Vulnerable	Despair	Guilty	Depressed	Hurt
Isolated Abandoned	Victimized Fragile	Grief Powerless	Ashamed Remorseful	Empty Inferior	Embarrassed Disappointed

SURPRISED			
Startled	Confused	Amazed	Excited
Shocked Dismayed	Disillusioned Perplexed	Astonished Awe	Eager Energetic

DISGUSTED			
Disapproving	Disappointed	Awful	Repelled
Judgmental Embarrassed	Apalled Revolted	Nauseated Destestable	Horrified Hesitant

BAD			
Bored	Busy	Stressed	Tired
Indifferent Apathetic	Pressured Rushed	Overwhelmed Out of Control	Sleepy Unfocused

THE FEELINGS LIST

A word of caution with regard to traumatic memories or mental illness:

If you do not feel ready to do this process on your own, please seek the assistance of a therapist. Only give this a go once you have done the forgiveness exercises and feel a sense of detachment. For more detailed guidelines, please refer to www.cheryneblom.com.

CHAPTER 27

QUESTION 2: WHY AM I FEELING WHAT I AM FEELING?

"Everything that irritates us about others can lead us to an understanding of ourselves."

Carl Jung

The second question of the Happiness Formula is *Why am I feeling what I am feeling?* This question is designed to draw us more deeply into self-reflection. It is not asked in the self-pitying tone of a victim, but with curiosity. As we gain conscious ego-awareness through feeling our feelings and beginning to question them, we can begin to adjust our filter. We are able to shift our perceptual experience and loosen the attachment to our feelings. Question 2 explores two types of stress triggers: external triggers and internal triggers.

EXTERNAL TRIGGERS

The external event is the trigger that pushes our "emotional button." The trigger is the person, event, sound, smell or taste that sets off our emotional reaction. Although we are not blaming this stressor, it is important to be aware of the external factors that trigger us. As Carl Jung reminds us in the above quotation, our external triggers can act as a mirror to help us become aware of what needs to be healed or attended to within us.

I used this process often to help me shift my attitude and manage my emotions during my interactions with my ex-husband. Instead of name calling, blaming or feeling intimidated around him, I began to view him as my Zen master, my most important teacher, the person who was helping me express my dormant virtues, such as grace and compassion. By holding such a positive focus within, I was able to remain calm, kind and graceful in my interactions with him. As a result, I demonstrated my virtues and aligned myself with my values. I allowed my essence to direct my focus. My ego-mind became a helpful employee in the service of my essence. All it needed was clear direction.

External triggers can be both subtle and obvious. An obvious trigger is a person or experience directly related to our pain—bumping into an ex-partner, having a sensitive conversation with a friend or reliving a past trauma can all elicit past emotions. A subtle smell can remind us of a loved one who has passed, and so can trigger emotions of grief. A song or particular tone of voice can remind us of a past event, such as a relationship breakup. So, as you reflect on what you are feeling, begin to notice who or what triggered your emotion.

In Chapter 15, I explained how trust is part of the essential nature of the essence. A component of trust is the idea that every person or situation is a teacher or messenger helping us grow or heal. If we hold this attitude that the people or events we feel are triggering us are actually here to enable our self-development, we can emotionally detach from the stress.

Think about the people who trigger you and contemplate the following questions:
- What is it about them that you do not like?
- What aspect of yourself does that reflect?
- What emotions do they bring up in you?
- What are they possibly mirroring back to you?
- What is this teaching you?

INTERNAL TRIGGERS

Internal triggers are the automatic negative thoughts (ANTs) we have that produce an emotional reaction. Thoughts such as *What if I fail?* or *What if they judge me?* are examples of questions that perpetuate our low self-esteem story.

As this is a mindfulness exercise, it is important for us to remain the observer of our feelings and thoughts rather than directly experiencing them. Three states of mind can help us disassociate from our thinking experience. They are *detachment, compassion and acceptance.*

1. **Detachment** reminds us to play the role of observer and reflect on our experiences from a more objective perspective. Detachment helps us identify what the mind attaches to and recognize if we are controlling, comparing, competing or compromising. Recognition of our inner gremlins offers us further awareness that our ego-patterns are present. So take the aerial view! Observe yourself from a distance, from above, for a more objective perspective on the situation.

2. **Compassion** reminds us to be nonjudgmental—to avoid criticism or defensiveness by being understanding of others as well as ourselves. Compassion helps us rein in the judgmental mind. It enables the inner critic to curb its acid tongue while you instead develop greater self-belief and courage.

3. **Acceptance** reminds us to have faith, to remember the perfection in our pain, let go of control and embrace uncertainty. It helps us forgive and release, and reminds us that our life lessons have a powerful purpose—they help us develop our core virtues. We are also reminded that the story we are narrating is directed by the delusions of our ego-self and therefore not representative of the complete truth.

STEPS TO WORKING THROUGH QUESTION 2:

1. Once you have written down or taken a mental note of your feelings, ask yourself what triggered your feelings. What was the external trigger?

2. Take note of how you recognized the trigger. For example, was it something you saw, such as a look a person gave you? Was it something you heard, such as criticism or an aggressive tone of voice? Or was it something you felt, such as a negative vibe from a person? Recognizing how you are triggered offers you greater self-awareness so you can more effectively manage your response to those external triggers in the future.

3. Now tune into your thoughts and notice what thoughts your feelings generate.

4. Write down your thoughts.

REFER TO THESE EXAMPLES FOR ASSISTANCE:

QUESTION 2: WHY AM I FEELING WHAT I AM FEELING?	QUESTION 2: WHY AM I FEELING WHAT I AM FEELING?	QUESTION 2: WHY AM I FEELING WHAT I AM FEELING?
A. WHAT IS THE EXTERNAL TRIGGER? The aggressive tone used by Sally's husband is her external trigger. **B. WHAT IS THE INTERNAL TRIGGER?** Sally tunes into her self-talk and notes the following thoughts: <ul><li>He is always so mean to me!</li><li>He doesn't appreciate me.</li><li>He doesn't understand me.</li><li>He is such an a-hole!</li><li>I can never do anything right by him.</li><li>He doesn't love me.</li></ul>	**A. WHAT IS THE EXTERNAL TRIGGER?** The upcoming speaking engagement is Paul's external trigger. **B. WHAT IS THE INTERNAL TRIGGER?** Paul tunes into his self-talk and notes the following thoughts: <ul><li>Do I know enough?</li><li>What if they see through me and discover that I really don't know that much?</li><li>What if I fail?</li><li>Will they fire me?</li><li>Will I humiliate myself?</li><li>Who am I to deliver this presentation?</li><li>Am I good enough?</li></ul>	**A. WHAT IS THE EXTERNAL TRIGGER?** The picture of Marnie's friends at a party she was not invited to is the external trigger. **B. WHAT IS THE INTERNAL TRIGGER?** Marnie tunes into her self-talk and notices the following thoughts: <ul><li>I am never invited anywhere.</li><li>I am always left out.</li><li>What is wrong with me?</li><li>What do the other girls have that I don't have?</li><li>What did I do wrong?</li><li>They make me feel worthless.</li></ul>

Once you are aware of your external trigger and internal thoughts, proceed to Question 3.

CHAPTER 28

QUESTION 3: WHAT IS THIS REALLY ABOUT?

*"The nature of illusion is that,
when you see through it, it disappears."*

Mooji

The third question of the Happiness Formula is *What is this really about?* Question 1 helped us identify our feelings. Question 2 helped us understand what triggered our emotions, both externally and internally. With Question 3 we go more deeply into our internal thoughts to recognize what is *really* being experienced. This crucial question is designed to help us break out of the ego's fear mindset before our emotions take control of our consciousness. This question acts like a butterfly net to catch the limiting beliefs of not being good enough, worthy or loved. "Catching" our thoughts allows us to observe them objectively.

Reflection enables us to remove the tainted filter of the ego-self. With a growth mindset fueled by courage, we can choose to let our fears go because we know that fear is an illusion: it is only a thought, a perception, a decision we made as a scared child. This decision does not define our identity and definitely does not represent our authentic self. Instead of attaching, we "catch and release."

Our ability to quickly defuse and distract our attention away from the trigger will, over time, break old conditioned associations. We can then retrain ourselves toward our desired emotional result. Think of this as the ability to short-circuit the pathway of the ego-self and quickly connect with your pure essence. This is the journey through your pain toward your inner light. This is a way to heal your inner child and help yourself grow.

Practicing mindfulness and utilizing the tools of detachment, compassion and acceptance are vitally important because they help us to defuse a full-blown emotional reaction. All we want to do here is observe, catch, detach and release. In the beginning, detaching from your emotions may feel difficult. However, with consistency you will break your past conditioning and learn a new behavioral pattern. With repetition, this new response will become your updated behavioral pattern.

STEPS TO WORKING THROUGH QUESTION 3:
1. As you feel your feelings and notice what is triggering you, focus on where *in the body you feel discomfort. Discomfort may show up in a number of areas: a cloudiness in your mind, a tightness in your throat, tightness or a fluttering sensation in your chest, butterflies in your belly, a general feeling of nausea or sickness.*
2. Notice what thoughts you have during this time. Notice what limiting beliefs are triggered, such as your own I'm-not-good-enough story.
3. Ask yourself, "What is this really about? What is my core fear? What is my mind attaching to?" These questions help you notice what beliefs and memories are triggered. In turn, you will become aware of your frightened inner child replaying the past or anticipating the future.
4. Direct your breath toward your pain or discomfort; as you do, you will soothe the inner turbulent emotions. Focus on your breath while tuning into your emotional centerline.
5. As per the previous questions, take a mental note or, better still, write them into your journal.
6. Continue to breathe and release your negative emotions. Refer to the energy clearing meditation in Chapter 20 as well as the forgiveness exercises in Chapter 13 for help with releasing negative emotions.

HERE ARE EXAMPLES OF HOW TO WORKSHOP QUESTION 3:

QUESTION 3: WHAT IS THIS REALLY ABOUT?	QUESTION 3: WHAT IS THIS REALLY ABOUT?
Sally catches her thought of not feeling loved and begins to reflect on its origin. She notices memories that were stored in her unconscious mind of her father yelling at her with a similarly aggressive tone. She hears him saying: "You can never do anything right! You will have big problems when you grow up if you don't improve." Sally notices the pain these words caused and realizes that she felt rejected and judged by her father. She realizes that in that moment she decided that she was not good enough and not worthy of being loved. She breathes into her emotions to soothe them. She attends to her inner child and helps her feel safe and loved again. She realizes that her husband is pushing this buried pain button. As she recognizes that she is reacting to him from her own inner wounds, she is able to hear her husband's tonality with greater awareness. She realizes that his upset is not about her; he is reacting to something in him—to one of his own emotional trigger points. As she detaches from her pain, she now feels a greater sense of calm and has greater clarity around what is happening between her husband and herself.	Paul catches his thought of not feeling good enough and begins to reflect on why he feels that way. He notices a memory from his childhood: He was seven years old and doing giving a presentation for to his class. He stumbled on his words, got flustered, and forgot what he was supposed to say. The children laughed at him and the teacher shook her head in dismay. Humiliated, Paul returned to his seat, thinking that he was stupid and pathetic. He made a pact with himself, that he would never put himself into that scenario situation again, and avoided public speaking at all costs from then on. Paul breathes into his stomach and into his panic to release his emotions. He attends to his inner child and thinks about all the inner strengths and capabilities he has. He helps his inner child resolve this painful memory by seeing the humor in the situation and not taking himself so seriously. He reminds himself that he is no longer a scared seven-year-old, but a man in his thirties who is ready to step into his confidence.

> **QUESTION 3: WHAT IS THIS REALLY ABOUT?**
>
> Marnie catches her thought of feeling worthless and begins to ask why this is triggering her so much.
>
> She notices a memory from primary (elementary) school. She was around nine years old and wanted desperately to be in the popular group. Nearby, a group of girls were talking amongst themselves. As Marnie approached them, they all went silent. She asked them what they were talking about and one of the girls said that it was her birthday party over the weekend, and they were talking about what happened at their sleepover. Marnie felt crushed that she had not been included and could not understand what the other girls "had" that she didn't have. Why had they been invited and she had not? What was wrong with her?
>
> She realizes that in that moment she decided that the other girls were better than her, that she was not good enough, did not belong anywhere, and that people would not accept her.
>
> Marnie breathes into her emotional centerline to soothe her inner child. She releases this inner pain by reminding herself how much love she has within her and who she really is.

Once you are aware of the memory your pain is attached to and what decisions you made in that moment, proceed to Question 4.

CHAPTER 29

QUESTION 4: WHAT ARE MY LESSONS?

"It takes courage . . . to endure the sharp pains of self-discovery rather than choose to take the dull pain of unconsciousness that would last the rest of our lives."

Marianne Williamson

The final question of the Happiness Formula is *What are my lessons?* This empowering question is designed to help us transcend our pain by learning from the event with an eye to purposeful growth. The first three questions took us into our feelings (our pain) to understand what internal pain button was being pushed. This final question helps us return to the present moment with greater awareness, strength and connection. It reminds us of the following:

- Happiness is not for chicken shits. It takes courage, commitment and conviction to make the moment-to-moment choices that move you toward what makes you truly happy.
- When we are in a mindset of fear, we are disconnected from our essence and therefore disconnected from our core virtues (character strengths).
- When we are in fear we are either replaying the past or anticipating the future—either way, we are not in the present moment.
- Our core fear is the toxic illusion that we are not good enough,

worthy or loved. We arrived at that belief as the result of an immature perceptual experience—it does not represent the truth.
- Our core fears trigger our fight, flight or freeze mode and make us reactive to people and situations. When in that state, we are not being the best version of who we can be; we are playing small and safe.
- Instead of focusing on our fear, we can focus on what is trying to emerge. We can ask ourselves, *How can I grow?*
- Nothing in nature that is alive is stationary. We are always growing.
- Every person or situation presents an opportunity for us to master our life purpose of actualizing the full potential of our virtues (the best version of ourselves).
- Pain, anxiety and emotional distress are warning signals that demand our attention. When we feel the distress and then consciously address it, we transcend our fear and pain and heal.
- To heal means we claim back the lost or fragmented parts of ourselves and become whole again.
- Remember: From pain comes growth—embrace your C.O.R.E. strength. (Courage, Optimism, Resilience, Energy)
- Remember: Do not take anything personally—be C.A.L.M. (Compassion, Acceptance, Love, Mindfulness)
- Remember: Detach from drama—be W.I.S.E. (Wisdom, Inspired-Action, Soul-Centered, Expression)
- Let your essence lead with trust, belief and faith.

HOW CAN I POSITIVELY REFRAME THIS MOMENT?

This question asks us to flip our focus toward a more optimistic perspective. We literally change the frame—we choose a new "filter" or "lens" to view our experiences differently. When we reframe successfully, we are able to observe the perfection in our pain as well as its purpose. This shift of mindset shrinks our fear, loosens the grip of its strangulation, and disempowers it. We experience our world with greater calm and clarity.

Changing our negative self-talk and looking for a more positive solution will instantly shift our mindset and emotions. This question helps to keep us solution-focused.

HOW CAN I GROW FROM THIS?

This question reminds us that every challenge is an opportunity to learn and grow. When we focus on our growth and what emerges within us as a result of the challenging situation, we activate our internal resources and begin to master those challenges.

WHAT VIRTUE(S) MUST I ACTIVATE IN THIS SITUATION?

This is an opportunity to put our Be-Do-Have plan into action and optimize our character strengths. Which of your virtues can you call upon to navigate your challenges? Which virtues will help you slay your fears and express self-love? Which will enable you to take responsibility and be the best version of yourself? As you do so, you realize your life purpose.

The three tools that help you address this question are vulnerability, openness and authenticity. By embracing vulnerability as an asset, we access the courage to break free of our fear. Vulnerability allows us to open ourselves honestly and reveal our deepest fears and desires. By communicating our truth openly, people can understand us and accept us because they don't feel threatened.

STEPS TO WORKING THROUGH QUESTION 4:

1. Connect with your essence. Question 3 will have helped you to release your negative emotions so that you now have a clear pathway to connecting with your essence. Focus on the innermost core of your being along your emotional centerline. Feel the warmth of your inner light and imagine expanding it. Imagine turning up an "inner dial" and seeing your light shining out of you. Remember that as you settle your fear and reach a state of calm, you activate the higher centers of your brain. This in turn activates your relaxation response and helps you problem-solve issues in an effective manner.

2. Remind yourself that you have everything you need within you and focus on your inner virtues and values. Decide to choose the higher path of your essence, your inner master, rather than submit to your fear.

3. Allow your resources and values to guide your response. If they had voices, what would they say? How would they guide you?
   - What would Courage guide you to do?
   - What would Trust guide you to do?
   - What would Love say?
   - What would Compassion say?
   - What would Grace say?
   - What would Calmness say?
   - What would Self-Worth say?
   - What would Patience say?

4. Tune into the voice of your intuition and allow this wisdom to guide your next choices. (Remember to use your Be-Do-Have list to remember the action steps you need to take. Ask yourself: Who do I need to be and what do I need to do in order to activate my virtues and align with my values?)

5. Express yourself freely and authentically. Notice how it feels to speak your truth and act on its wisdom. Embrace those feelings, embody them and let the vibration of your truth settle into your cells. Remember that the more you eliminate behaviors that result in fear, the more integrity you have. This "wholeness"—this soundness, this congruence—fosters greater levels of self-respect, self-worth, clarity and certainty, and will result in self-empowerment.

6. Continue to practice these steps in all the challenging moments ahead; the more consistent you are, the more competent you will become. With greater competency, you will have greater confidence and courage to be your truth instead of your fear.

Here are examples of how to workshop Question 4:

QUESTION 4: WHAT IS MY LESSON HERE?

Sally reflects on her personal list of virtues, which are: accepting, beautiful, empathetic, forgiving, peaceful, spiritual, open-hearted, kind, confident and honest.
Her three highest values are peace, love and freedom.
Now that she has soothed the emotional tantrum belonging to her inner child and she feels a greater sense of connection and calmness, she is reminded of the power that exists within her.
She asks herself the following questions:
- If I were being empathetic, what would I do now? How would I respond?
- If I were accepting, how would I respond?
- If I were kind, forgiving and honest, how would I respond?

She focuses on her values of peace, love and freedom, and realizes that if she wants to experience those values, she needs to follow the guidance of her virtues.
Sally returns to a conversation with her husband and with courageous vulnerability explains that the tone she heard triggered her father issues. It reminded her of the way her father spoke to her as a child and how much that brought her down. She explains that as a result she became conditioned to shut down or defend herself.
She realizes now that Sam feels frustrated and stressed and asks him what he needs and how she can help him. Sam responds by opening up and revealing his own vulnerabilities and explains what he needs to feel more supported by Sally.
As a result Sam and Sally can attend to each other on a deeper level with greater love.

QUESTION 4: WHAT IS MY LESSON HERE?	QUESTION 4: WHAT IS MY LESSON HERE?
Paul reflects on his personal list of virtues, which are: ambitious, authentic, aware, courageous, enthusiastic, creative, passionate, playful, resourceful and inspiring. His three highest values are achievement, confidence and self-worth. By soothing his inner child and embracing his maturity and confidence, Paul is reminded of a higher purpose that drives him to achieve. He connects with his virtues and asks himself the following questions: • Am I being passionate? • Am I being resourceful? • Am I being inspiring? • If I were completely authentic and courageous, how would I respond to this opportunity? Paul focuses on his values of achievement, confidence and self-worth, and recognizes that he has everything within him to succeed and make a difference to his team and his company. Paul uses his virtues of playfulness, creativity and passion to construct an inspiring presentation for his team. As a result he feels greater self-confidence and self-worth, and knows that he can achieve whatever he puts his mind to. With the help of an ambitious and inspirational presentation, Paul is promoted to the role of head trainer and achieves one of his greatest goals.	Marnie reflects on her personal list of virtues, which are: caring, considerate, compassionate, flexible, fun, generous, happy, grateful, wise, and sensitive. Her three highest values are love, freedom and compassion. Marnie connects with her inner child by "hugging" her with the warmth of her breath. She reminds her "hurt child" that she is pure love and is accepted and loved by many people. She realizes that perhaps she is being overly sensitive. When she focuses on how much love she offers the right people, she feels a greater sense of peace and happiness. She realizes that it is only when she compares herself to others and competes for their approval that she feels disempowered. As she releases the painful memory from her past, she is more present in the here and now and embraces the opportunities in front of her. As she focuses on being fun, generous, caring, grateful and wise, she begins to relax. Marnie recognizes that the crowd that did not invite her was similar to the popular group in school; neither group has the same interests or values that she has. She knows that she has her own group of people and does not need to be included in everything to feel accepted. She feels a greater sense of forgiveness, love, freedom and compassion.

As you can see from these scenarios, the four questions of the Happiness Formula offered each individual a way to manage their emotions in a resilient and optimistic manner. They journeyed into their emotional pain and "played" with it in a way that helped them recognize what past events and limiting decisions were stuck in their emotional body.

The ability to self-connect and reflect offered them greater awareness of what pain buttons were present and needing to be released. As they each shifted their focus toward their lessons, toward their virtues, they were able to reframe their fear-based limiting histories into empowered narratives grounded in the values of personal growth, freedom and empowerment.

CHAPTER 30

IMPLEMENTING AND PRACTICING THE HAPPINESS FORMULA: BE YOUR OWN GURU

"Remember, to learn and not to do is really not to learn. To know and not to do is really not to know."

Stephen R. Covey

Practicing compassion toward ourselves is of vital importance in the process of committing to self-mastery. It is important to remember that our habitual behaviors are deeply imprinted and take time to unlearn. We therefore need to be patient, kind and nonjudgmental toward ourselves as we take steps to change our habits. The most important element is intention. As long as we keep on intending to change and grow, we will embrace all the ups and downs along the way. Baby steps are all we need. In time we will transform without consciously working at it. We only need to remember to connect with our essence and activate its guidance. In each moment that we do, we transform and grow.

Your first attempt at the four questions of the Happiness Formula could take a few hours, days or even weeks to process. If you observe your reactions over time, you will begin to note your ego-self's patterns. To begin with, allow at least one hour to work through the questions. Once you have been through all four questions a few times, you will be able to process them within a few minutes, fast-tracking directly to your lessons and activating your virtues instinctively. So, next time you feel emotionally triggered, use these four questions to help you navigate through your fear, through your pain, and return to a state of self-love.

A journal allows you to look back on your answers and add to them as you gain further awareness. I also recommend the four questions as a meditation in which you silently contemplate each question.

When you have outlined your questions and understood *what* is triggering you and *why*, you can fast-track straight from Question 1 to Question 4. Once you have awareness of the cause of your inner pain and distress, you do not need to keep revisiting it. You can practice mindfulness to observe your feelings and memories without activating a mental story. This means you can observe your feelings, notice they stem from your hurt inner child, recognize the beliefs of not feeling good enough, worthy or loved, and then instantly focus on your lessons or positive reframing.

When you notice yourself reacting to a person or a situation, STOP, and ask yourself the four questions. Every time you use them, you soothe your inner child and settle turbulent emotions. You break the cycle of negative thoughts and behaviors that drain your energy and foster shame, blame, guilt and fear. You eliminate defensiveness, criticism and the urge to withdraw. You stop fighting, fleeing or freezing in stressful moments and you keep yourself calm and connected.

Your success with the Happiness Formula lies in its implementation. Every time you stop, observe, catch, detach, release and embrace, you manage your reactions and take responsibility for your responses. Every time you allow your virtues to guide you, you align with your values. As you align with your values, you express your authentic self. Over time, situations or people who challenged you in the past will be easy to deal with. You will have greater resilience and experience emotional equilibrium.

As a result of your calmness, you will have more energy and clarity. You can now direct your energy to what you are passionate about. Not only will you master the lessons you were meant to learn in your lifetime, but you will also realize your higher purpose and contribute to our world in an empowering and significant way. This will cultivate a calmer world, a compassionate world, a world motivated by love rather than fear.

CHAPTER 31

MY BLESSING TO YOU

"Understand that the right to choose your own path is a sacred privilege. Use it. Dwell in possibility."

Oprah Winfrey

It is with a heart filled with love and gratitude that I thank you for reading this book and allowing me to share my thoughts with you. I trust you will have great success in implementing the tools I offered you here, and I wish you strength and courage on your journey of self-transformation and mastery.

Remember, the ego itself is not the problem. The limiting beliefs we formed along our timelines have intoxicated us with fear and tainted the ego-self. You do not need to believe these ideas; they are not your true identity. They were the beliefs formed by a scared child with a limited perspective. Who you are is your authentic self, your essence, which expresses your core virtues (strengths), your values, passion and ultimate purpose. You can give up the draining thoughts and behaviors that belong to the ego-self as they no longer serve you.

Give up the need to be right.
Give up worrying what other people think.
Give up the need to please and be liked or accepted.
Give up defensiveness.

Give up comparing yourself to others.
Give up competing and trying to prove your worth.
Give up compromising yourself by people-pleasing.
Give up the need to control yourself, other people and outcomes.
Give up the fear of change.
Give up the fear of uncertainty.
Give up self-pity, self-doubt, self-sabotage, self-loathing, self-righteousness, self-indulgence, self-harm, self-preservation, self-denial, self-absorption, self-withdrawal and self-consciousness.
Give up the dysfunctional terms and conditions of your self-worth.
Give up the need to be loved.
Give up the need for more "stuff."
Give up the need for validation, recognition and attention.
Give up judgement, criticism and blame.

There is no need to prove yourself any longer. It is time to BE YOU. *Proving* breeds pressure; *being* breeds bliss. Get to know your virtues and values. Embody them. They represent your full potential and will guide you to your greatness and purpose. Tune in and listen to the calling of your soul. How can you significantly contribute to the world with your own unique gifts? How can you light up the world and help restore balance and love?

Your mastery lies in your moment-to-moment choices. You empower your life one thought at a time. You are the alchemist. You are the architect of your achievements, the engineer of your emotions, and the designer of your destiny. Every time you flip your fear and embrace authenticity is a moment of triumph.

Embrace vulnerability.
Embrace your core virtues as your greatest strengths.
Embrace your values as your top priorities.
Embrace the daily habits and goals that align with your values and express your virtues.
Embrace your *personal purpose proposition.*
Embrace trust, belief and faith.
Embrace a growth mindset.
Embrace self-awareness, self-acceptance, self-belief, self-respect, self-trust, self-esteem, self-worth, self-confidence, self-sufficiency, self-care, self-management and self-love.
Embrace yourself.

Embrace your passions.
Embrace the essence of you.
You have everything you need within you and can now activate the courage to be YOU.

To your truth and freedom, with lots of love,
Cheryne

CHAPTER 32

ADDITIONAL RESOURCES

*"We are what we repeatedly do.
Excellence, then, is not an act, but a habit."*

Aristotle

Here are a few of my favorite meditations. For each meditation find a quiet space where you can sit, lie down, or stand peacefully. Ensure your phone is on silent. Close your eyes and focus on the present moment.

1. Basic Mind Focus Meditation
- Think of the desired emotional state you want to achieve. You may like to refer to your virtues and values exercise and focus on aligning yourself with your core resources.
- Create a visual image in your mind's eye. Take note of all the details in your picture: the colors, shapes and textures. Notice where you are and who is with you.
- Use a positive statement to focus your mind on your desired emotion. "I am . . ."
- Begin to focus on your breath. Notice the feel of your breath. Is it restricted to your upper chest or sinking deeply into your abdomen? Feel the rhythm of your breath moving up and down your body. Feel your chest rise and your belly expand with each inhalation, and feel your chest fall and your belly

flatten as you exhale. Use your breath to soften any tension in the body. Just imagining your breath in a particular part of your body automatically sends it there.
- Move your focus to your internal picture, your self-talk and your feelings, and build that connection with your desired values and virtues.
- Hold your desired state in your body and mind for at least eight breaths before gently opening your eyes.

2. Body Relaxation
- Begin by focusing on your breath. Notice where in your body you feel your breath and observe the rhythm of your breath as it moves through your body. Feel the gentle rise and fall of each inhalation and exhalation. Notice the space and lightness in your breath.
- Bring your focus to the top of your head and slowly soften your body all the way down. Relax your mind, your face—in particular, your jaw. Separate your teeth slightly and rest your tongue in your mouth. Relax your neck and feel your shoulders drop away from your ears. Feel your arms relax all the way down to the palms of your hands and your fingertips. Slowly release all the tension in your body. Relax your torso, your chest and your stomach. Feel more space around your organs. Slowly relax your spine, vertebra by vertebra. Relax your upper back, your middle back and your lower back. Feel any tension along your spine melting. Relax through your pelvis, down your legs, and all the way to the tips of your toes.
- Feel your whole body softening and relaxing.
- Feel your breath moving easily throughout your body.
- For a more energized feeling, start at your feet and move your awareness up your body, finishing at the top of your head.

3. Quick and Easy Breathing Technique
- Begin by focusing on your breath. Notice where in your body you feel your breath and observe the rhythm of your breath as it moves through your body. Feel the gentle rise and fall of each inhalation and exhalation. Notice the space and lightness in your breath.

- Inhale slowly for the count of four.
- Hold your breath at the "top" of your body for two counts.
- Exhale slowly for six counts. Ensure you are completely emptying your lungs by breathing to the full completion of your breath.
- Hold your breath at the "bottom" of your body for three counts and then repeat the same cycle.
- Practice eight breath cycles. This will give you two minutes of deep, cleansing breathing.

4. Energy Clearing (Release Negative Emotions/Energy)
- Begin by focusing on your breath. Notice where in your body you feel your breath and observe the rhythm of your breath moving through your body. Feel the gentle rise and fall of each inhalation and exhalation. Notice the space and lightness in your breath.
- Imagine your breath is a vacuum cleaner with a powerful suction.
- As you inhale, feel your breath sucking up any negative feelings, tightness or tension in your body.
- As you exhale, imagine expelling those toxins out of your body. Focus on the words *let go,* and release whatever the body no longer needs.
- Imagine your inhalation loosening any negative thoughts.
- Imagine your exhalation letting them go.
- Repeat until your mind and body feel clear and energized.

5. Connection to Mother Earth (ME) Guided Meditation:

This meditation is best done standing so that you can easily feel the connections and work with gravity. You can do this meditation outside in the garden or on the beach. It is also effective in the shower. If you are uncomfortable standing, you can sit or lie down and use your imagination to visualize the connections.

- Begin standing with your feet shoulder width apart. Bend your knees slightly. Tilt your pelvis to ensure your back is straight, and create an arch with your arms in front of your body. Ensure your hands are at the level of your heart (as per illustration).

- Focus on your breath as per the previous meditations and relax your body.
- As you exhale, imagine your breath is a coffee plunger pushing down any negative feelings or tension in your body. Keep on "plunging" the negativity down your body until you reach your feet. From there, release those feelings out through the soles of your feet.
- As you focus on your feet, imagine roots growing out the soles of your feet and plunging deep into the earth. You can even imagine the different layers of the earth as you stretch your roots all the way to the center of Earth.
- As you imagine arriving at the nucleus of the Earth, imagine this to be the heart of Mother Earth and feel the pulsation of her beating heart.
- Attach your roots to her "heart." Think of this connection as an umbilical cord connecting a mother and child.
- Slowly inhale her pulsation up your roots and feel the vibrating energy enter your body.
- Imagine the buzzing energy from Mother Earth to be unconditional love entering your body. Inhale this life force energy all the way up your body and into your heart. Connect the cord from her heart to yours.
- Feel the connection between you and Mother Earth. Feel your heart beating in sync with her pulse, and feel the love and safety of this connection.
- Observe the energy filling your body. What qualities does it have? What are its virtues? Perhaps those virtues are the same ones you described as your own core virtues—compassion, wisdom, courage, graciousness, serenity, acceptance, playfulness. And now say to yourself, "As I connect with Mother Earth, I connect with ME. As she breathes life into me, I can feel the virtues of my essence. This is self-love. This is me."
- Imagine your breath sending those feelings all around your body. Feel your essence in your breath. Hold this connection for a few more breaths and then slowly open your eyes.

If you have trouble relating to any of these meditations, search for a meditation podcast, use an application on your phone, or find one on

YouTube. You may like to try my meditation podcast called Peace in My Pocket—Guided Meditations, which you can find on Apple Podcasts.

For assistance with the exercises I have included in this book, please refer to worksheets and video tutorials in the Self Discovery Hub at www.cheryneblom.com.

ABOUT CHERYNE

Cheryne (pronounced Shireen) Blom has worked as a self-empowerment coach and Mindfulness teacher for over a decade. She is passionate about helping you rediscover your unique strengths, virtues and purpose so that you can actualize your full potential. In 2009 Cheryne published her first book, *Be Enthused—52 Weeks of Enthusiasm*, which encapsulates the diversity of her message. Her blog, Be You Be True, has had close to 500,000 views and her podcast Peace in My Pocket has been enjoyed by over 50,000.

Born in South Africa, raised in the United States and living now in Australia, Cheryne considers herself a biltong-burger loving Ugg-boot fanatic. When she is not life-coaching, writing, course-creating, podcasting, speaking or meditating, Cheryne can be found with her three children and beloved boxer, Chester, playing at a bayside beach with her feet immersed in water.

CONNECT WITH CHERYNE

Please visit Cheryne's website: www.cheryneblom.com

Look for Peace in My Pocket Meditation Podcast on Apple, Spotify and YouTube for FREE guided meditations

Follow Cheryne:
Facebook: cheryneblomauthor
Instagram: cheryneblomauthor

ACKNOWLEDGMENTS

I want to thank all the special souls who helped me write this book. Thank you for showing up at exactly the right time.

To Joanne Fedler, thank you for your mentorship, guidance and kick up the a**. I am forever grateful for your gift in bringing out the best in your writers.

To Liliane Grace, my editor. With lightning speed, you took my words to another level. It was an honor and a blessing to work with you.

To all the beautiful women in the author liftoff program- thank you for your love, encouragement and sisterhood. Your courage to share your truth inspired me to do the same. For my writing-pod Sisters Lisa, Claire and Athina thank you for all your feedback, suggestions and wisdom.

To the brilliant Brigitte Benge, you made the impossible possible.

To Koehler Books for finding me on Publishizer and making my dream of publishing this book a reality.

To my mother and sisters whose unconditional love makes me feel limitless.

To my father, who passed over just before this book was published, thank you for helping me discover my greatness. You introduced me to the world of spirituality and taught me to look deeply into the world and myself.

To my children for showing me that I CAN create magnificence.

To my soul-sisters (you know who you are) thank you for your friendship. Thank you for standing by me no matter what, for holding me when I need to cry and then laughing it all away.

To my social media tribes and family, thank you for your likes, shares and cyber-connections.

A special thanks to all the clients I have worked with since 2007. Through our conversations, the content of this book was created. It has been an honor to walk beside you on your journey towards empowerment. Not only did you help create my coaching model, but you also helped me heal the parts of myself that mirrored your pain. With every coaching session, I get to live my life's purpose and for that, I will be forever grateful.

And for you, the reader, thank you for choosing this book.

PUBLISHIZER PATRON SUPPORT

Thank you to everyone who supported my Publishizer campaign—I could not have done this without you!

Nan Abbot, Marcia Abboud, Lorraine Abraham, Emma Alsop, Andrea Ash, Franca Azzato, Anne Barnett, Brigitte Benge, Lisa Benson, Claire Bienvenu, Ann Billington, Karen Blom, Xanti Bootcov, Amanda Boyd, Melanie Brooks, Lynne Brown, Michele Brown, Janet Brydon, Judy Campbell, Andrea Cannon, Angelina Cirelli Salomone, Sheryl Cleminson, Pip Cody, Di Colacino, Mylee Collins, Sarah Crighton, Peter English, Lisa Farber, Joanne Fedler, Michele Fernadez, Sarah Findley, Suzie Forbes, Tanya Goldin, Angela Hallam, Jenni Harding, Miranda Harwood, Anita Henderson, Dana Herbert, Justine Hirshowitz, Lance Hirson, Evan Hoff, Sue Hoffman, Suzi Hommelhof, Sandra Jason, Kylie Jones, Natalie Jones, Jack Kagan, Ashley Kahan, Shannah Kennedy, Kylie Khouri, Becc Kimm, Michele Korn, Tanja Kovacic, Jo-Ann Lim, Vanessa Lontos, Tony Lotzof, Peter Lustig, Mal McKechnie, Suzie McMillan, Lisa Myers, Susan Nailon, Jennifer Newton, Julia Nichols, Sydnie Olsen, Rose Parsons, Stephanie Payne, Debra Peck, Arnold Price, Dawn Pye, Delwyn Rayner, Emily Reid, Ernesto Rennella, Jaenette Rink, Margaret Rolla, Susan Rose, Anna Rossi, Nicole Salinger, Judy Salthouse, Sylvia Schwall, Kate Seemann, Bec Smith, Charlotte Spatz, Mihaela Stefanovic, Belinda Stone, Warren Szybkowski, Alana Tendler, Gwen Thompson-Wellington, Annie Toscher, Susan Rose Trakman, Nicole Tran, Joanna Treweek, Lucy Van Der Riet, Craig Van Zeil, Jess Van Zeil, Nikki Vati, Myfanwy Walker, Laine Walsch, Simone Walsch, Kim Wark, Lisa Weinstein, Bradley White and Denise Zagni

www.ingramcontent.com/pod-product-compliance
Lightning Source LLC
Chambersburg PA
CBHW060517080526
44586CB00012B/520